THE TRUTH
ROGER CASEMENT

THE TRIAL OF ROGER CASEMENT

Written and illustrated by
Fionnuala Doran

SELF MADE HERO

DEDICATION

For Granny and Granda

First published in 2016
by SelfMadeHero
139-141 Pancras Road
London NW1 1UN
www.selfmadehero.com

Written and Illustrated by Fionnuala Doran

Publishing Director: Emma Hayley
Sales & Marketing Manager: Sam Humphrey
Publishing Assistant: Guillaume Rater
UK Publicist: Paul Smith
US Publicist: Maya Bradford
Designer: Txabi Jones
Editor: Dan Lockwood

A CIP record for this book is available from the British Library

ISBN: 978-1-910593-20-2

10 9 8 7 6 5 4 3 2 1

Printed and bound in Slovenia

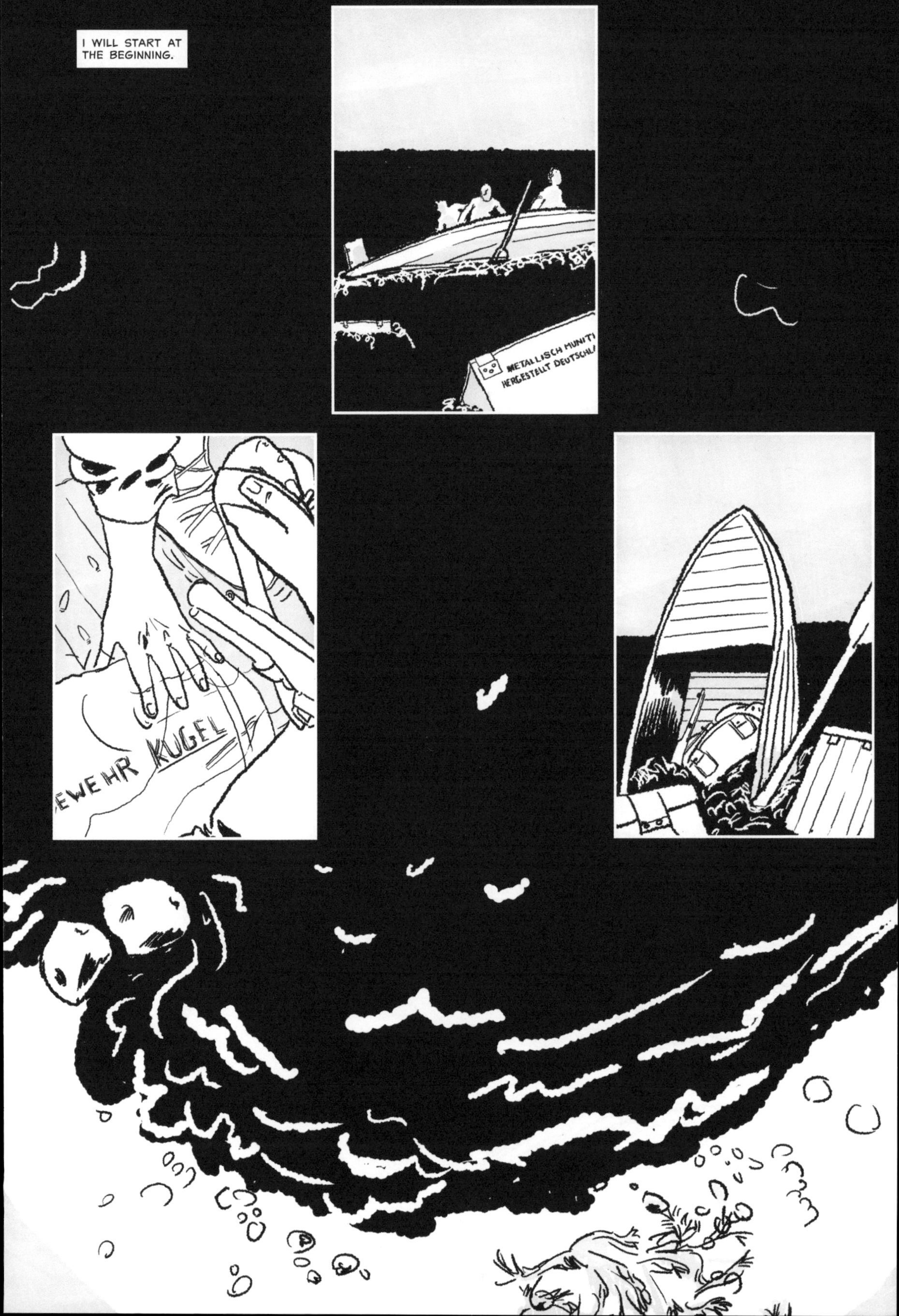
I WILL START AT THE BEGINNING.
METALLISCH MUNITI
HERGESTELLT DEUTSCHLA
EWEHR KUGEL

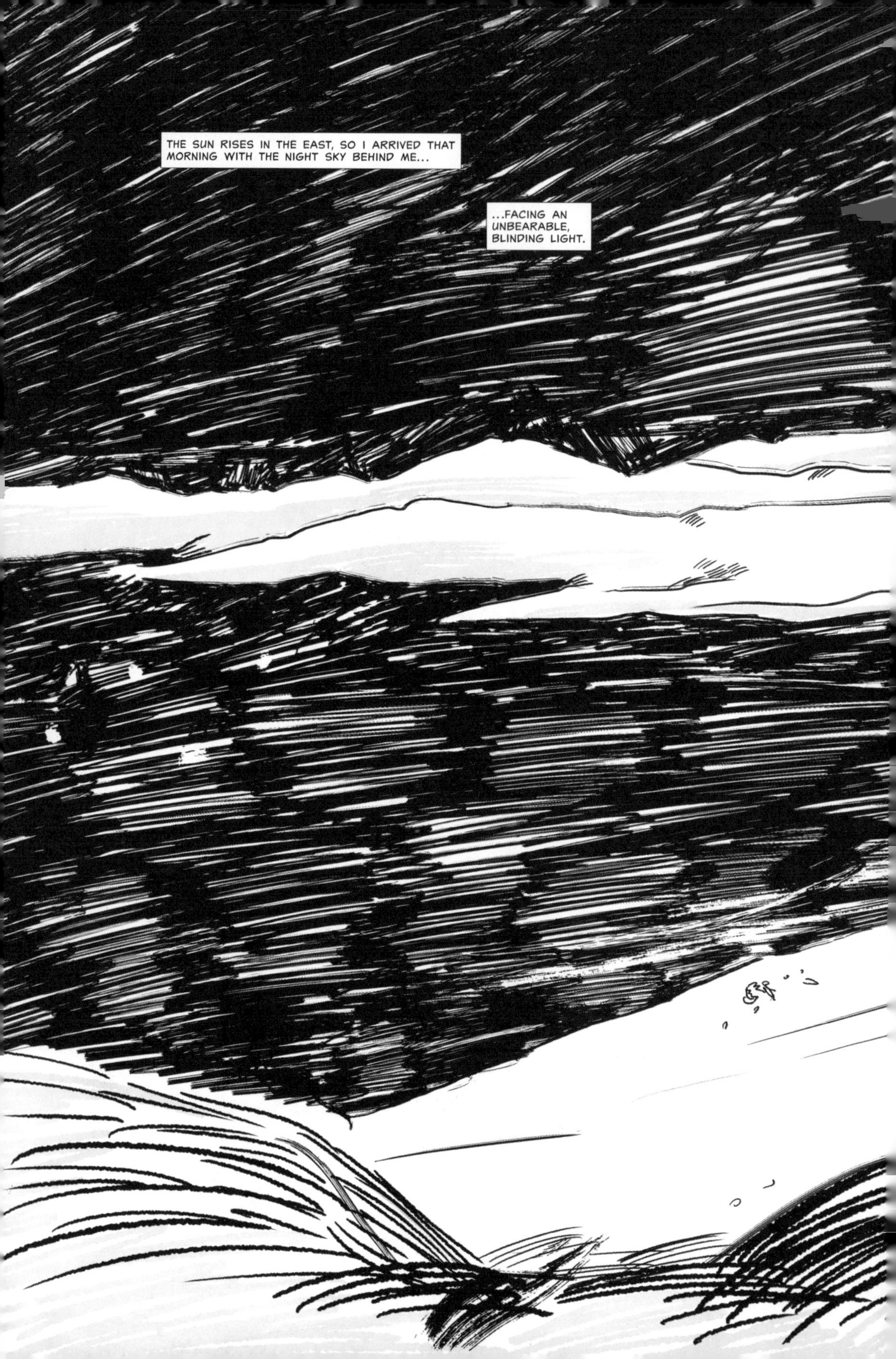
THE SUN RISES IN THE EAST, SO I ARRIVED THAT MORNING WITH THE NIGHT SKY BEHIND ME...
...FACING AN UNBEARABLE, BLINDING LIGHT.

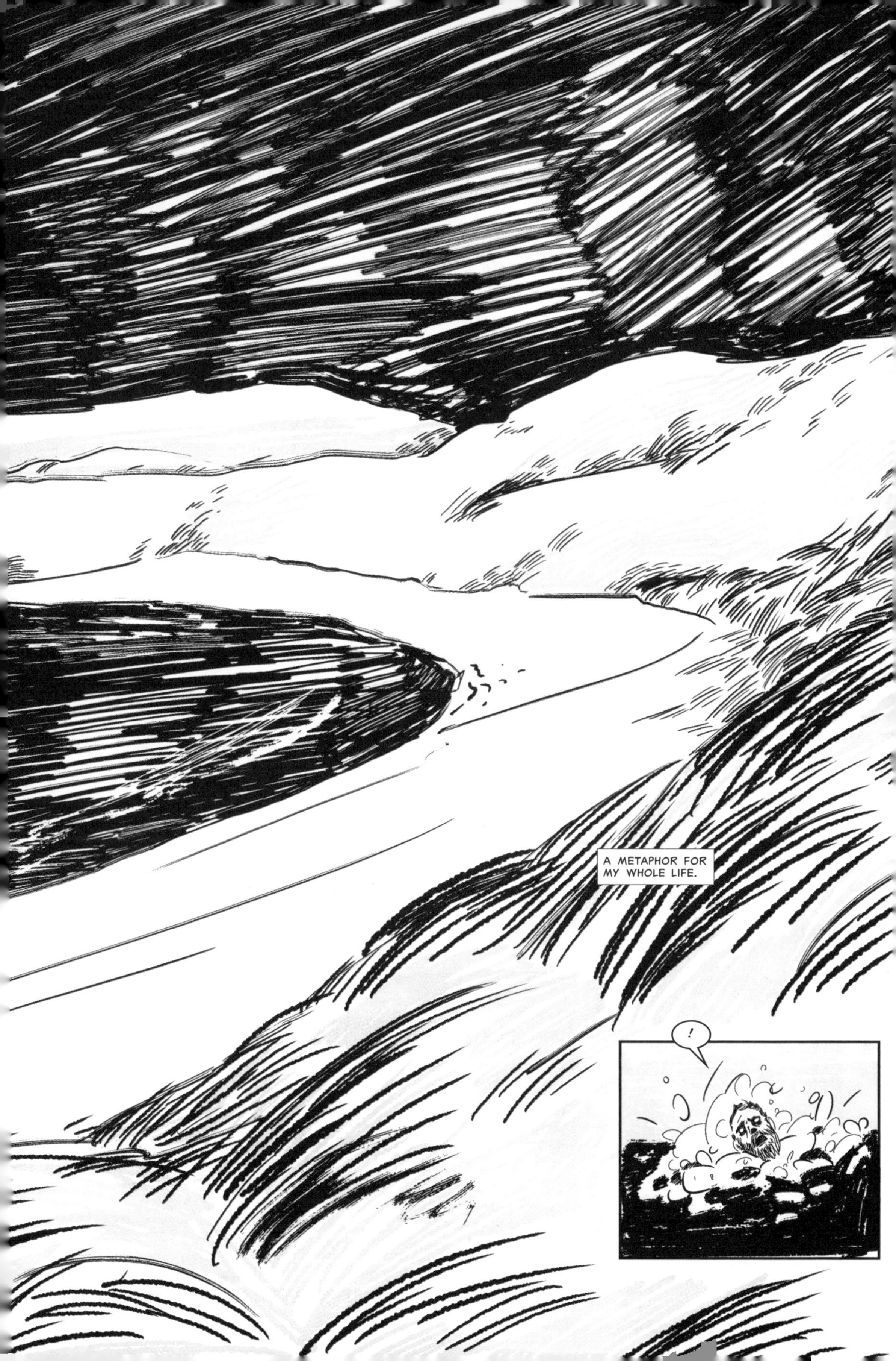
A METAPHOR FOR
MY WHOLE LIFE.
!

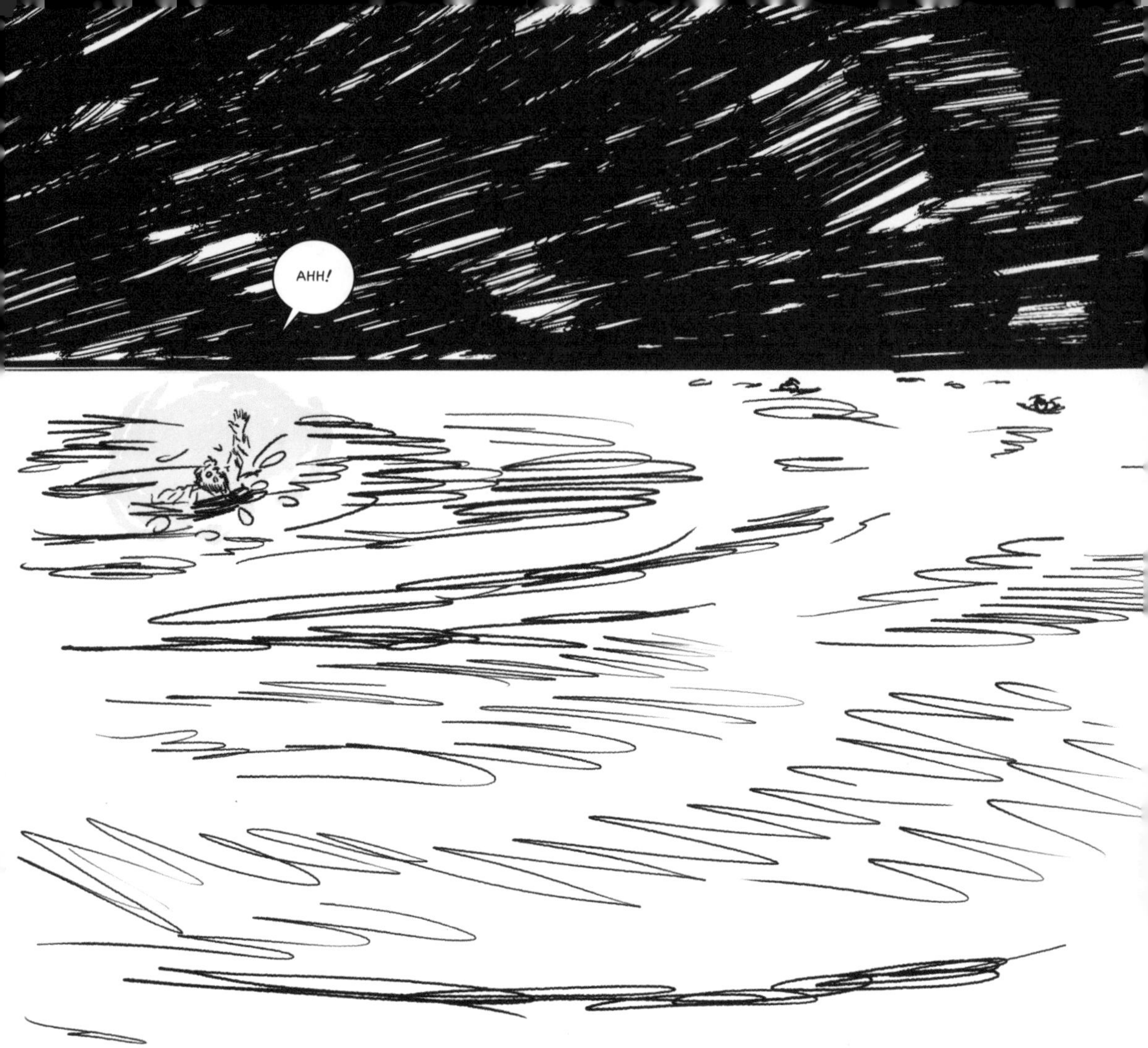
AHH!

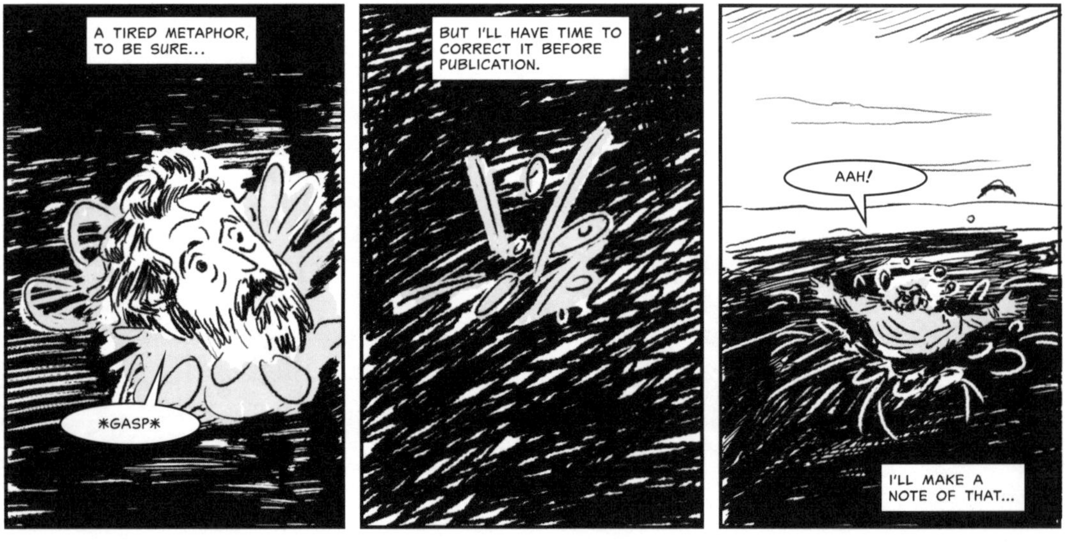
A TIRED METAPHOR, TO BE SURE...
GASP
BUT I'LL HAVE TIME TO CORRECT IT BEFORE PUBLICATION.
AAH!
I'LL MAKE A NOTE OF THAT...

PERHAPS AN ALTERNATE OPENING WOULD BE SOMETHING THEMED AFTER LIGHT, OR NEW DAWNS...

SOMETHING MORE ORIGINAL AND STRIKING...

TO MAKE THE READER EXCLAIM: "AH!"

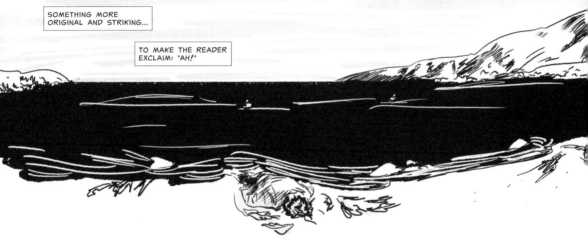

PUFT

"I HAD NOT THOUGHT OF THAT BEFORE!"

WHEEZE

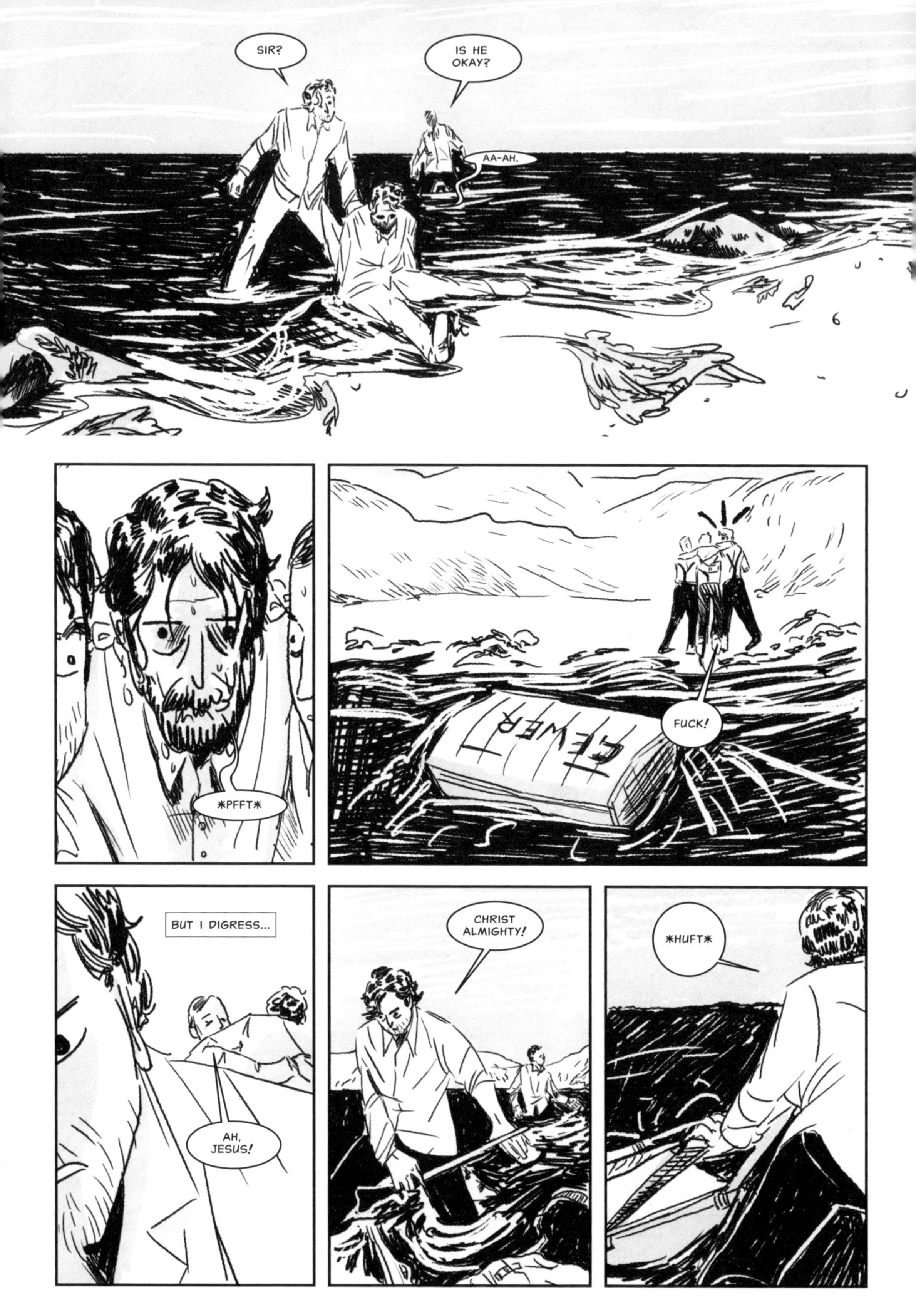
SIR?
IS HE OKAY?
AA-AH.
PFFT
FUCK!
FEWER
BUT I DIGRESS...
AH, JESUS!
CHRIST ALMIGHTY!
HUFT

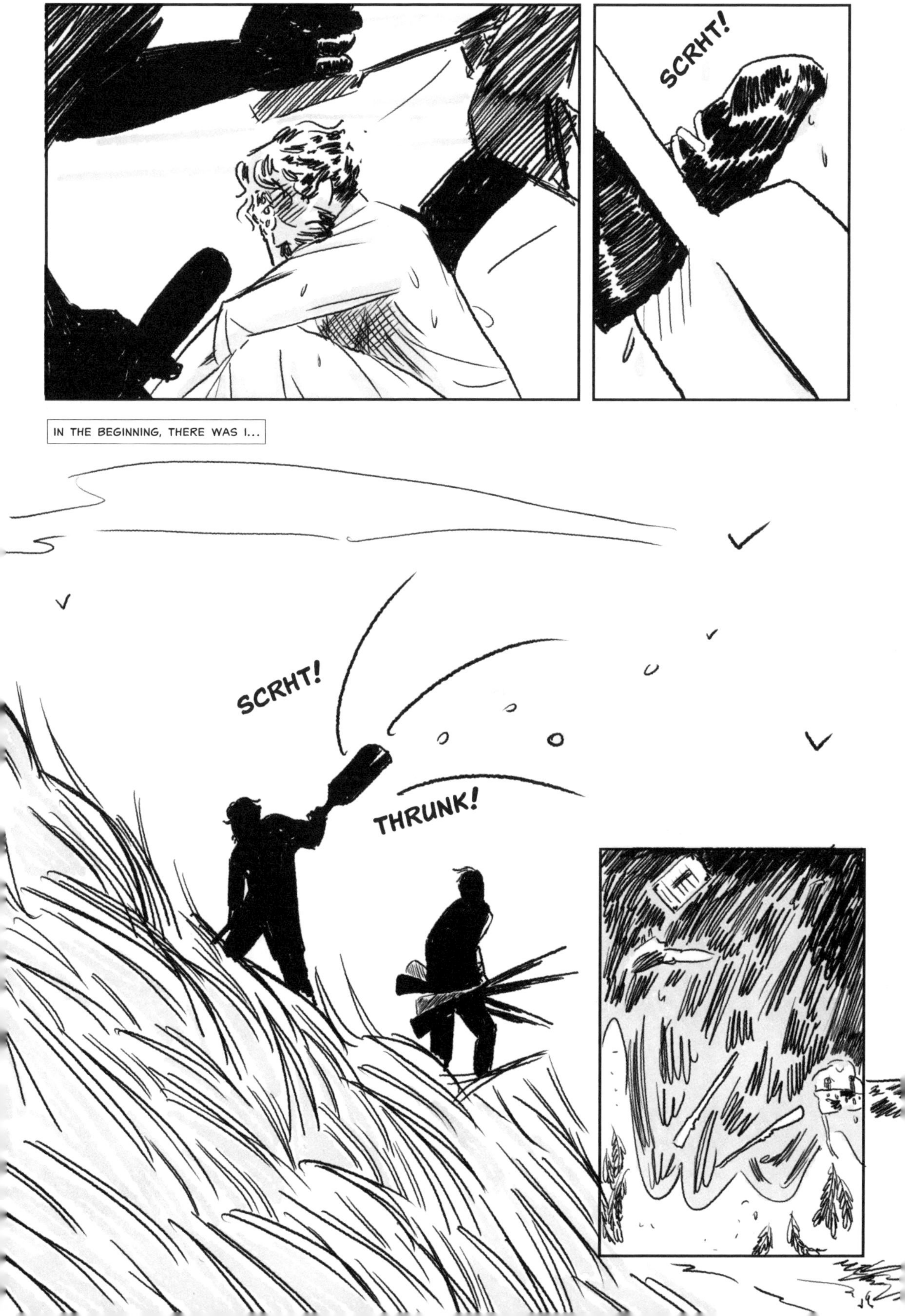
SCRHT!
IN THE BEGINNING, THERE WAS I...
SCRHT!
THRUNK!

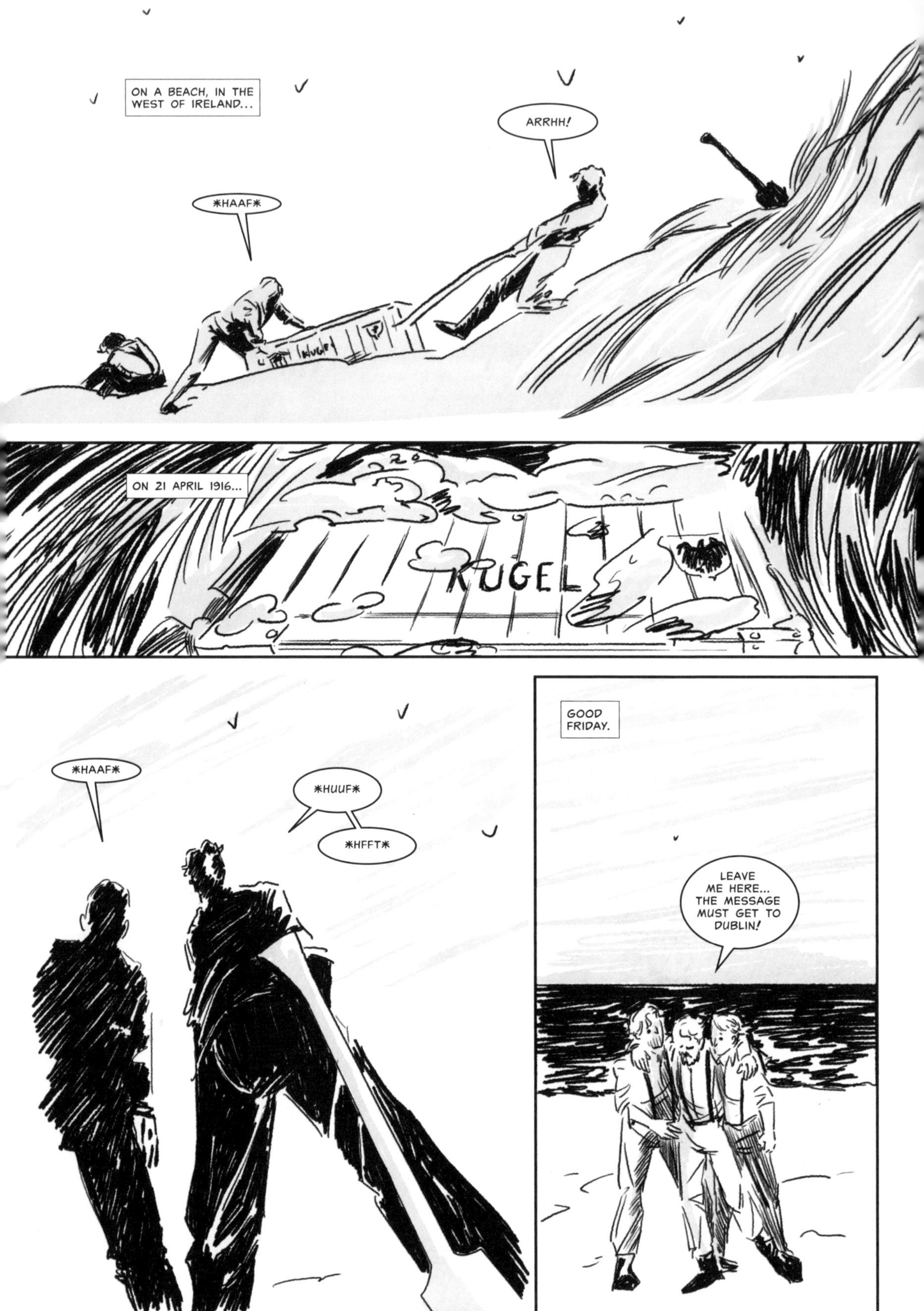
ON A BEACH, IN THE WEST OF IRELAND...
HAAF
ARRHH!
ON 21 APRIL 1916...
KUGEL
HAAF
HUUF
HFFT
GOOD FRIDAY.
LEAVE ME HERE... THE MESSAGE MUST GET TO DUBLIN!

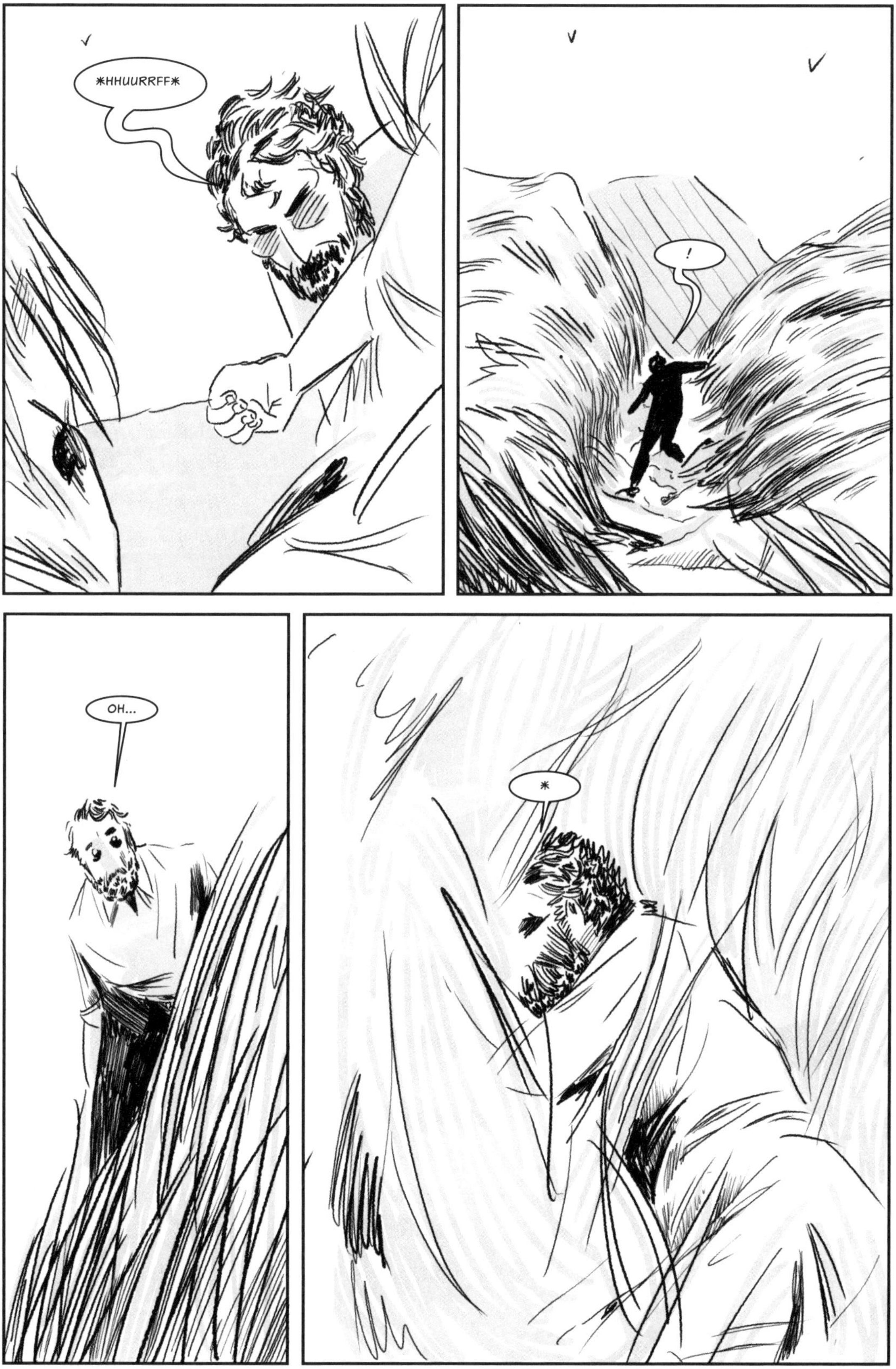
HHUURRFF
!
OH...
*

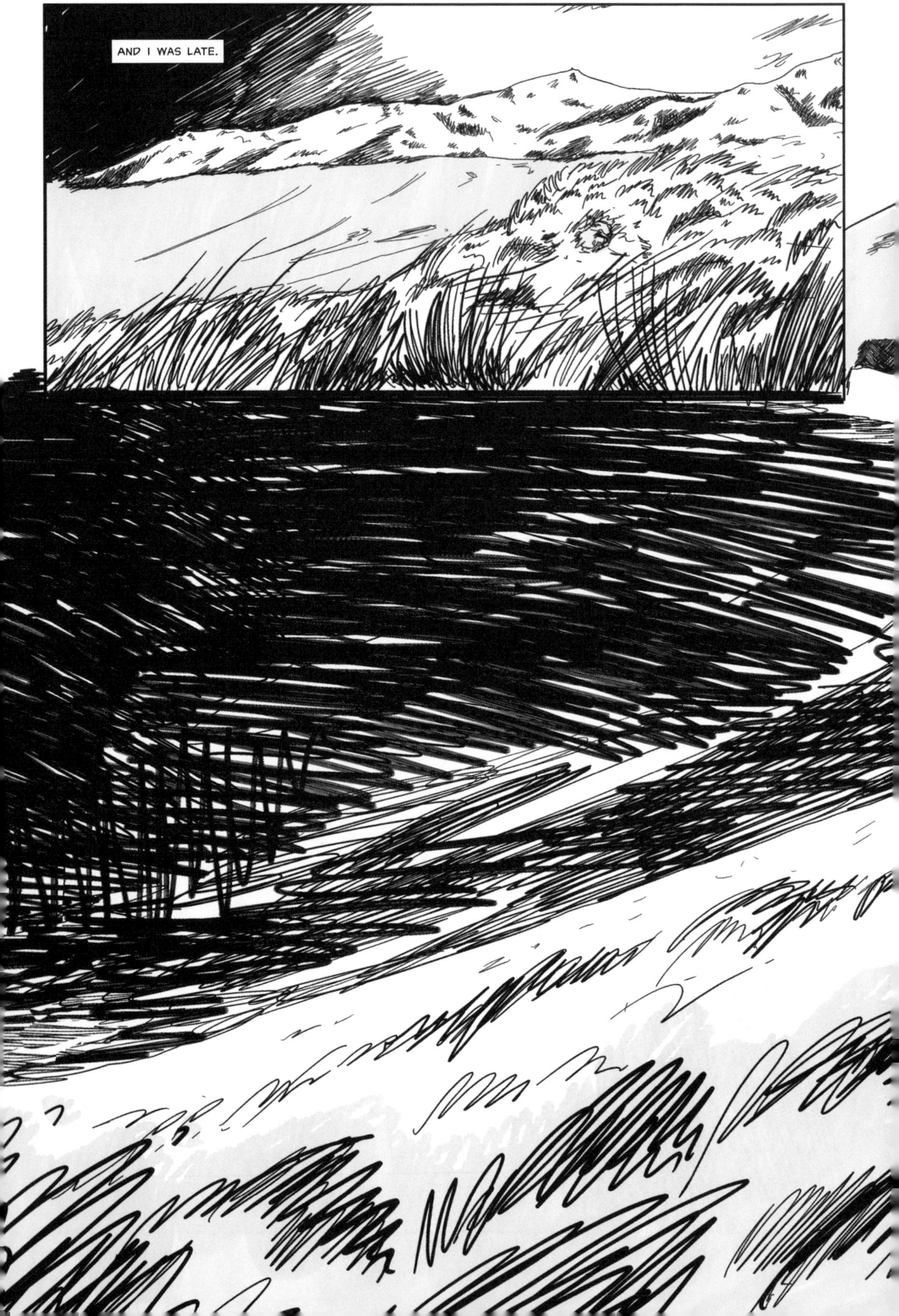
AND I WAS LATE.

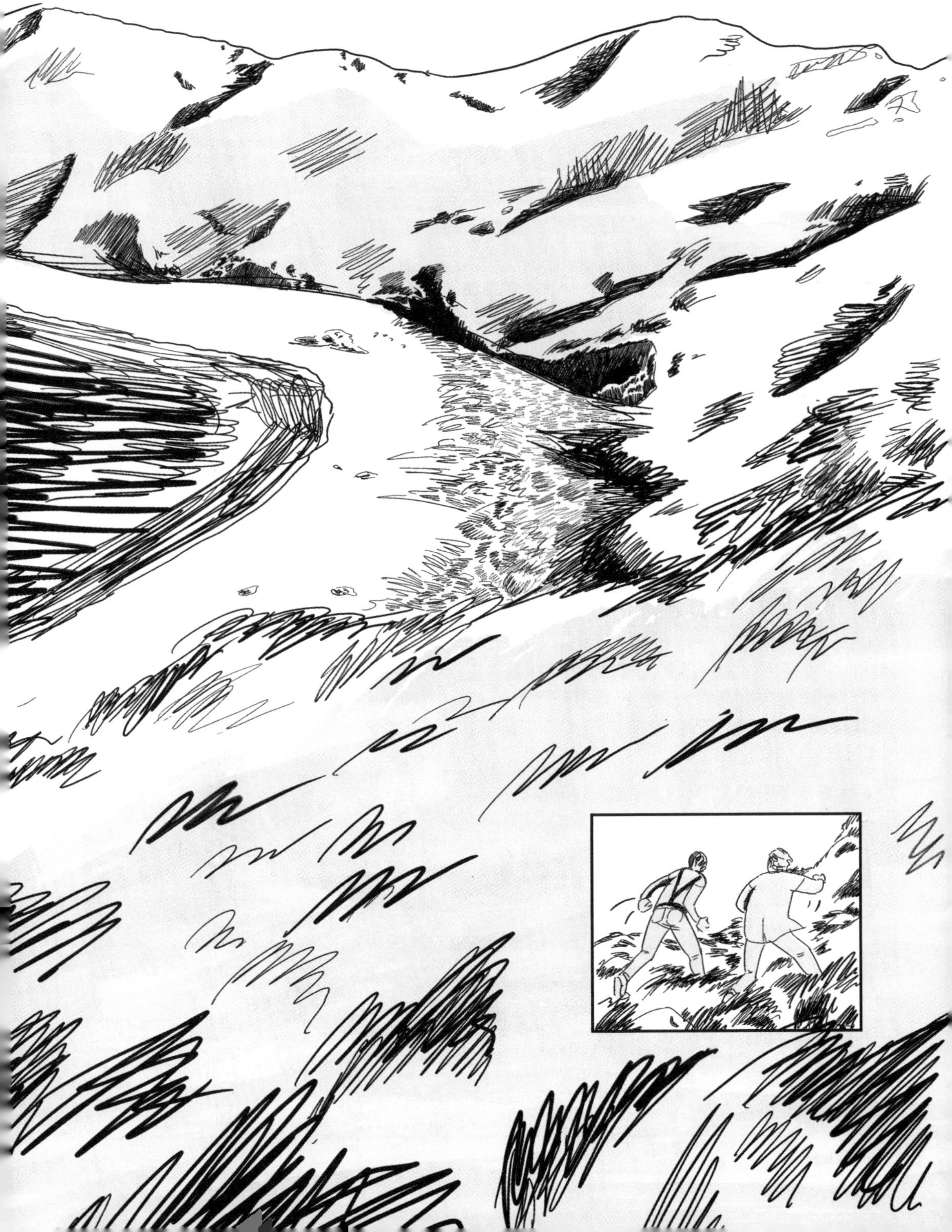

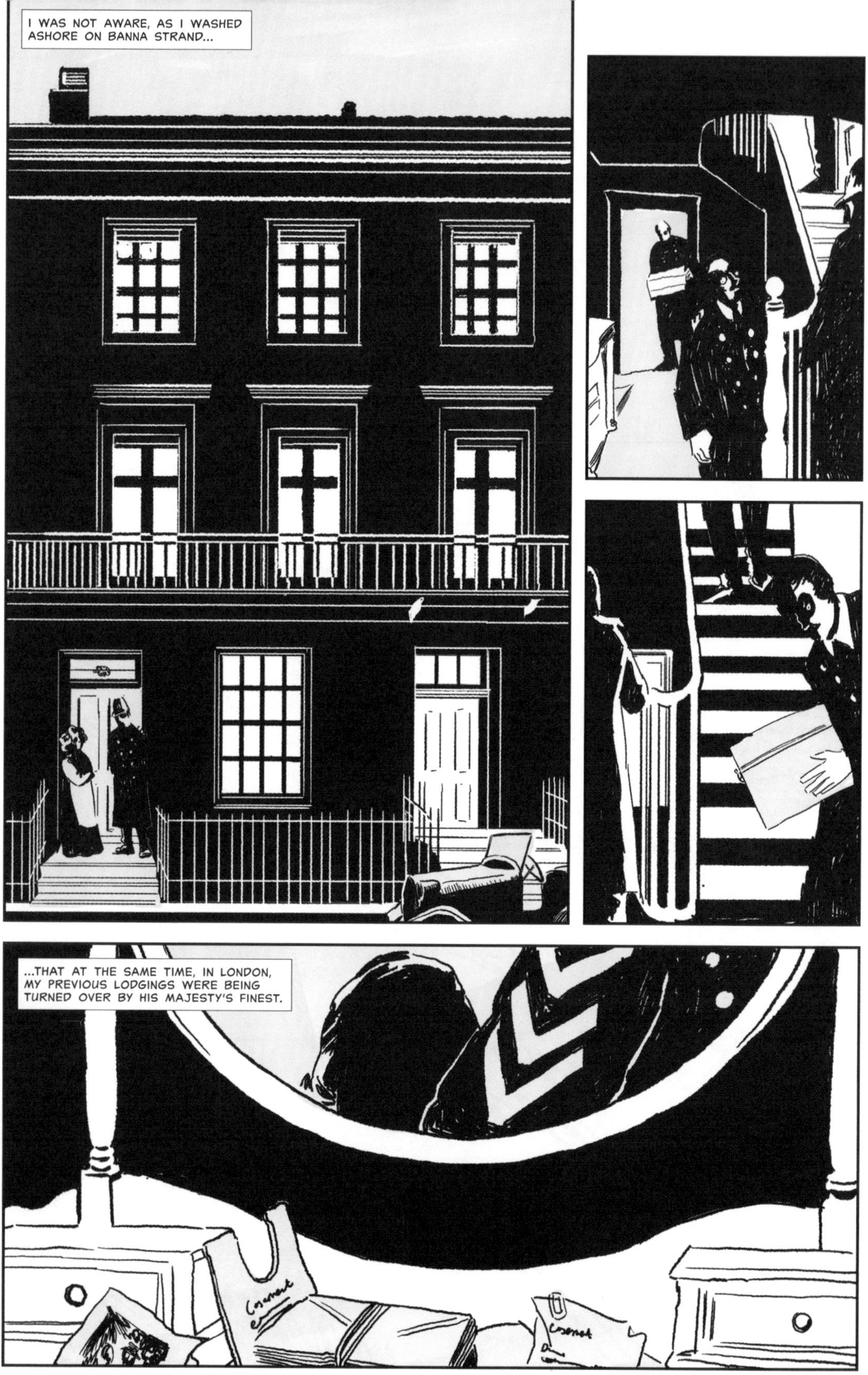
I WAS NOT AWARE, AS I WASHED ASHORE ON BANNA STRAND...
...THAT AT THE SAME TIME, IN LONDON, MY PREVIOUS LODGINGS WERE BEING TURNED OVER BY HIS MAJESTY'S FINEST.

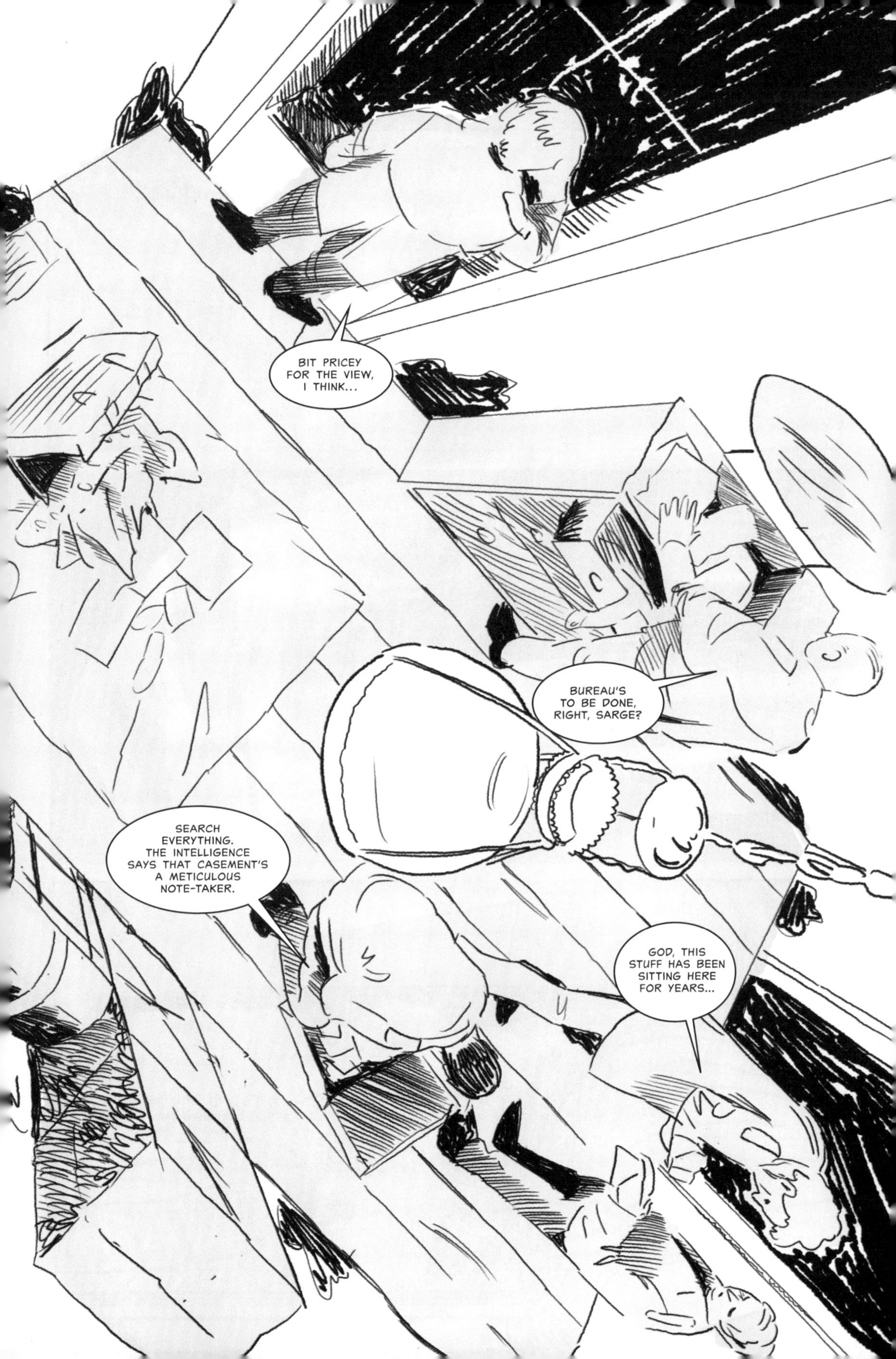
BIT PRICEY FOR THE VIEW, I THINK...
BUREAU'S TO BE DONE, RIGHT, SARGE?
SEARCH EVERYTHING. THE INTELLIGENCE SAYS THAT CASEMENT'S A METICULOUS NOTE-TAKER.
GOD, THIS STUFF HAS BEEN SITTING HERE FOR YEARS...

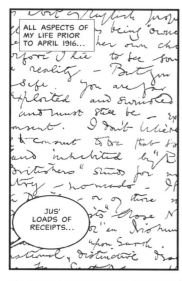

ALL ASPECTS OF MY LIFE PRIOR TO APRIL 1916...

JUS' LOADS OF RECEIPTS...

OLD LEDGERS, STUFF LIKE THAT.

!

...WERE TO BE INVESTIGATED FOR EVIDENCE OF TREACHERY.

DUNNO WHAT USE THEY'RE GOIN' TO BE TO SCOTLAND YARD.

MAYBE THEY'RE FOR PIECING TOGETHER HIS MOVEMENTS OR SOMETHING LIKE THAT.

YOU KNOW, LIKE WHAT SHERLOCK HOLMES DOES.

YOU'RE PUTTIN' A LOT OF FAITH IN OUR SUPERIORS THERE...

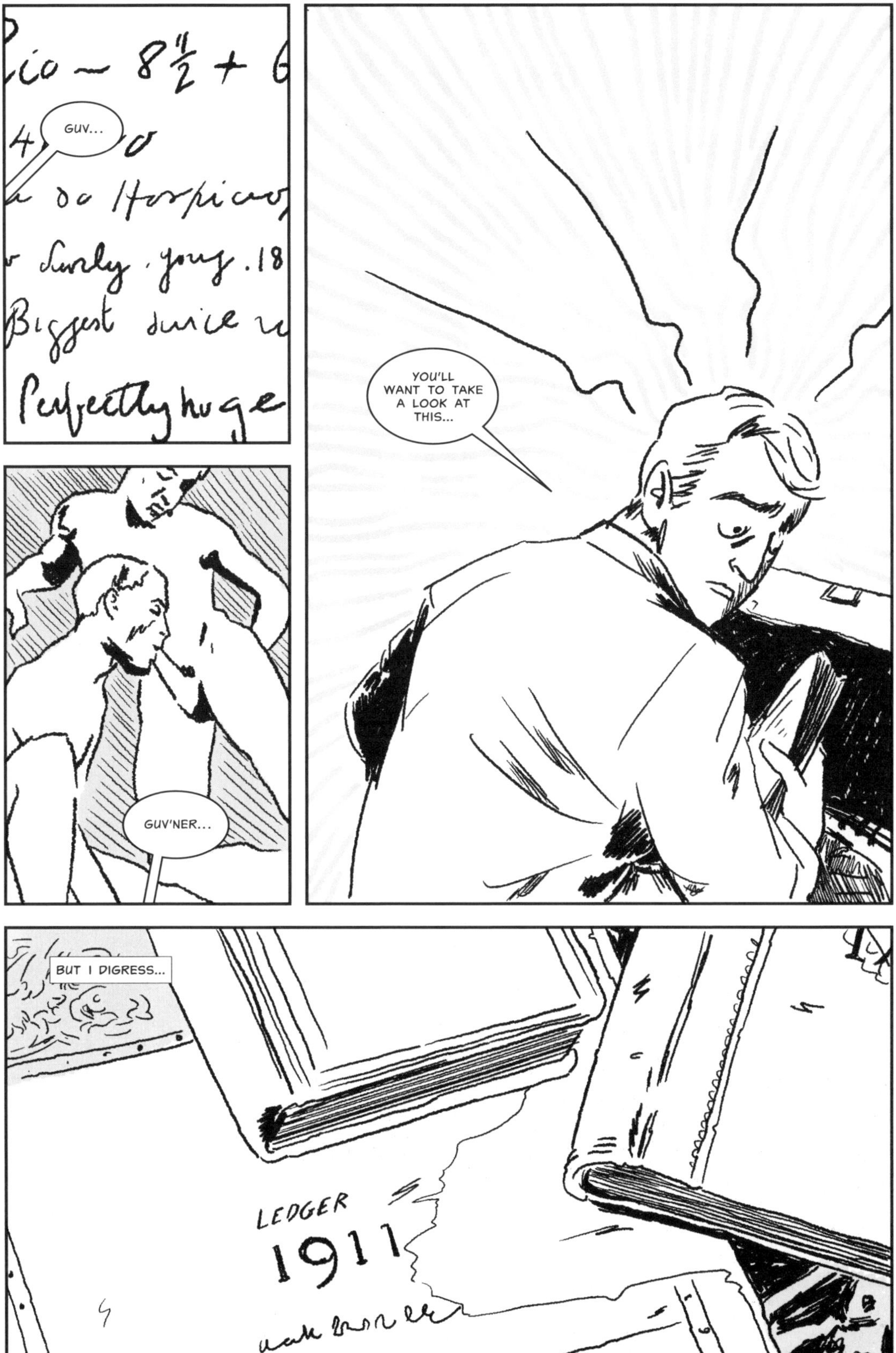

GUV...
Perfectly huge
GUV'NER...
YOU'LL WANT TO TAKE A LOOK AT THIS...
BUT I DIGRESS...
LEDGER
1911

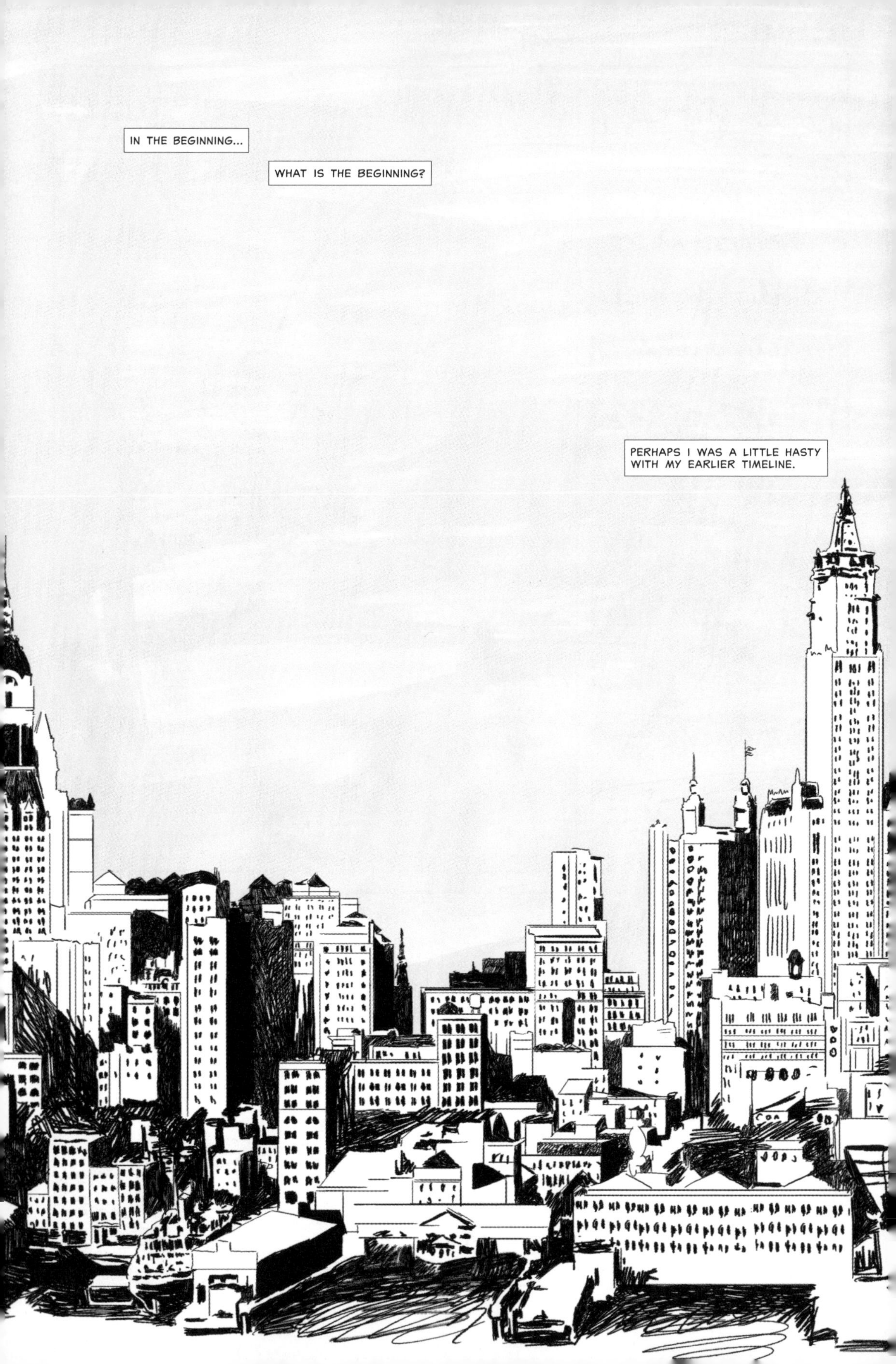
IN THE BEGINNING...
WHAT IS THE BEGINNING?
PERHAPS I WAS A LITTLE HASTY WITH MY EARLIER TIMELINE.

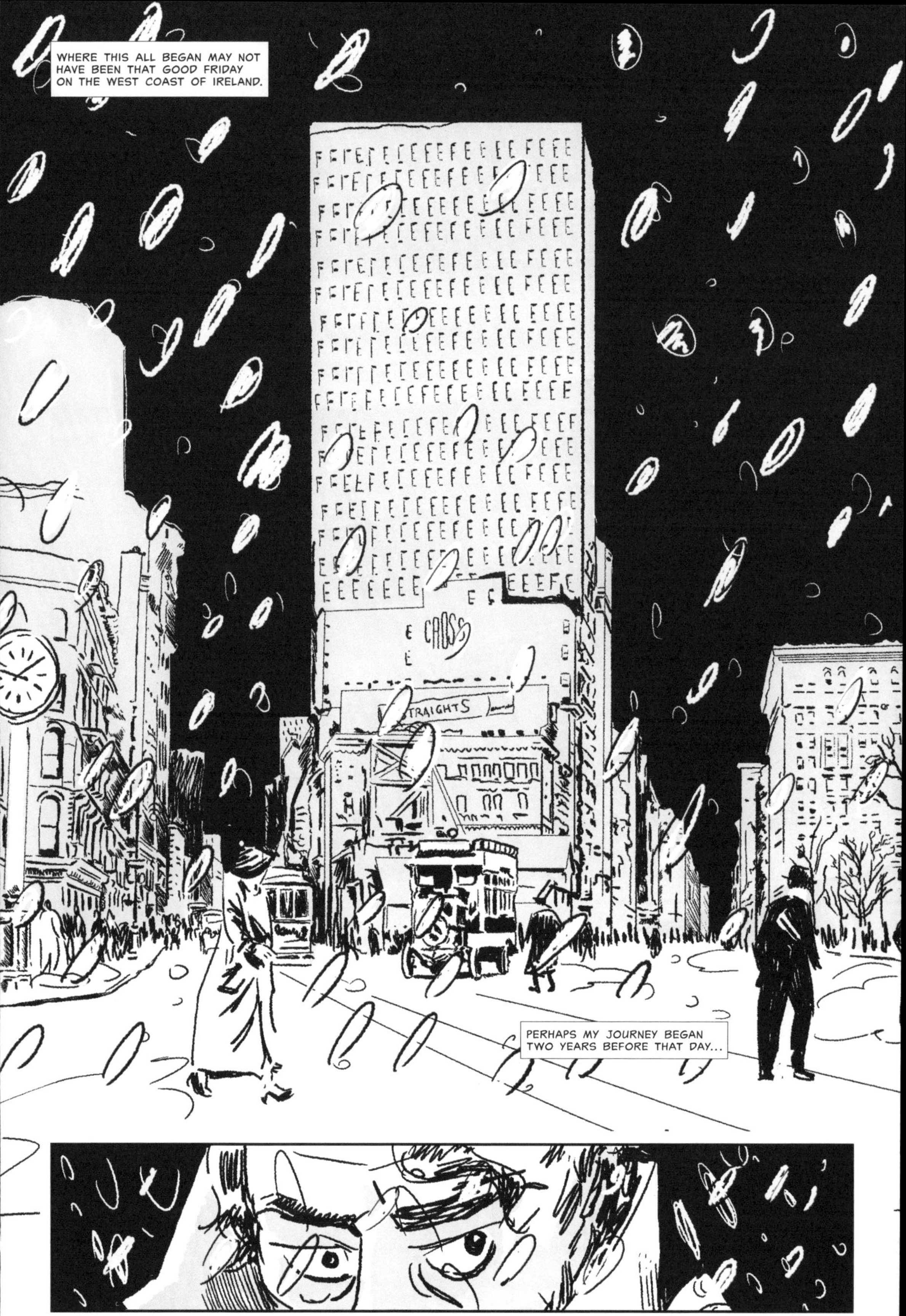
WHERE THIS ALL BEGAN MAY NOT HAVE BEEN THAT GOOD FRIDAY ON THE WEST COAST OF IRELAND.
PERHAPS MY JOURNEY BEGAN TWO YEARS BEFORE THAT DAY...

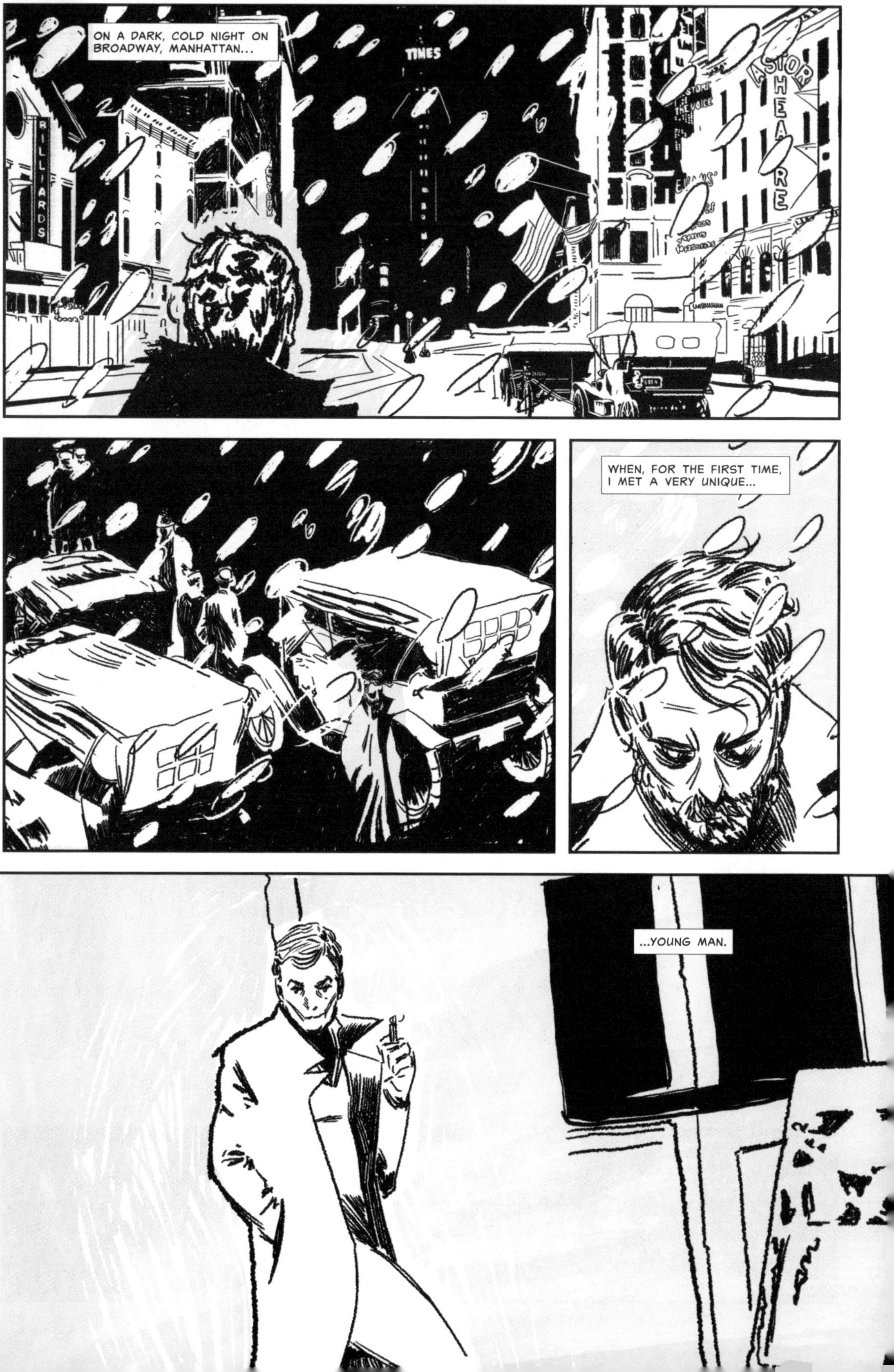

ON A DARK, COLD NIGHT ON BROADWAY, MANHATTAN...
TIMES
BILLIARDS
ASTOR
WHEN, FOR THE FIRST TIME, I MET A VERY UNIQUE...
...YOUNG MAN.

FOREIGN AND NEW
TO THE CITY...

...ALONE, STRANDED...

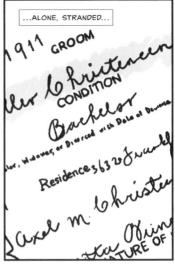

...IN NEED OF HELP.

I'M LOST.

MY REGIMENT SAILED SOME DAYS AGO.
I AM LEFT HERE, ALONE.
AND I AM SO DESPERATELY IN NEED...
...OF YOUR HELP.
PERHAPS I'M A FOOL.

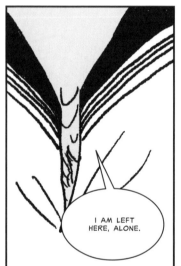

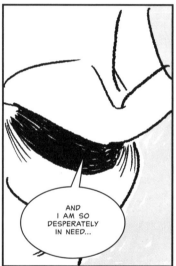

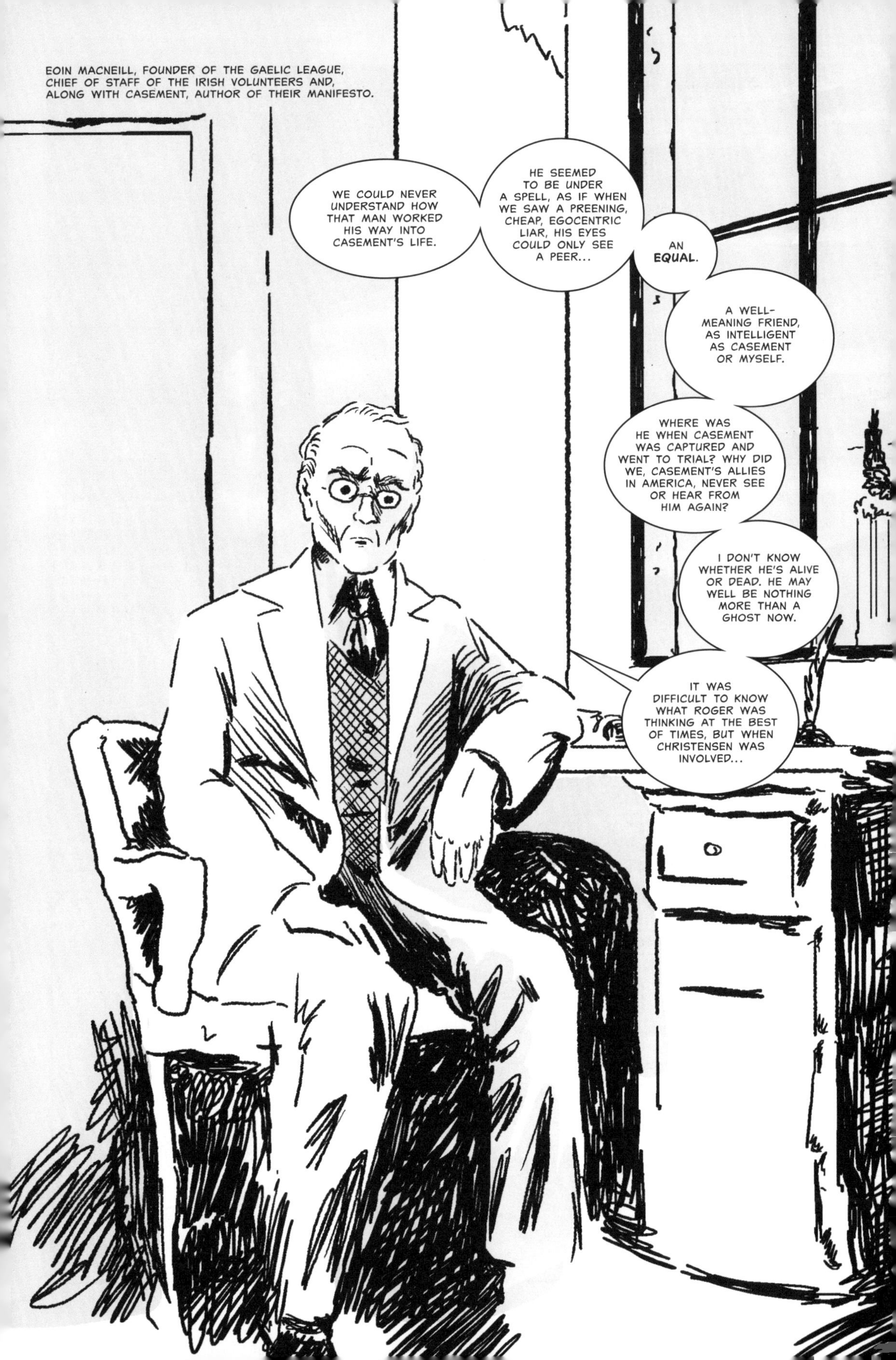
EOIN MACNEILL, FOUNDER OF THE GAELIC LEAGUE, CHIEF OF STAFF OF THE IRISH VOLUNTEERS AND, ALONG WITH CASEMENT, AUTHOR OF THEIR MANIFESTO.
WE COULD NEVER UNDERSTAND HOW THAT MAN WORKED HIS WAY INTO CASEMENT'S LIFE.
HE SEEMED TO BE UNDER A SPELL, AS IF WHEN WE SAW A PREENING, CHEAP, EGOCENTRIC LIAR, HIS EYES COULD ONLY SEE A PEER...
AN **EQUAL**.
A WELL-MEANING FRIEND, AS INTELLIGENT AS CASEMENT OR MYSELF.
WHERE WAS HE WHEN CASEMENT WAS CAPTURED AND WENT TO TRIAL? WHY DID WE, CASEMENT'S ALLIES IN AMERICA, NEVER SEE OR HEAR FROM HIM AGAIN?
I DON'T KNOW WHETHER HE'S ALIVE OR DEAD. HE MAY WELL BE NOTHING MORE THAN A GHOST NOW.
IT WAS DIFFICULT TO KNOW WHAT ROGER WAS THINKING AT THE BEST OF TIMES, BUT WHEN CHRISTENSEN WAS INVOLVED...

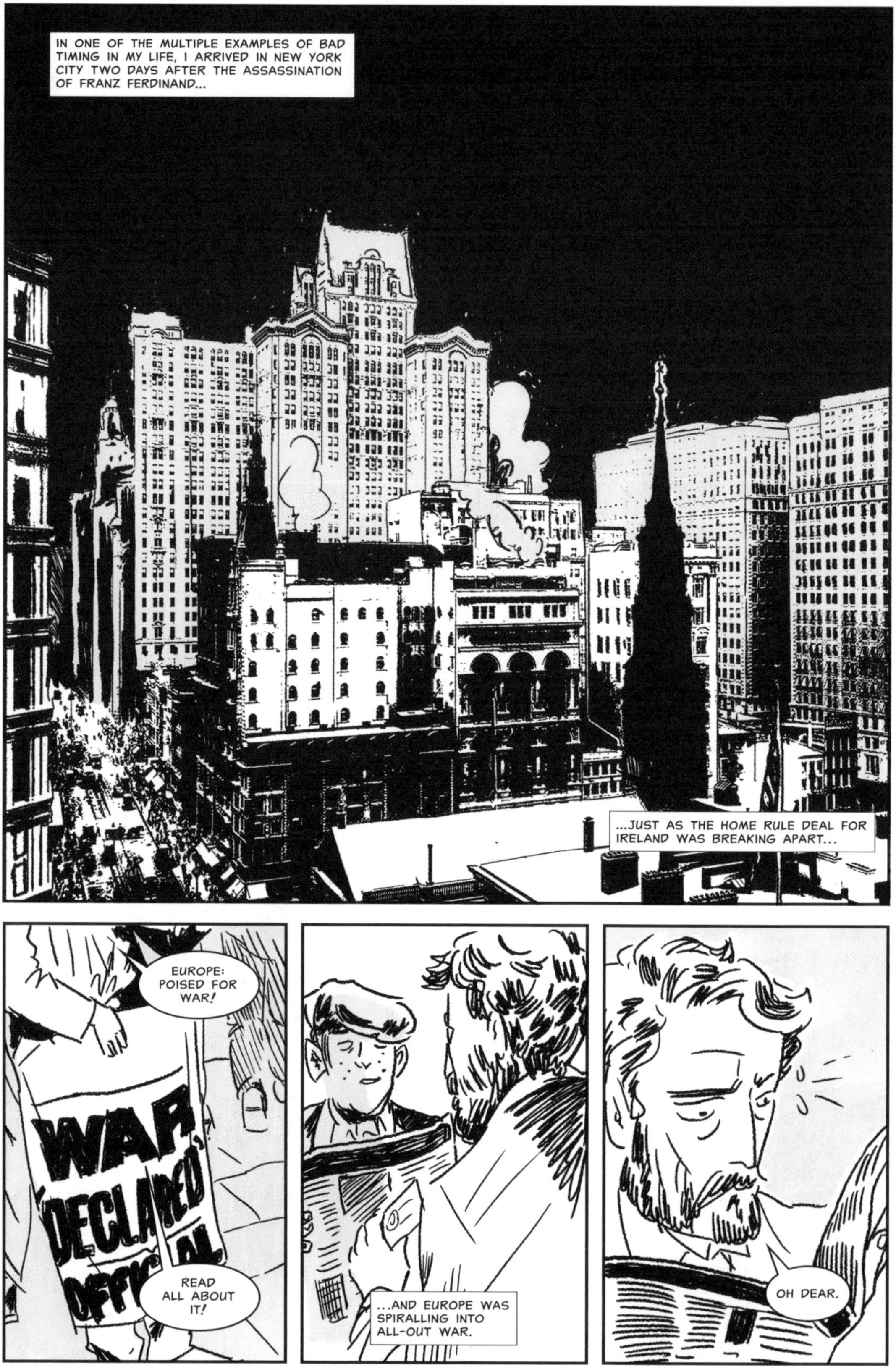
IN ONE OF THE MULTIPLE EXAMPLES OF BAD TIMING IN MY LIFE, I ARRIVED IN NEW YORK CITY TWO DAYS AFTER THE ASSASSINATION OF FRANZ FERDINAND...
...JUST AS THE HOME RULE DEAL FOR IRELAND WAS BREAKING APART...
EUROPE: POISED FOR WAR!
WAR DECLARED
READ ALL ABOUT IT!
...AND EUROPE WAS SPIRALLING INTO ALL-OUT WAR.
OH DEAR.

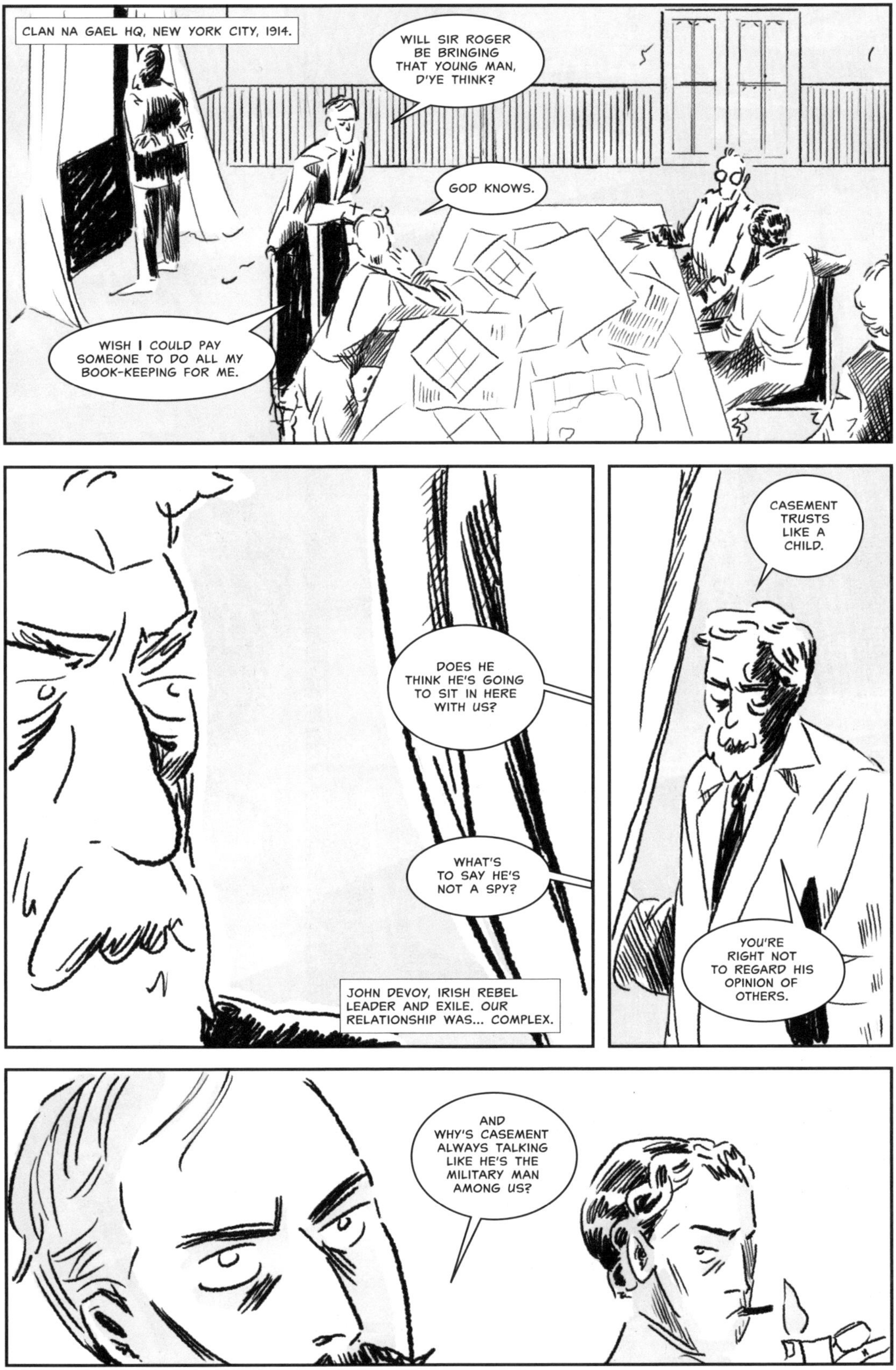
CLAN NA GAEL HQ, NEW YORK CITY, 1914.
WILL SIR ROGER BE BRINGING THAT YOUNG MAN, D'YE THINK?
GOD KNOWS.
WISH I COULD PAY SOMEONE TO DO ALL MY BOOK-KEEPING FOR ME.
DOES HE THINK HE'S GOING TO SIT IN HERE WITH US?
WHAT'S TO SAY HE'S NOT A SPY?
JOHN DEVOY, IRISH REBEL LEADER AND EXILE. OUR RELATIONSHIP WAS... COMPLEX.
CASEMENT TRUSTS LIKE A CHILD.
YOU'RE RIGHT NOT TO REGARD HIS OPINION OF OTHERS.
AND WHY'S CASEMENT ALWAYS TALKING LIKE HE'S THE MILITARY MAN AMONG US?

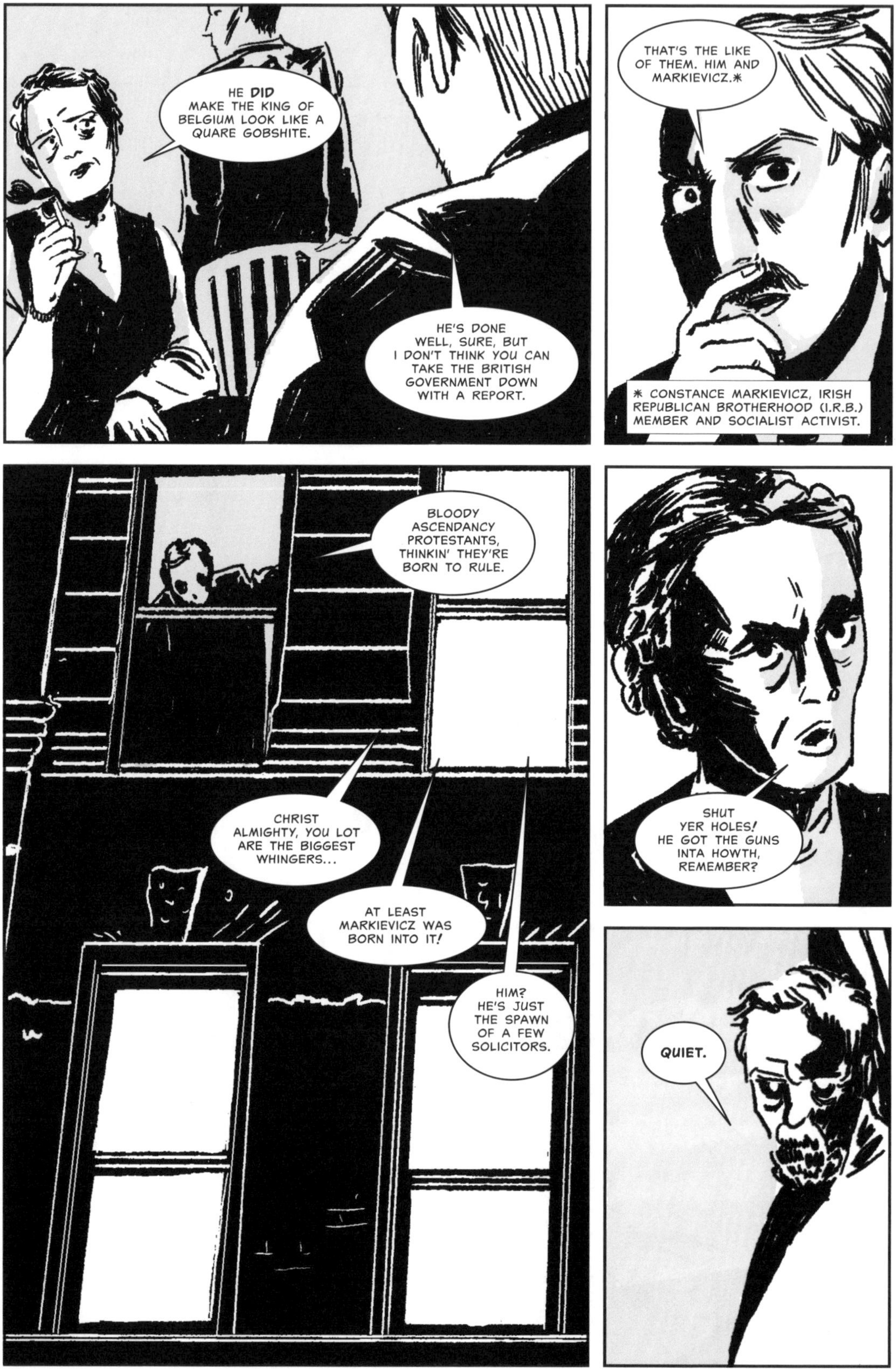
HE DID MAKE THE KING OF BELGIUM LOOK LIKE A QUARE GOBSHITE.
HE'S DONE WELL, SURE, BUT I DON'T THINK YOU CAN TAKE THE BRITISH GOVERNMENT DOWN WITH A REPORT.
THAT'S THE LIKE OF THEM. HIM AND MARKIEVICZ.*
* CONSTANCE MARKIEVICZ, IRISH REPUBLICAN BROTHERHOOD (I.R.B.) MEMBER AND SOCIALIST ACTIVIST.
BLOODY ASCENDANCY PROTESTANTS, THINKIN' THEY'RE BORN TO RULE.
CHRIST ALMIGHTY, YOU LOT ARE THE BIGGEST WHINGERS...
AT LEAST MARKIEVICZ WAS BORN INTO IT!
HIM? HE'S JUST THE SPAWN OF A FEW SOLICITORS.
SHUT YER HOLES! HE GOT THE GUNS INTA HOWTH, REMEMBER?
QUIET.

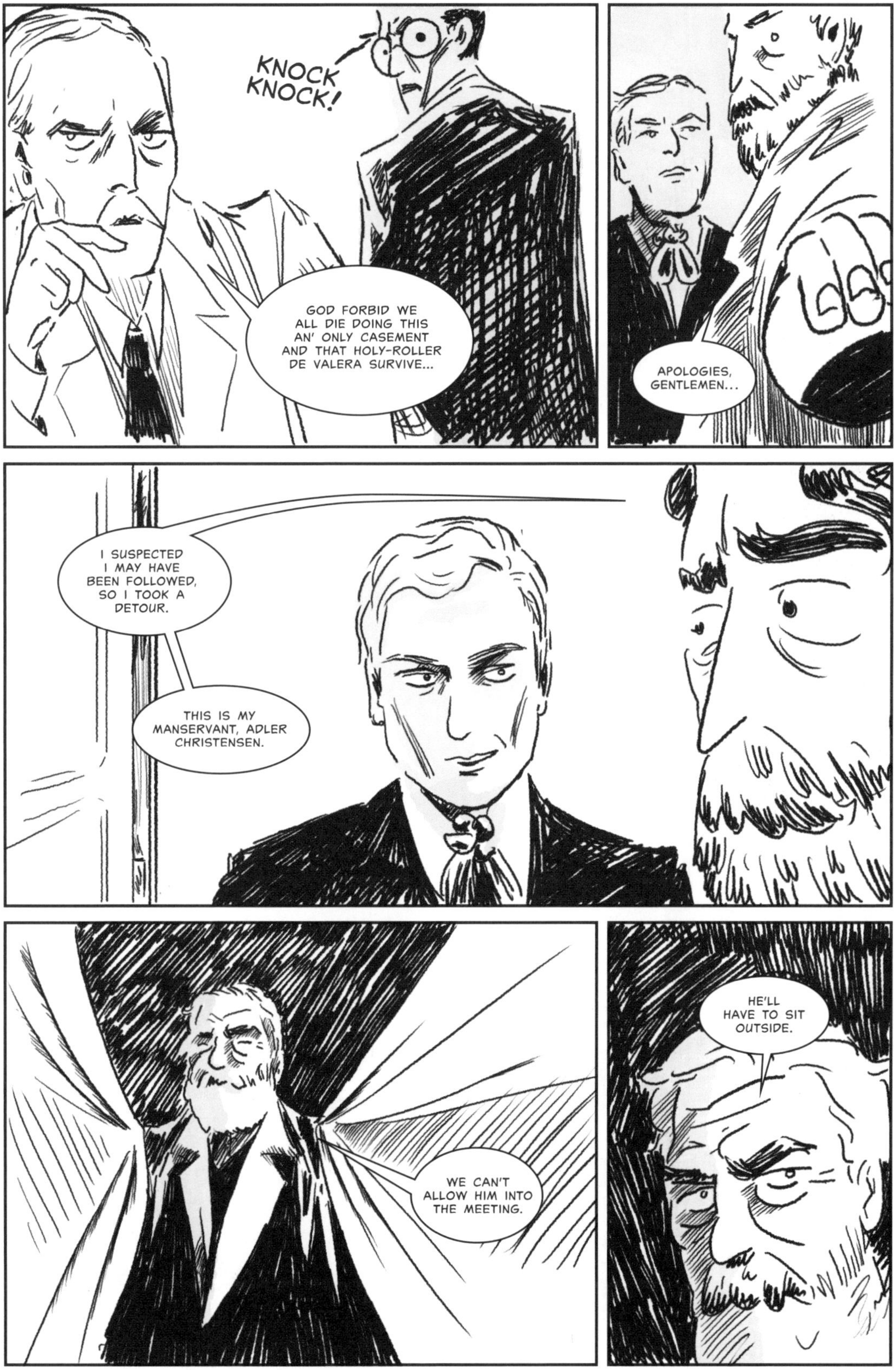
KNOCK KNOCK!
GOD FORBID WE ALL DIE DOING THIS AN' ONLY CASEMENT AND THAT HOLY-ROLLER DE VALERA SURVIVE...
APOLOGIES, GENTLEMEN...
I SUSPECTED I MAY HAVE BEEN FOLLOWED, SO I TOOK A DETOUR.
THIS IS MY MANSERVANT, ADLER CHRISTENSEN.
WE CAN'T ALLOW HIM INTO THE MEETING.
HE'LL HAVE TO SIT OUTSIDE.

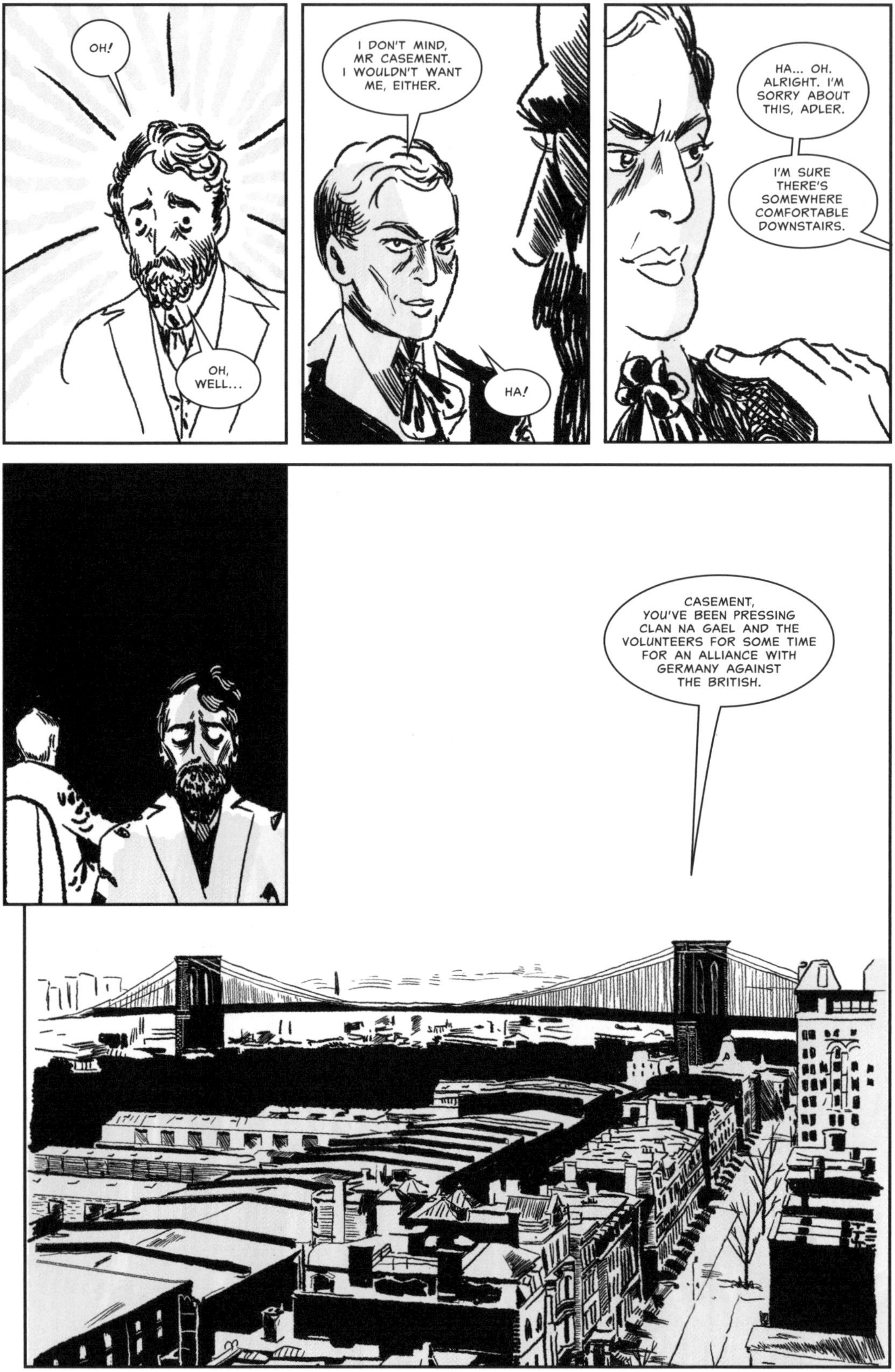
OH!
OH, WELL...
I DON'T MIND, MR CASEMENT. I WOULDN'T WANT ME, EITHER.
HA!
HA... OH. ALRIGHT. I'M SORRY ABOUT THIS, ADLER.
I'M SURE THERE'S SOMEWHERE COMFORTABLE DOWNSTAIRS.
CASEMENT, YOU'VE BEEN PRESSING CLAN NA GAEL AND THE VOLUNTEERS FOR SOME TIME FOR AN ALLIANCE WITH GERMANY AGAINST THE BRITISH.

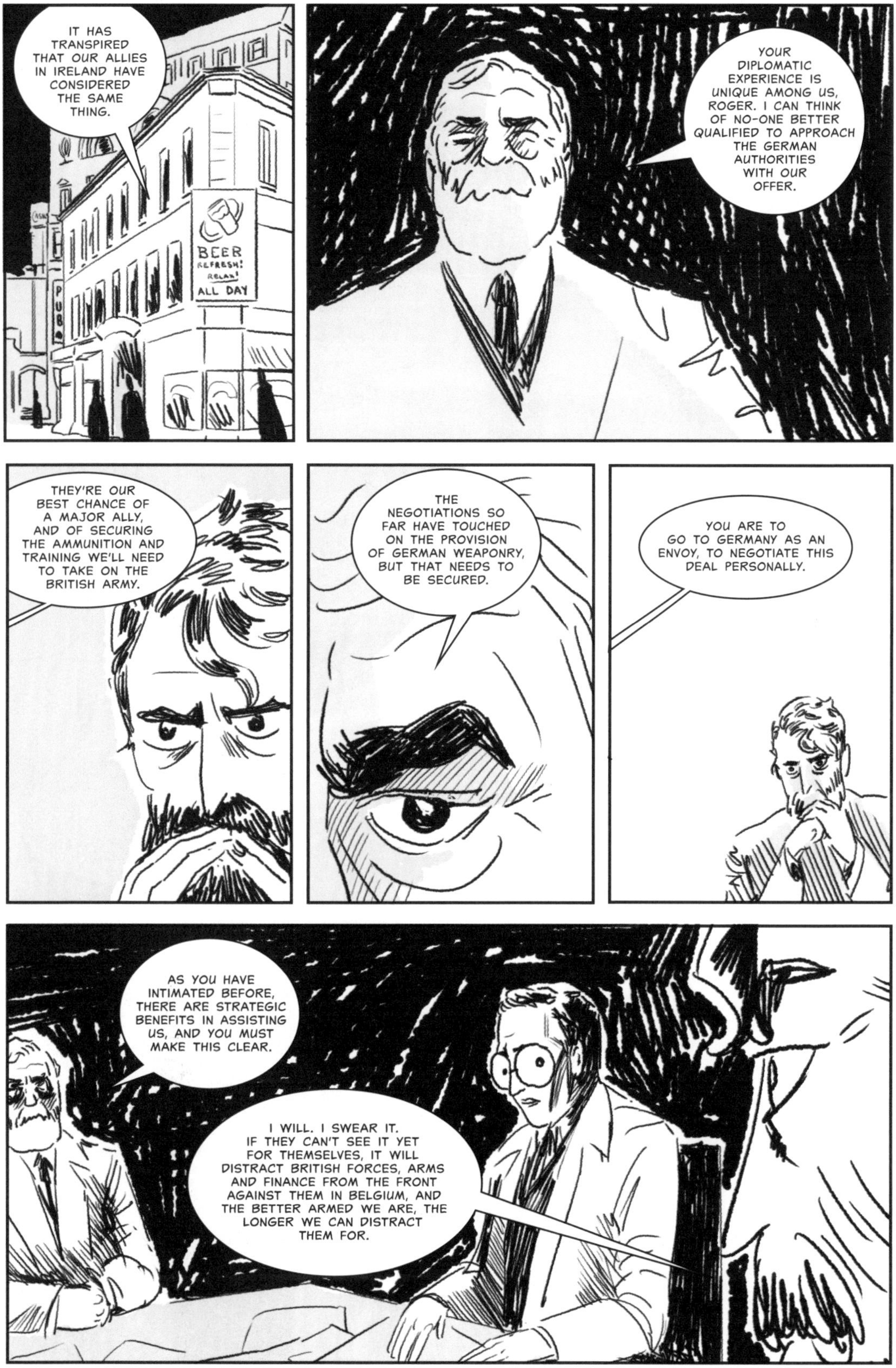
IT HAS TRANSPIRED THAT OUR ALLIES IN IRELAND HAVE CONSIDERED THE SAME THING.
BEER
REFRESH! RELAX!
ALL DAY
PUB
YOUR DIPLOMATIC EXPERIENCE IS UNIQUE AMONG US, ROGER. I CAN THINK OF NO-ONE BETTER QUALIFIED TO APPROACH THE GERMAN AUTHORITIES WITH OUR OFFER.
THEY'RE OUR BEST CHANCE OF A MAJOR ALLY, AND OF SECURING THE AMMUNITION AND TRAINING WE'LL NEED TO TAKE ON THE BRITISH ARMY.
THE NEGOTIATIONS SO FAR HAVE TOUCHED ON THE PROVISION OF GERMAN WEAPONRY, BUT THAT NEEDS TO BE SECURED.
YOU ARE TO GO TO GERMANY AS AN ENVOY, TO NEGOTIATE THIS DEAL PERSONALLY.
AS YOU HAVE INTIMATED BEFORE, THERE ARE STRATEGIC BENEFITS IN ASSISTING US, AND YOU MUST MAKE THIS CLEAR.
I WILL. I SWEAR IT. IF THEY CAN'T SEE IT YET FOR THEMSELVES, IT WILL DISTRACT BRITISH FORCES, ARMS AND FINANCE FROM THE FRONT AGAINST THEM IN BELGIUM, AND THE BETTER ARMED WE ARE, THE LONGER WE CAN DISTRACT THEM FOR.

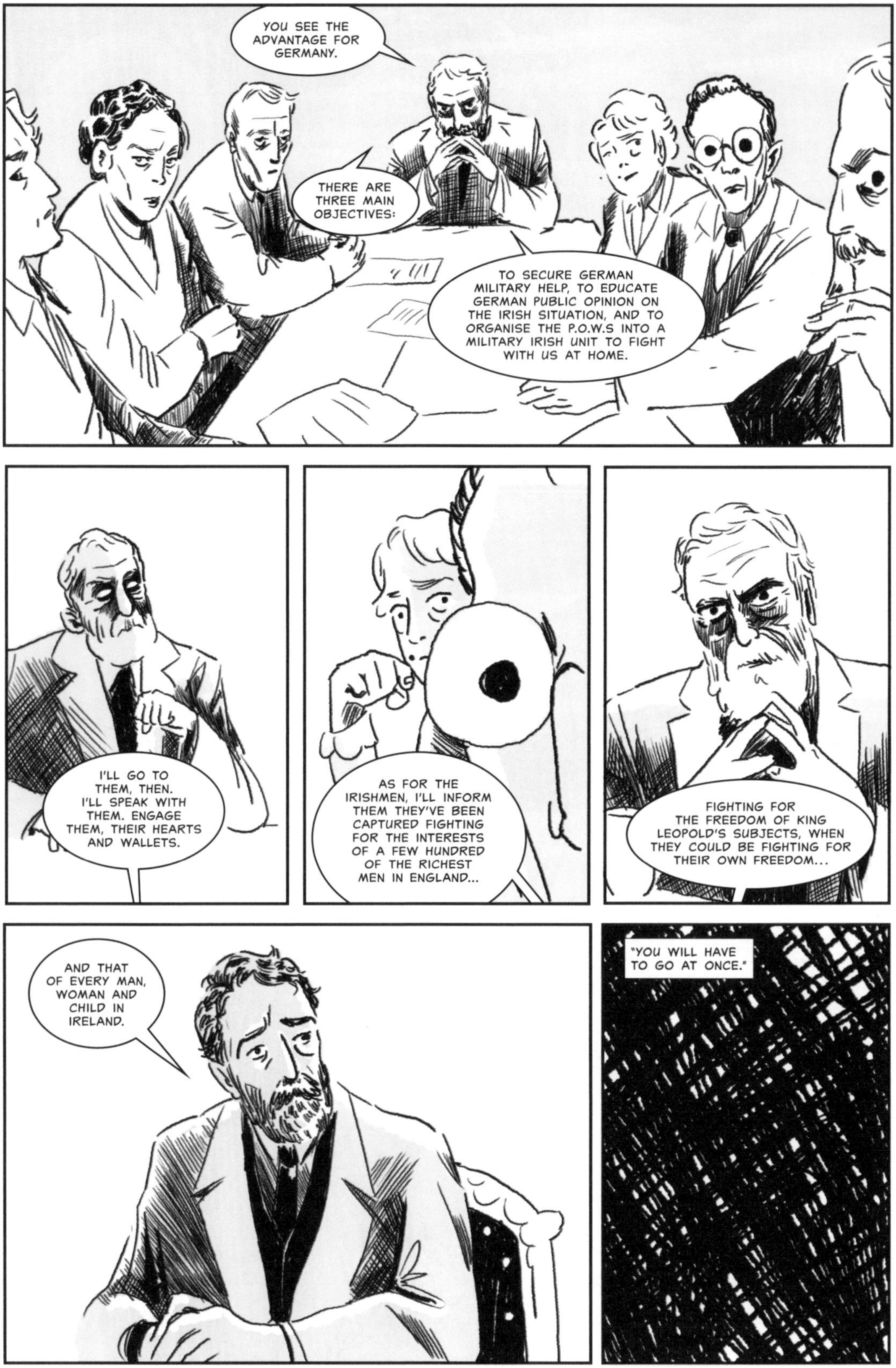

YOU SEE THE ADVANTAGE FOR GERMANY.
THERE ARE THREE MAIN OBJECTIVES:
TO SECURE GERMAN MILITARY HELP, TO EDUCATE GERMAN PUBLIC OPINION ON THE IRISH SITUATION, AND TO ORGANISE THE P.O.W.S INTO A MILITARY IRISH UNIT TO FIGHT WITH US AT HOME.
I'LL GO TO THEM, THEN. I'LL SPEAK WITH THEM. ENGAGE THEM, THEIR HEARTS AND WALLETS.
AS FOR THE IRISHMEN, I'LL INFORM THEM THEY'VE BEEN CAPTURED FIGHTING FOR THE INTERESTS OF A FEW HUNDRED OF THE RICHEST MEN IN ENGLAND...
FIGHTING FOR THE FREEDOM OF KING LEOPOLD'S SUBJECTS, WHEN THEY COULD BE FIGHTING FOR THEIR OWN FREEDOM...
AND THAT OF EVERY MAN, WOMAN AND CHILD IN IRELAND.
"YOU WILL HAVE TO GO AT ONCE."

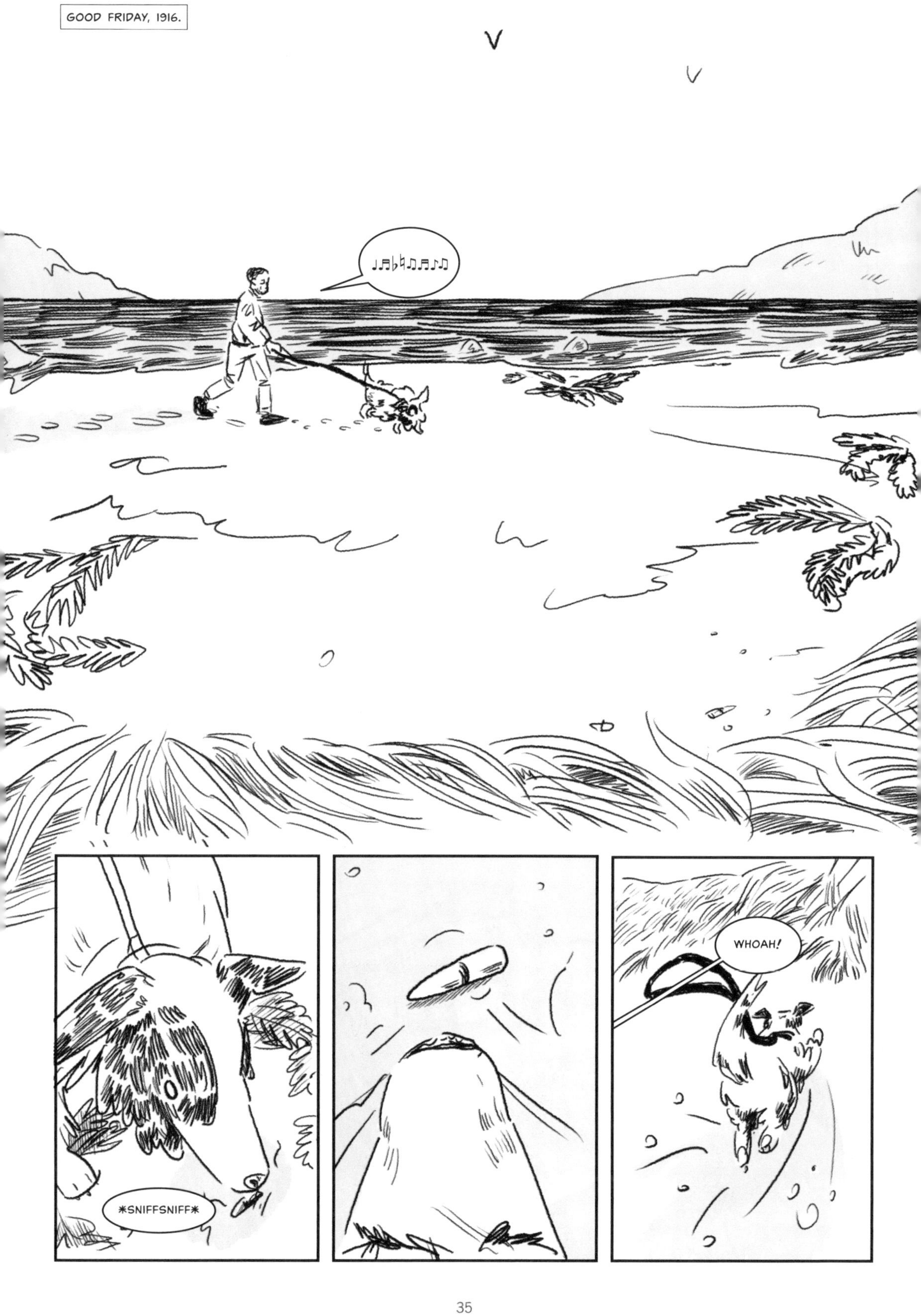
GOOD FRIDAY, 1916.
SNIFFSNIFF
WHOAH!

COME BACK, YOU!
WHAT THE HELL ARE YE DOING?
RUF?
?

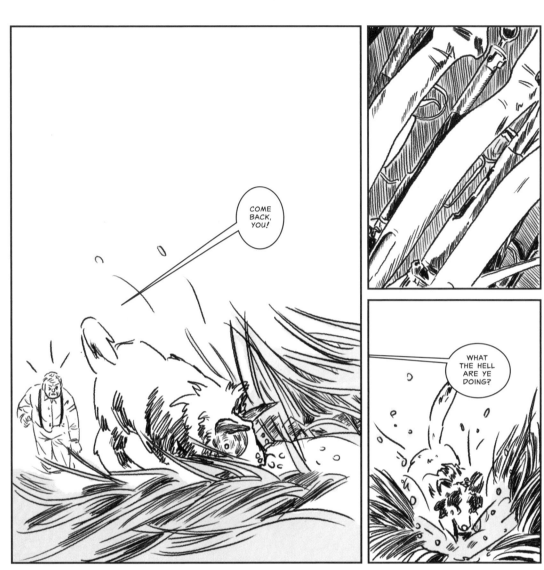

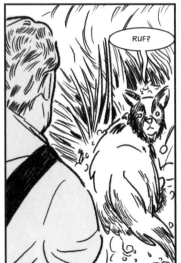

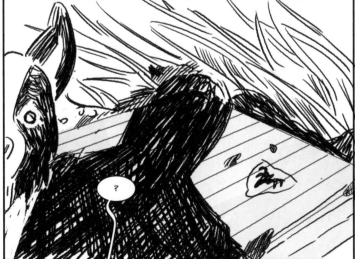

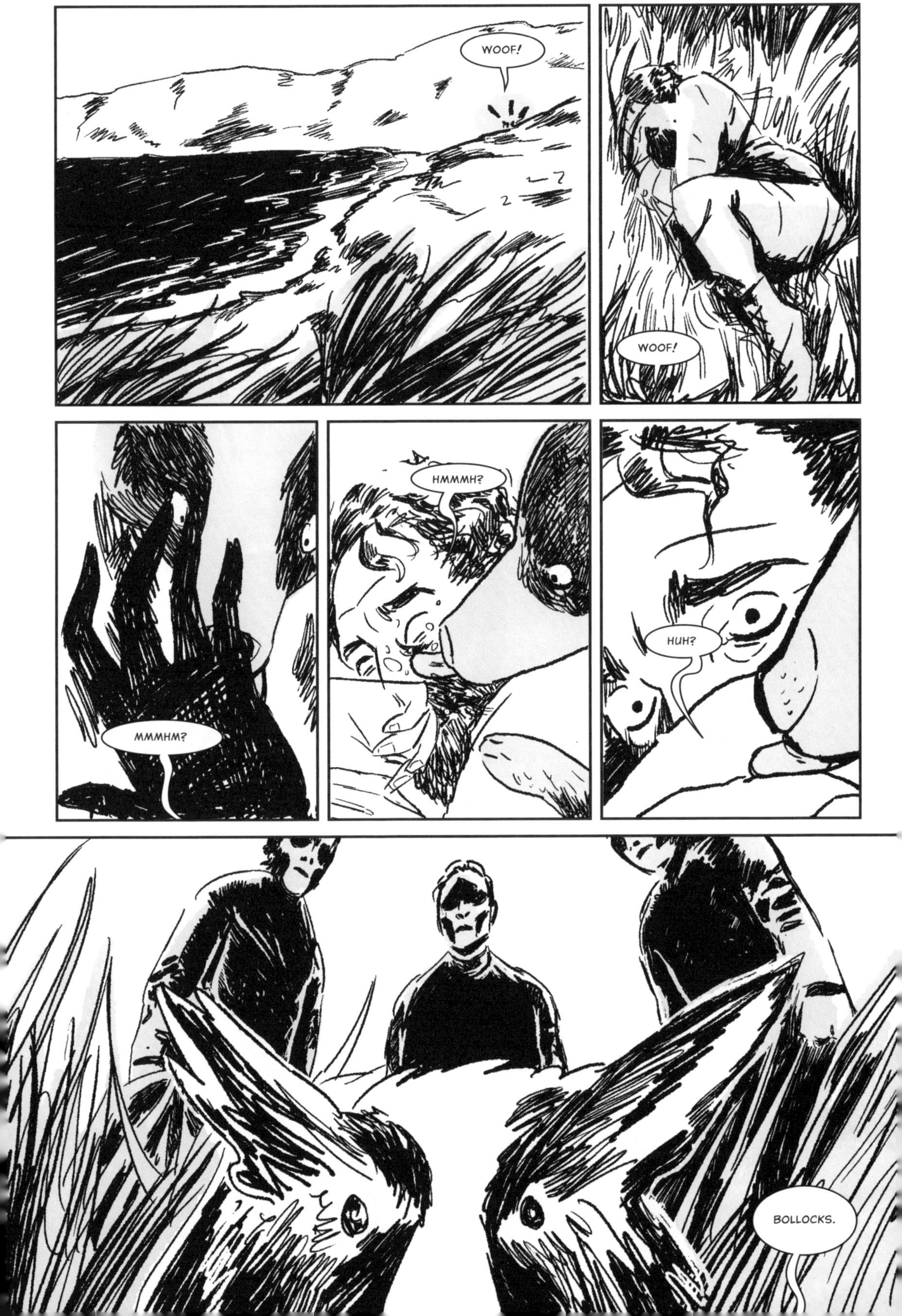
WOOF!
WOOF!
MMMHM?
HMMMH?
HUH?
BOLLOCKS.

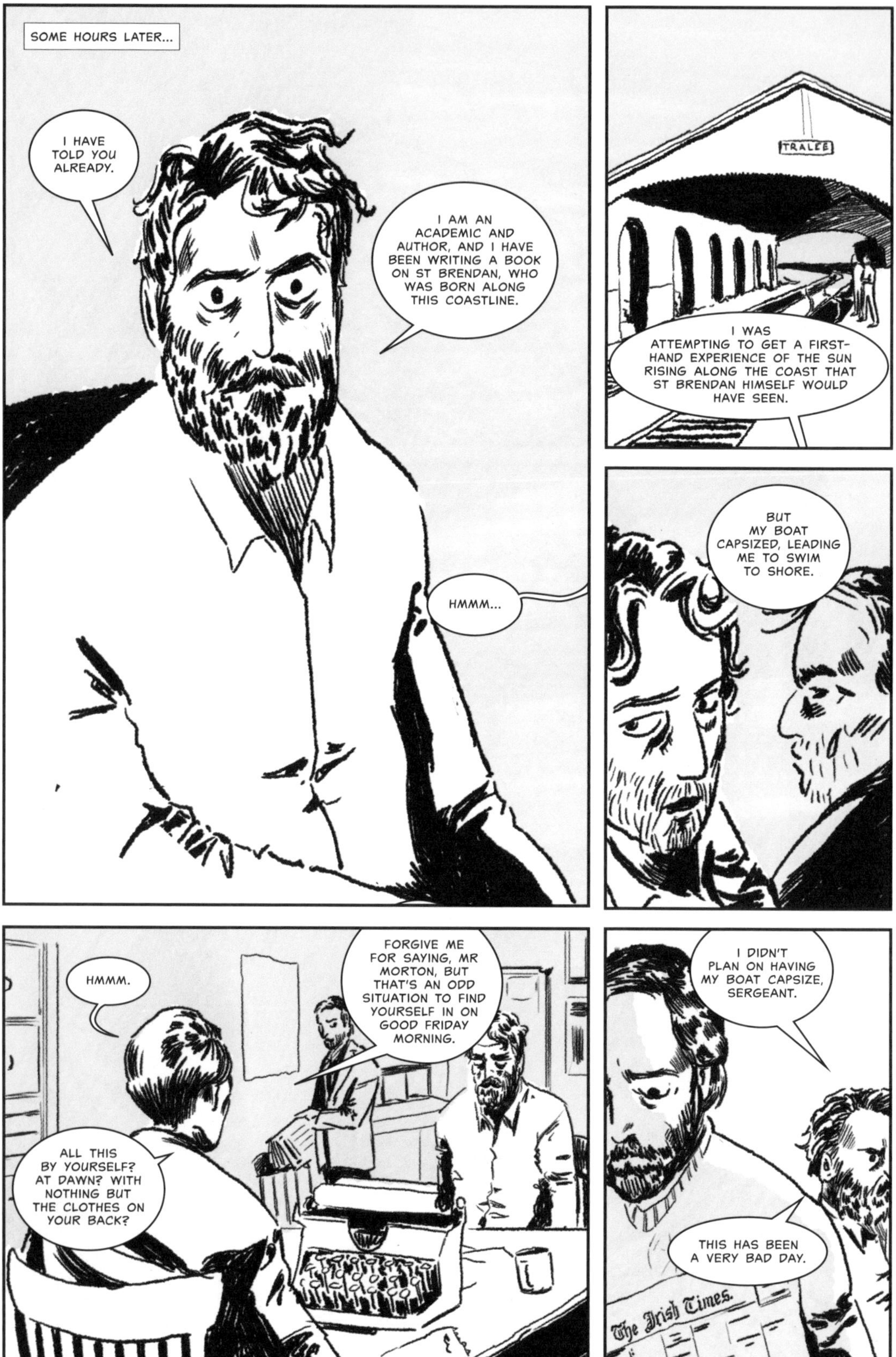
SOME HOURS LATER...
I HAVE TOLD YOU ALREADY.
I AM AN ACADEMIC AND AUTHOR, AND I HAVE BEEN WRITING A BOOK ON ST BRENDAN, WHO WAS BORN ALONG THIS COASTLINE.
HMMM...
TRALEE
I WAS ATTEMPTING TO GET A FIRST-HAND EXPERIENCE OF THE SUN RISING ALONG THE COAST THAT ST BRENDAN HIMSELF WOULD HAVE SEEN.
BUT MY BOAT CAPSIZED, LEADING ME TO SWIM TO SHORE.
HMMM.
FORGIVE ME FOR SAYING, MR MORTON, BUT THAT'S AN ODD SITUATION TO FIND YOURSELF IN ON GOOD FRIDAY MORNING.
ALL THIS BY YOURSELF? AT DAWN? WITH NOTHING BUT THE CLOTHES ON YOUR BACK?
I DIDN'T PLAN ON HAVING MY BOAT CAPSIZE, SERGEANT.
THIS HAS BEEN A VERY BAD DAY.
The Irish Times.

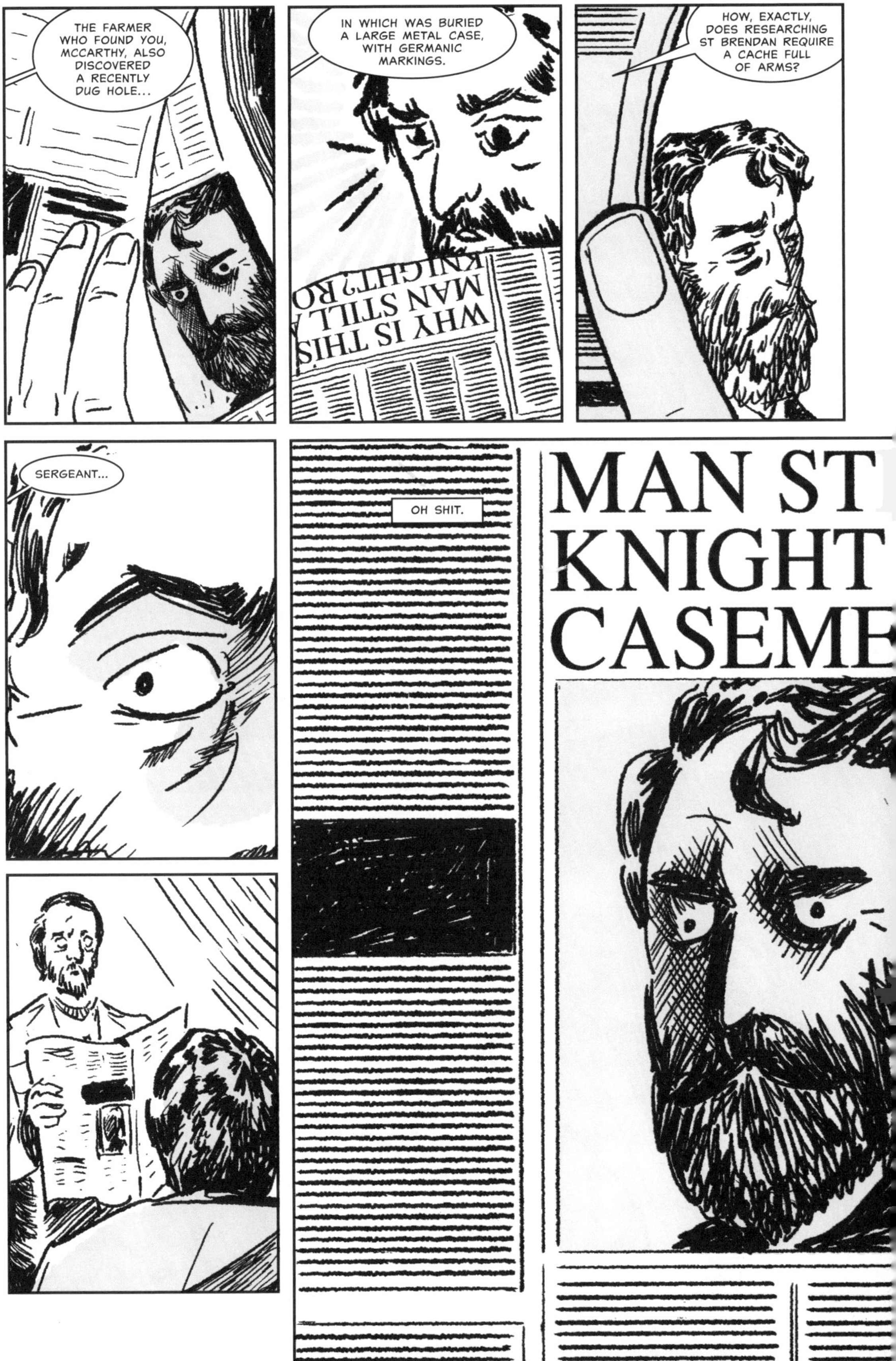
THE FARMER WHO FOUND YOU, MCCARTHY, ALSO DISCOVERED A RECENTLY DUG HOLE...
IN WHICH WAS BURIED A LARGE METAL CASE, WITH GERMANIC MARKINGS.
HOW, EXACTLY, DOES RESEARCHING ST BRENDAN REQUIRE A CACHE FULL OF ARMS?
SERGEANT...
OH SHIT.
KNIGHT

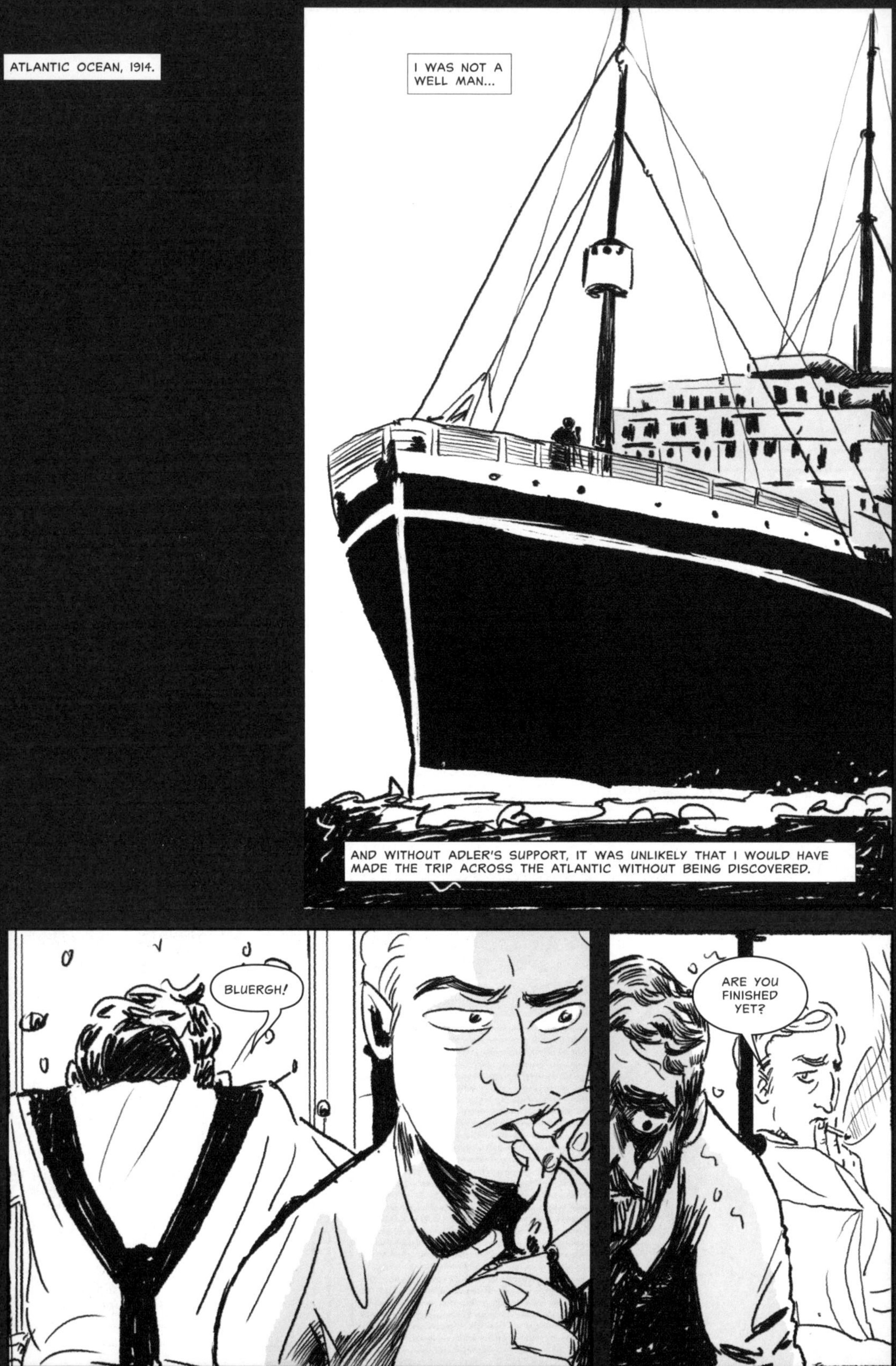

ATLANTIC OCEAN, 1914.
I WAS NOT A WELL MAN...
AND WITHOUT ADLER'S SUPPORT, IT WAS UNLIKELY THAT I WOULD HAVE MADE THE TRIP ACROSS THE ATLANTIC WITHOUT BEING DISCOVERED.
BLUERGH!
ARE YOU FINISHED YET?

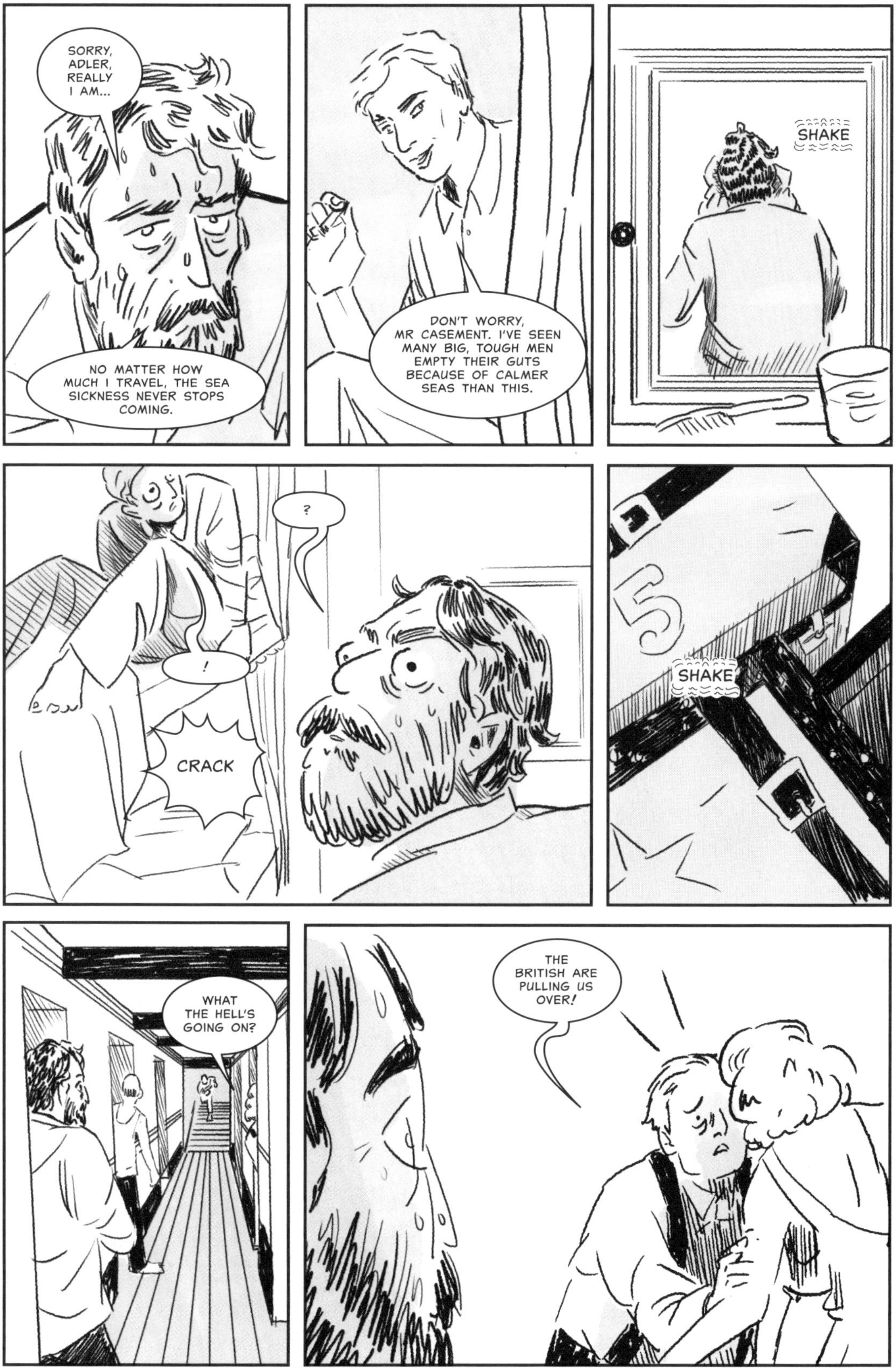
SORRY, ADLER, REALLY I AM...
NO MATTER HOW MUCH I TRAVEL, THE SEA SICKNESS NEVER STOPS COMING.
DON'T WORRY, MR CASEMENT. I'VE SEEN MANY BIG, TOUGH MEN EMPTY THEIR GUTS BECAUSE OF CALMER SEAS THAN THIS.
SHAKE
?
!
CRACK
SHAKE
WHAT THE HELL'S GOING ON?
THE BRITISH ARE PULLING US OVER!

...epublican Brotherho...

German Ambassador t...

United States of Ameri...

...ed plan for our action...

s,

...ernment has bee...

...ur two amb...

...cement

...ainst the British e...

...yranny inflicted up...

...xchange of weapons...

...ained men, prepare...

...rike at heart of Brit...

...ublin, and at strateg...

...ross island.

...ucial to the suc...

...tual interest...

Casement

WE'VE GOT INSTRUCTIONS TO SEARCH EVERYONE ON BOARD.

A LOOK AT YOUR PASSENGER MANIFEST, PLEASE.

CHUCK IT OVERBOARD!

I'M NOT GETTING CAUGHT SMUGGLING **YOUR** CRAP!

HIDE IT!

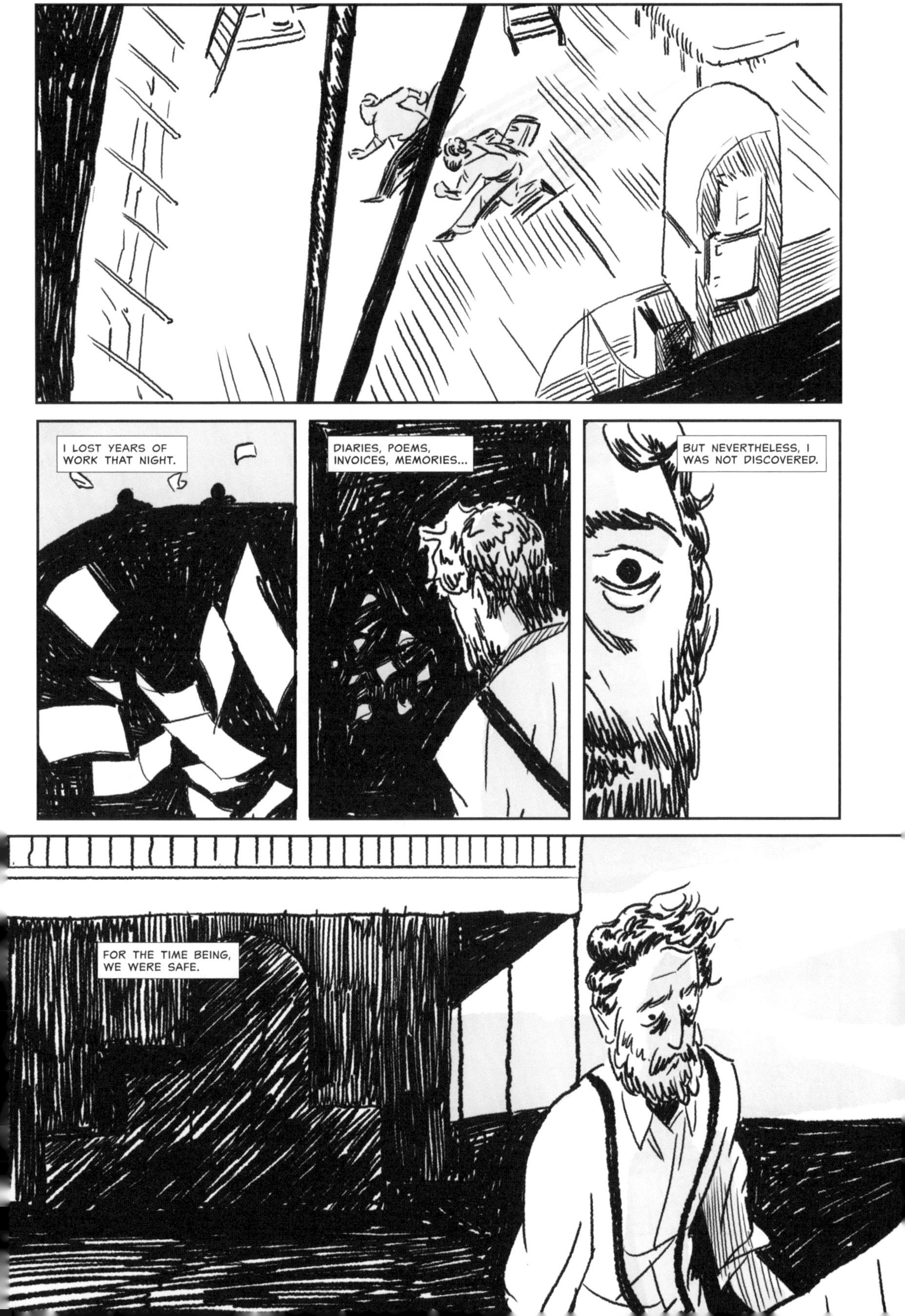
I LOST YEARS OF WORK THAT NIGHT.
DIARIES, POEMS, INVOICES, MEMORIES...
BUT NEVERTHELESS, I WAS NOT DISCOVERED.
FOR THE TIME BEING, WE WERE SAFE.

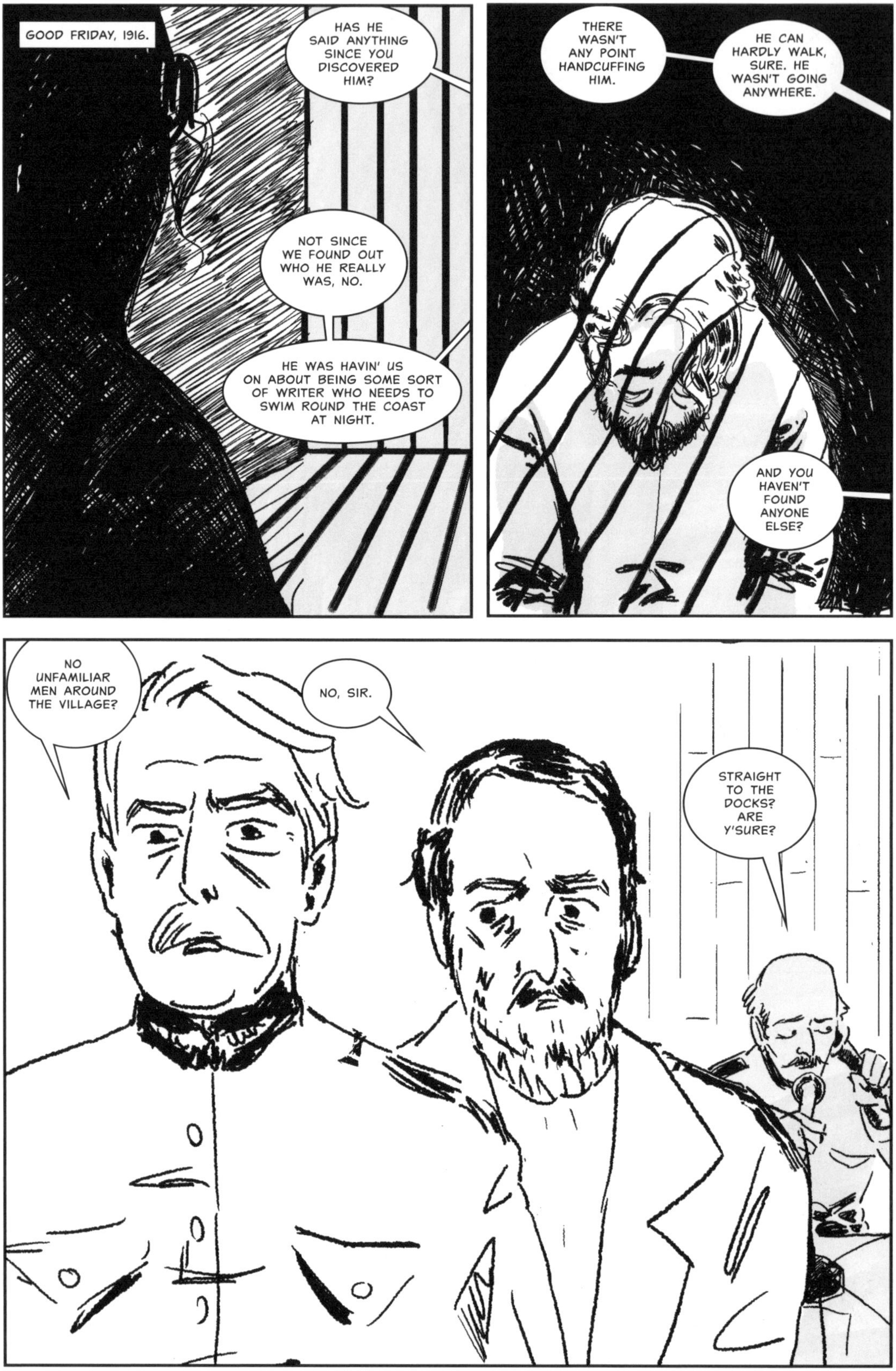
GOOD FRIDAY, 1916.
HAS HE SAID ANYTHING SINCE YOU DISCOVERED HIM?
NOT SINCE WE FOUND OUT WHO HE REALLY WAS, NO.
HE WAS HAVIN' US ON ABOUT BEING SOME SORT OF WRITER WHO NEEDS TO SWIM ROUND THE COAST AT NIGHT.
THERE WASN'T ANY POINT HANDCUFFING HIM.
HE CAN HARDLY WALK, SURE. HE WASN'T GOING ANYWHERE.
AND YOU HAVEN'T FOUND ANYONE ELSE?
NO UNFAMILIAR MEN AROUND THE VILLAGE?
NO, SIR.
STRAIGHT TO THE DOCKS? ARE Y'SURE?

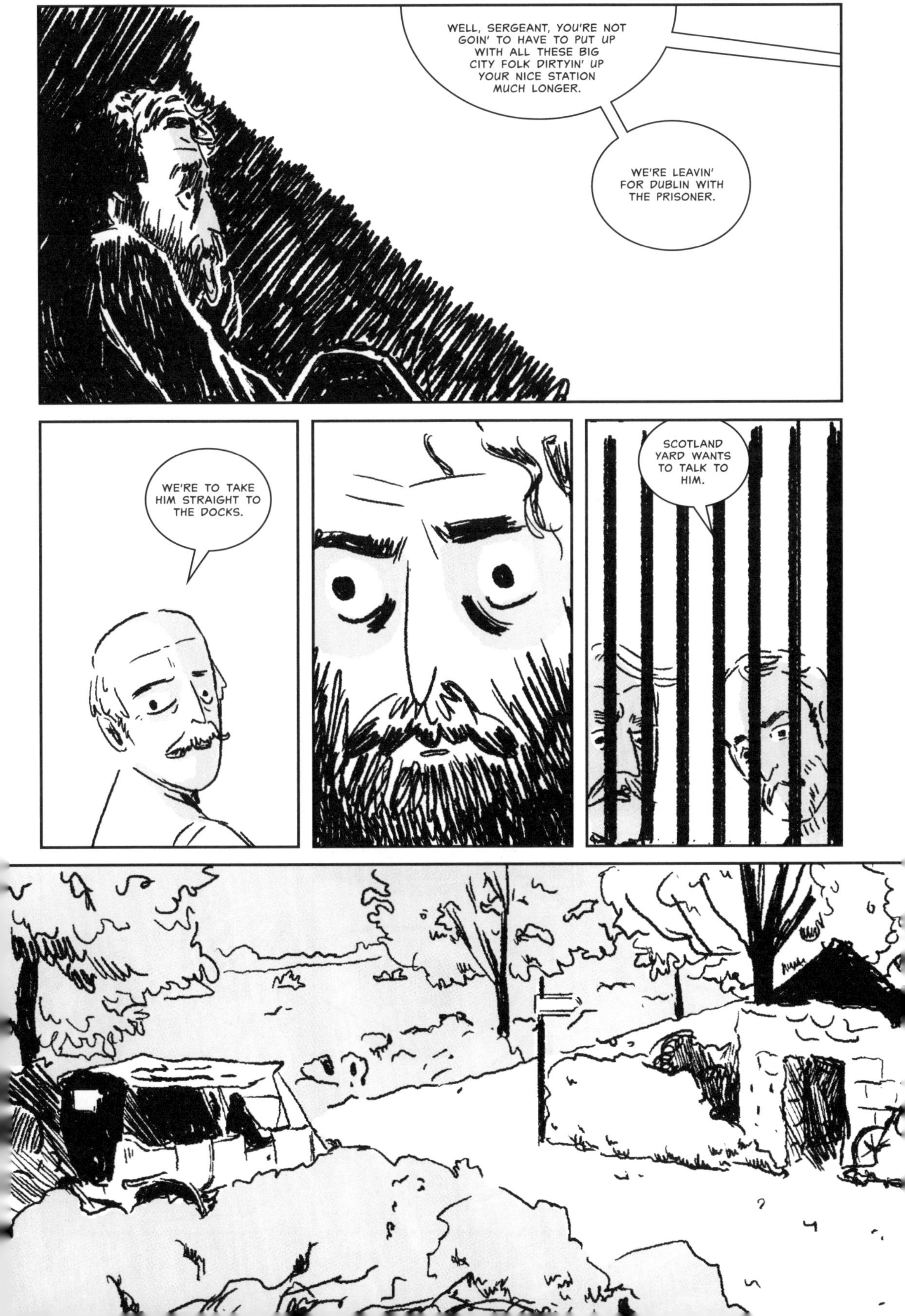
WELL, SERGEANT, YOU'RE NOT GOIN' TO HAVE TO PUT UP WITH ALL THESE BIG CITY FOLK DIRTYIN' UP YOUR NICE STATION MUCH LONGER.
WE'RE LEAVIN' FOR DUBLIN WITH THE PRISONER.
WE'RE TO TAKE HIM STRAIGHT TO THE DOCKS.
SCOTLAND YARD WANTS TO TALK TO HIM.

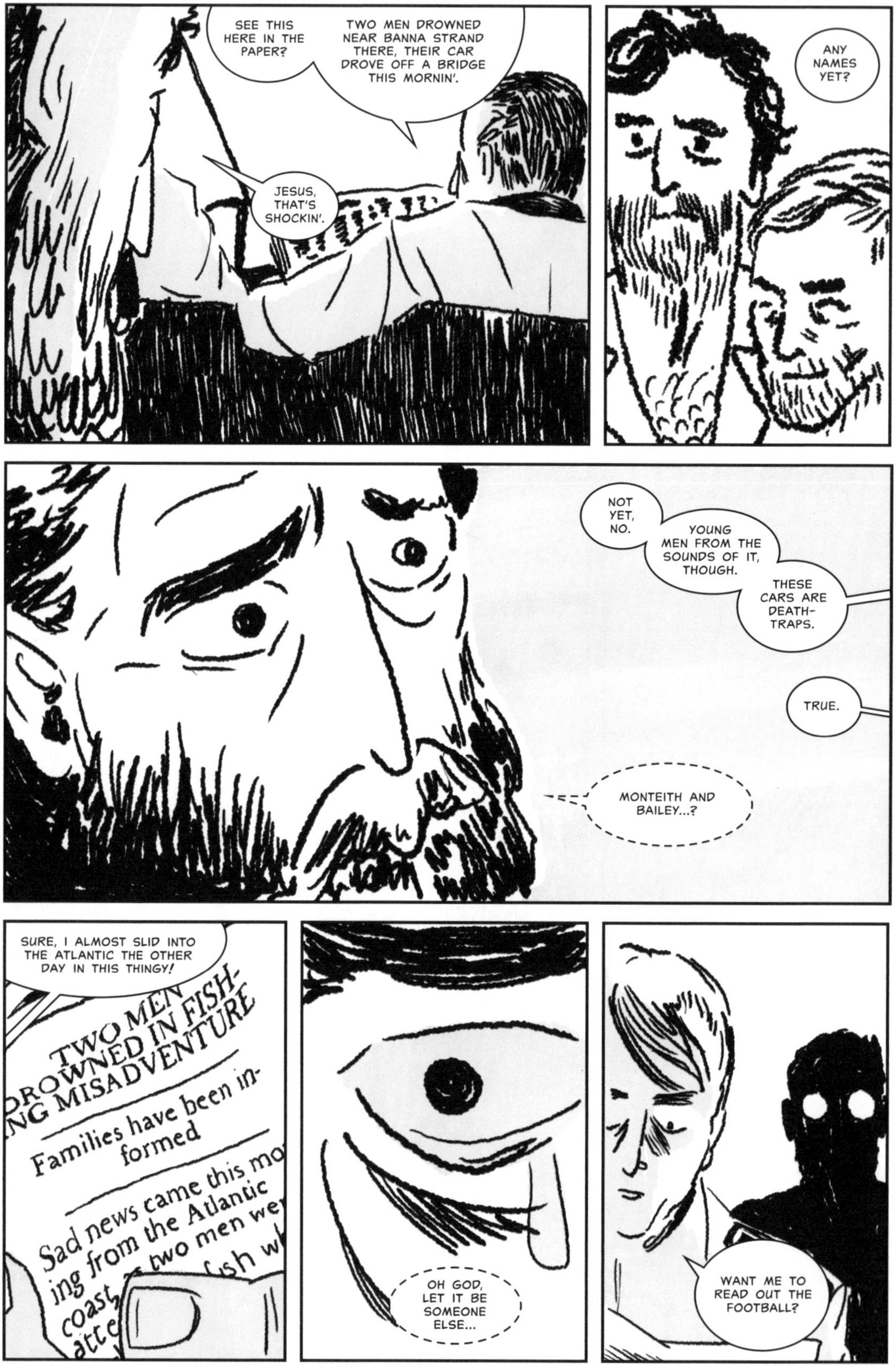
SEE THIS HERE IN THE PAPER?
TWO MEN DROWNED NEAR BANNA STRAND THERE, THEIR CAR DROVE OFF A BRIDGE THIS MORNIN'.
JESUS, THAT'S SHOCKIN'.
ANY NAMES YET?
NOT YET, NO.
YOUNG MEN FROM THE SOUNDS OF IT, THOUGH.
THESE CARS ARE DEATH-TRAPS.
TRUE.
MONTEITH AND BAILEY...?
SURE, I ALMOST SLID INTO THE ATLANTIC THE OTHER DAY IN THIS THINGY!
TWO MEN DROWNED IN FISHING MISADVENTURE
Families have been informed
Sad news came this mo
ing from the Atlantic
coast, two men we
OH GOD, LET IT BE SOMEONE ELSE...
WANT ME TO READ OUT THE FOOTBALL?

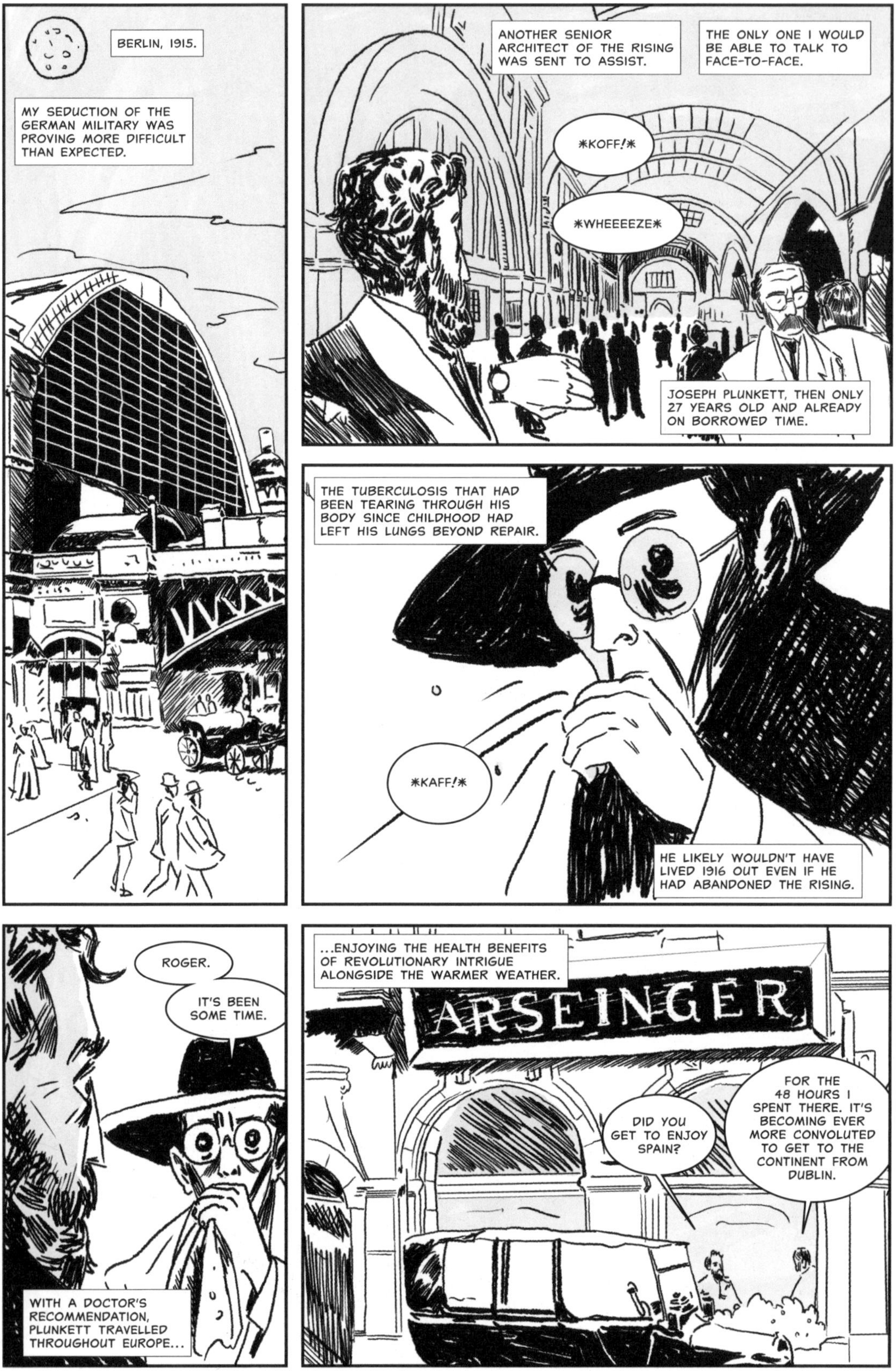
BERLIN, 1915.
MY SEDUCTION OF THE GERMAN MILITARY WAS PROVING MORE DIFFICULT THAN EXPECTED.
ANOTHER SENIOR ARCHITECT OF THE RISING WAS SENT TO ASSIST.
THE ONLY ONE I WOULD BE ABLE TO TALK TO FACE-TO-FACE.
KOFF!
WHEEEEZE
JOSEPH PLUNKETT, THEN ONLY 27 YEARS OLD AND ALREADY ON BORROWED TIME.
THE TUBERCULOSIS THAT HAD BEEN TEARING THROUGH HIS BODY SINCE CHILDHOOD HAD LEFT HIS LUNGS BEYOND REPAIR.
KAFF!
HE LIKELY WOULDN'T HAVE LIVED 1916 OUT EVEN IF HE HAD ABANDONED THE RISING.
ROGER.
IT'S BEEN SOME TIME.
WITH A DOCTOR'S RECOMMENDATION, PLUNKETT TRAVELLED THROUGHOUT EUROPE...
...ENJOYING THE HEALTH BENEFITS OF REVOLUTIONARY INTRIGUE ALONGSIDE THE WARMER WEATHER.
ARSEINGER
DID YOU GET TO ENJOY SPAIN?
FOR THE 48 HOURS I SPENT THERE. IT'S BECOMING EVER MORE CONVOLUTED TO GET TO THE CONTINENT FROM DUBLIN.

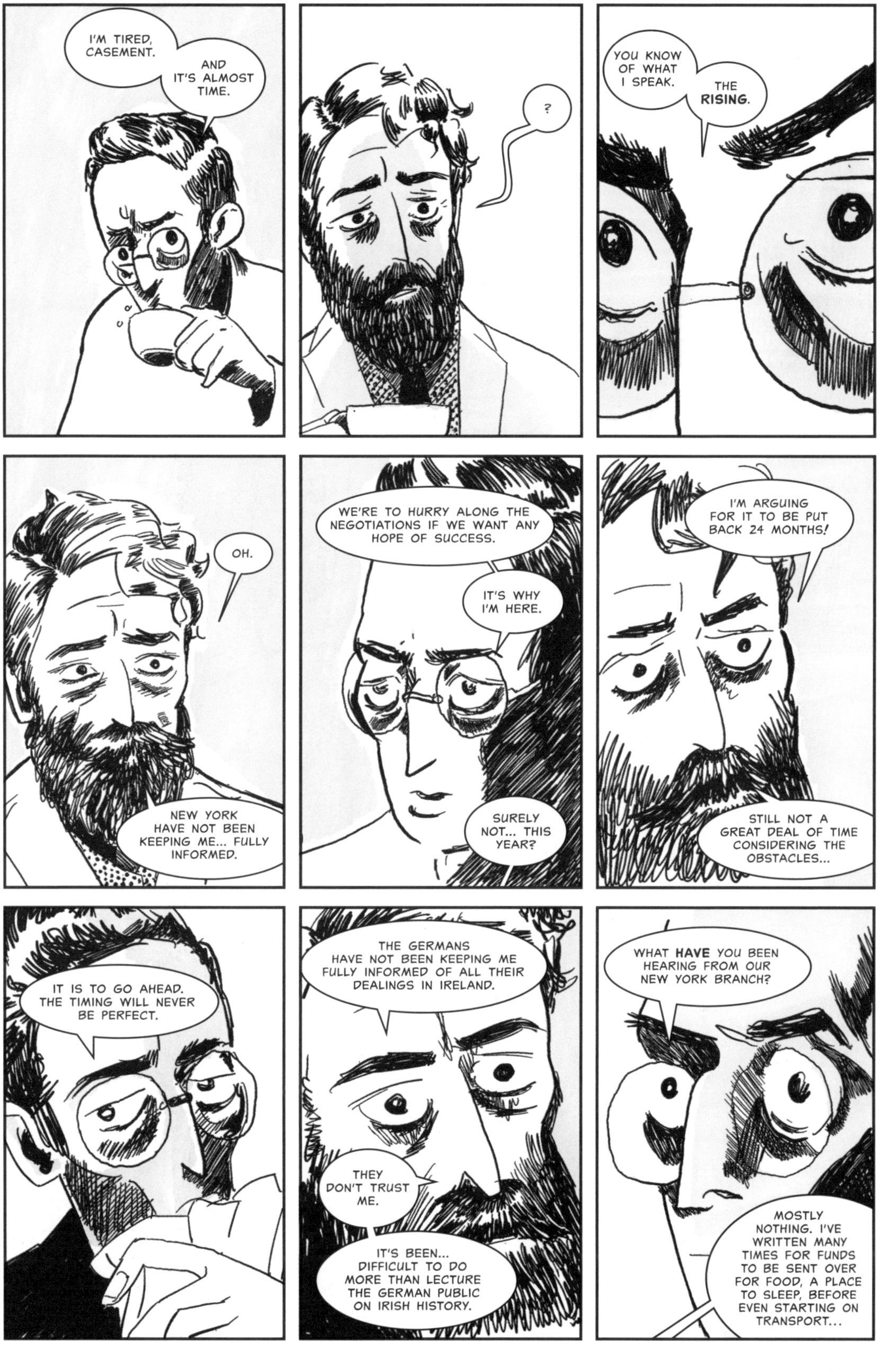
I'M TIRED, CASEMENT.
AND IT'S ALMOST TIME.
?
YOU KNOW OF WHAT I SPEAK.
THE **RISING**.
OH.
NEW YORK HAVE NOT BEEN KEEPING ME... FULLY INFORMED.
WE'RE TO HURRY ALONG THE NEGOTIATIONS IF WE WANT ANY HOPE OF SUCCESS.
IT'S WHY I'M HERE.
SURELY NOT... THIS YEAR?
I'M ARGUING FOR IT TO BE PUT BACK 24 MONTHS!
STILL NOT A GREAT DEAL OF TIME CONSIDERING THE OBSTACLES...
IT IS TO GO AHEAD. THE TIMING WILL NEVER BE PERFECT.
THE GERMANS HAVE NOT BEEN KEEPING ME FULLY INFORMED OF ALL THEIR DEALINGS IN IRELAND.
THEY DON'T TRUST ME.
IT'S BEEN... DIFFICULT TO DO MORE THAN LECTURE THE GERMAN PUBLIC ON IRISH HISTORY.
WHAT **HAVE** YOU BEEN HEARING FROM OUR NEW YORK BRANCH?
MOSTLY NOTHING. I'VE WRITTEN MANY TIMES FOR FUNDS TO BE SENT OVER FOR FOOD, A PLACE TO SLEEP, BEFORE EVEN STARTING ON TRANSPORT...

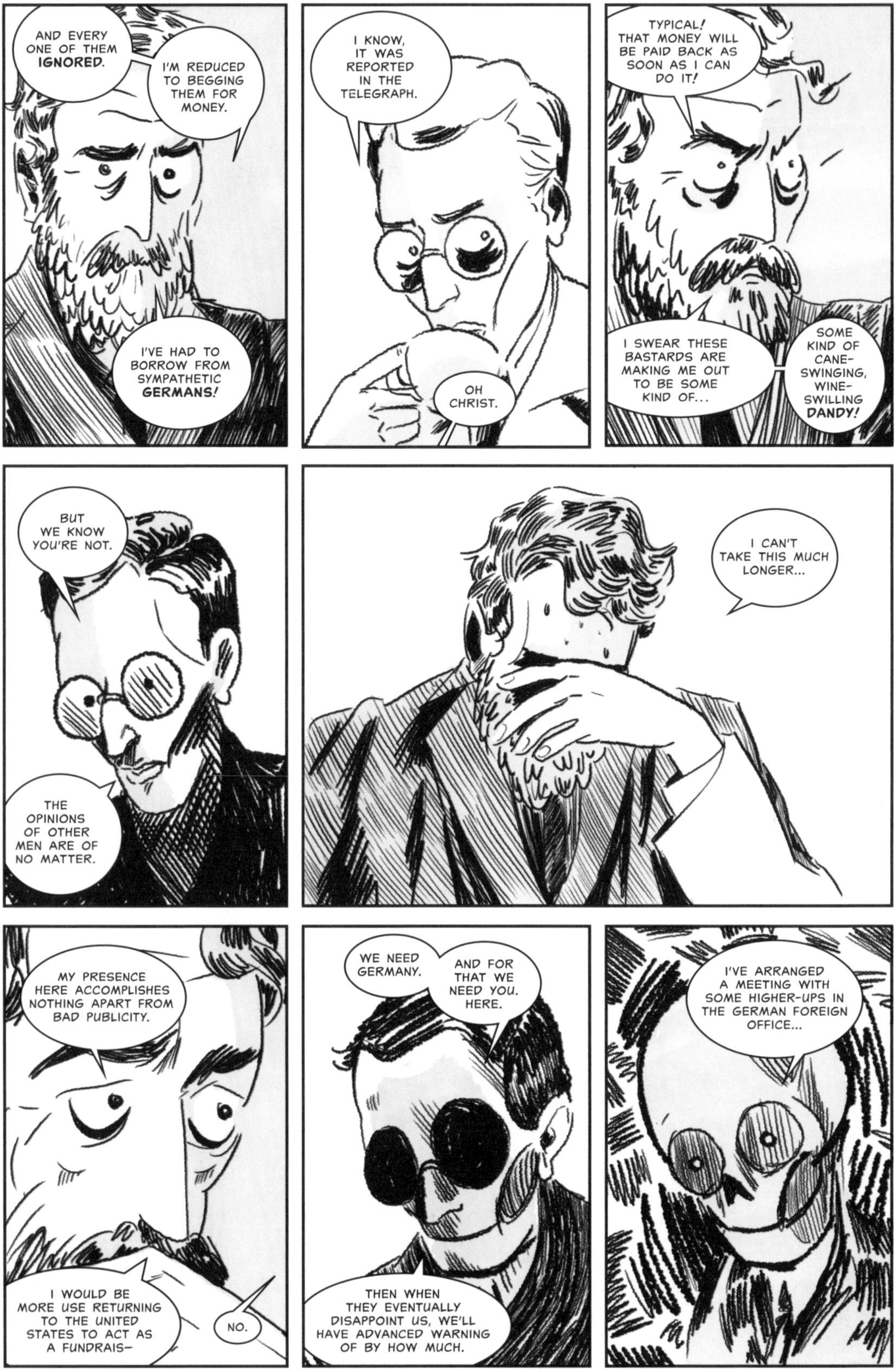
AND EVERY ONE OF THEM **IGNORED**.
I'M REDUCED TO BEGGING THEM FOR MONEY.
I'VE HAD TO BORROW FROM SYMPATHETIC **GERMANS!**
I KNOW, IT WAS REPORTED IN THE TELEGRAPH.
OH CHRIST.
TYPICAL! THAT MONEY WILL BE PAID BACK AS SOON AS I CAN DO IT!
I SWEAR THESE BASTARDS ARE MAKING ME OUT TO BE SOME KIND OF...
SOME KIND OF CANE-SWINGING, WINE-SWILLING **DANDY!**
BUT WE KNOW YOU'RE NOT.
THE OPINIONS OF OTHER MEN ARE OF NO MATTER.
I CAN'T TAKE THIS MUCH LONGER...
MY PRESENCE HERE ACCOMPLISHES NOTHING APART FROM BAD PUBLICITY.
I WOULD BE MORE USE RETURNING TO THE UNITED STATES TO ACT AS A FUNDRAIS—
NO.
WE NEED GERMANY.
AND FOR THAT WE NEED YOU. HERE.
THEN WHEN THEY EVENTUALLY DISAPPOINT US, WE'LL HAVE ADVANCED WARNING OF BY HOW MUCH.
I'VE ARRANGED A MEETING WITH SOME HIGHER-UPS IN THE GERMAN FOREIGN OFFICE...

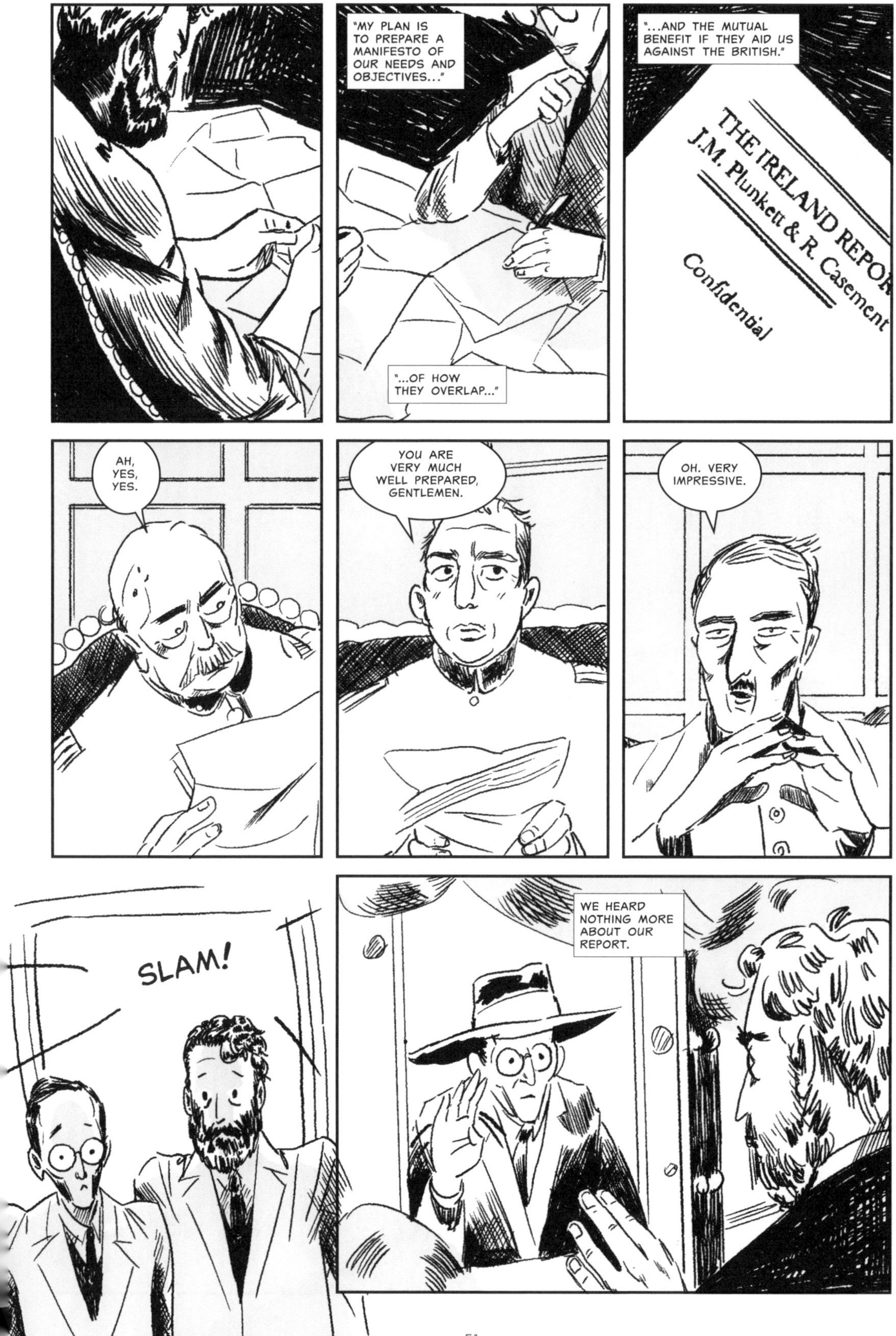
"MY PLAN IS TO PREPARE A MANIFESTO OF OUR NEEDS AND OBJECTIVES..."
"...OF HOW THEY OVERLAP..."
"...AND THE MUTUAL BENEFIT IF THEY AID US AGAINST THE BRITISH."
THE IRELAND REPOR
J.M. Plunkett & R. Casement
Confidential
AH, YES, YES.
YOU ARE VERY MUCH WELL PREPARED, GENTLEMEN.
OH. VERY IMPRESSIVE.
SLAM!
WE HEARD NOTHING MORE ABOUT OUR REPORT.

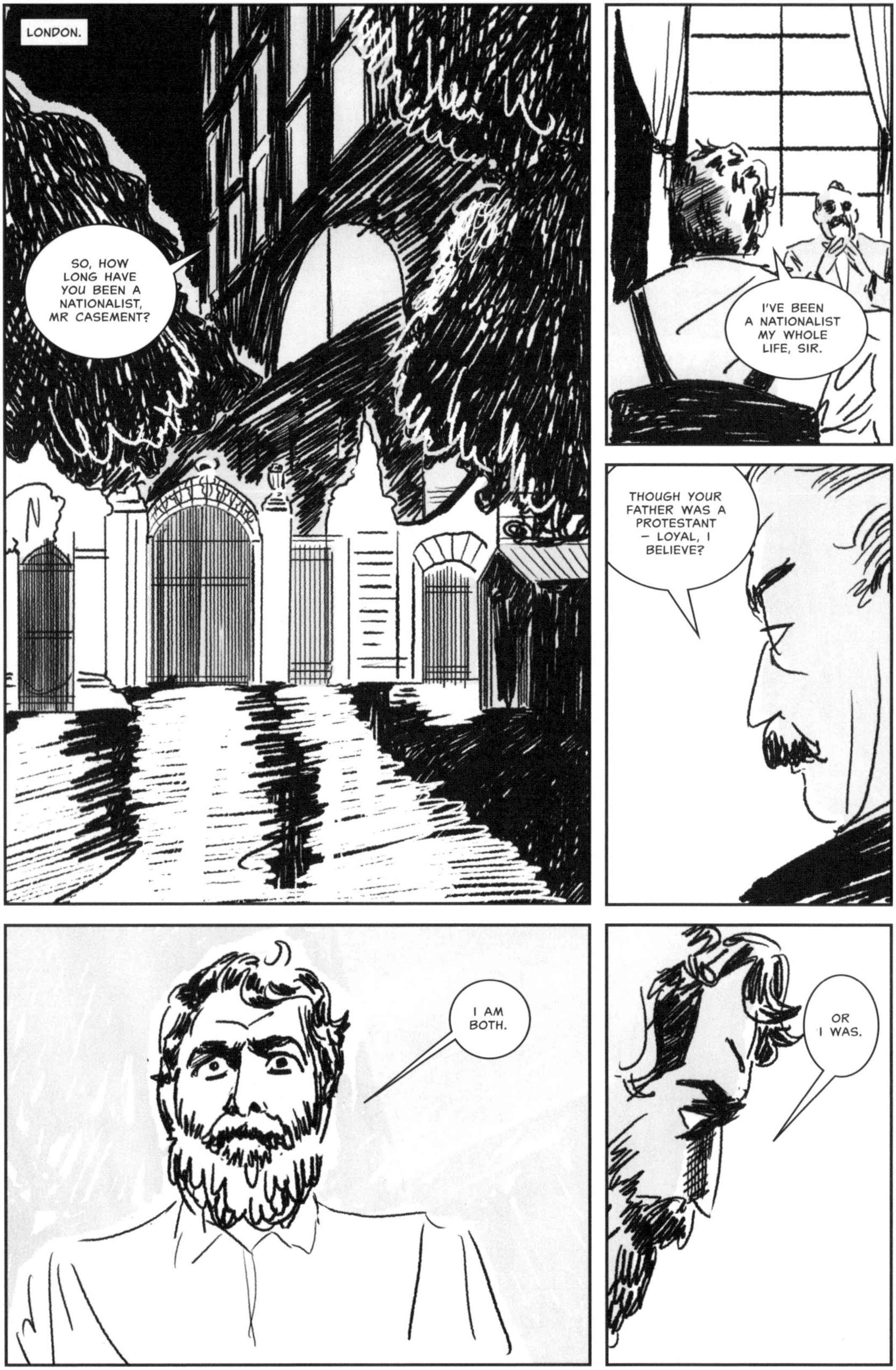
LONDON.
SO, HOW LONG HAVE YOU BEEN A NATIONALIST, MR CASEMENT?
I'VE BEEN A NATIONALIST MY WHOLE LIFE, SIR.
THOUGH YOUR FATHER WAS A PROTESTANT – LOYAL, I BELIEVE?
I AM BOTH.
OR I WAS.

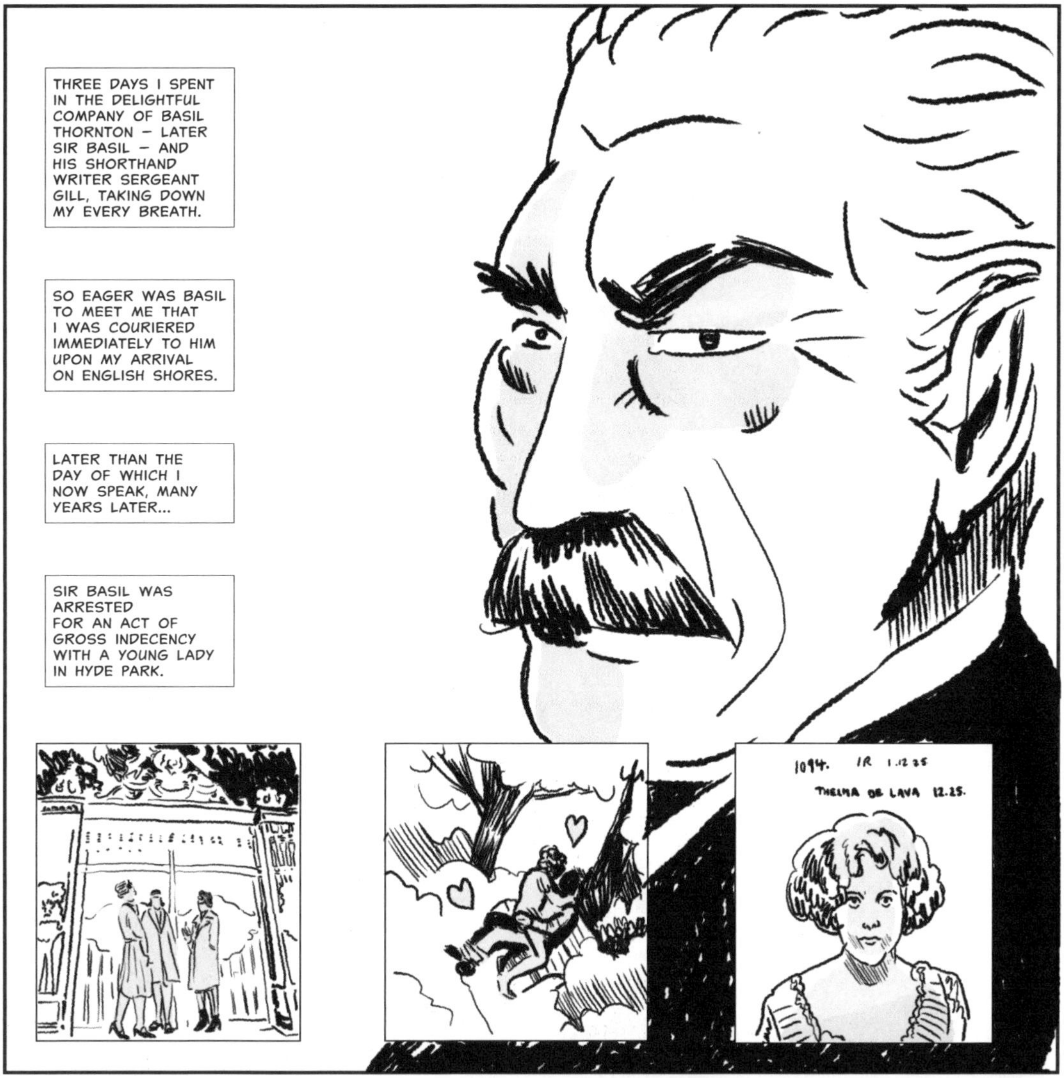
THREE DAYS I SPENT IN THE DELIGHTFUL COMPANY OF BASIL THORNTON – LATER SIR BASIL – AND HIS SHORTHAND WRITER SERGEANT GILL, TAKING DOWN MY EVERY BREATH.
SO EAGER WAS BASIL TO MEET ME THAT I WAS COURIERED IMMEDIATELY TO HIM UPON MY ARRIVAL ON ENGLISH SHORES.
LATER THAN THE DAY OF WHICH I NOW SPEAK, MANY YEARS LATER...
SIR BASIL WAS ARRESTED FOR AN ACT OF GROSS INDECENCY WITH A YOUNG LADY IN HYDE PARK.
1094. IR 1.12.25
THELMA DE LAVA 12.25.

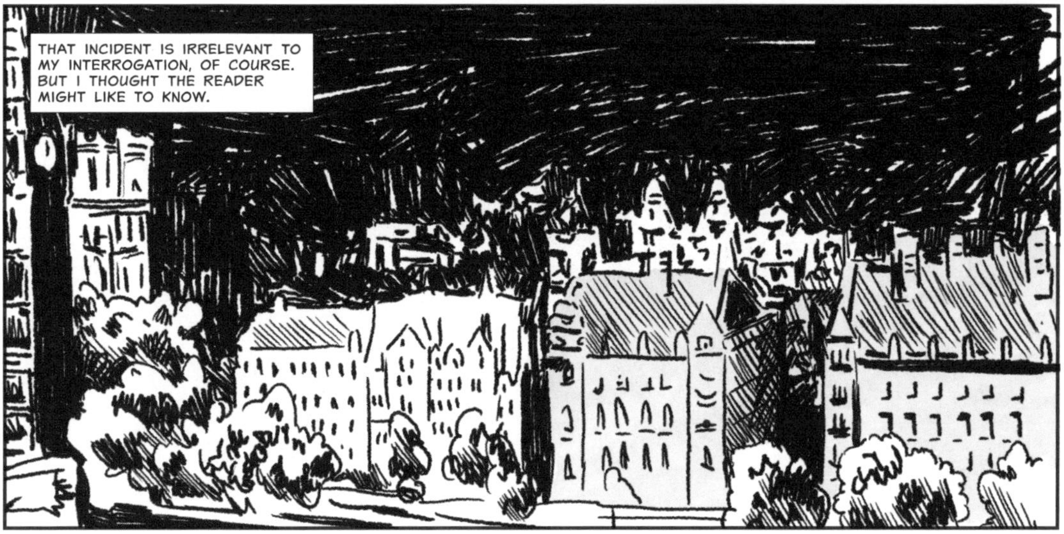
THAT INCIDENT IS IRRELEVANT TO MY INTERROGATION, OF COURSE. BUT I THOUGHT THE READER MIGHT LIKE TO KNOW.

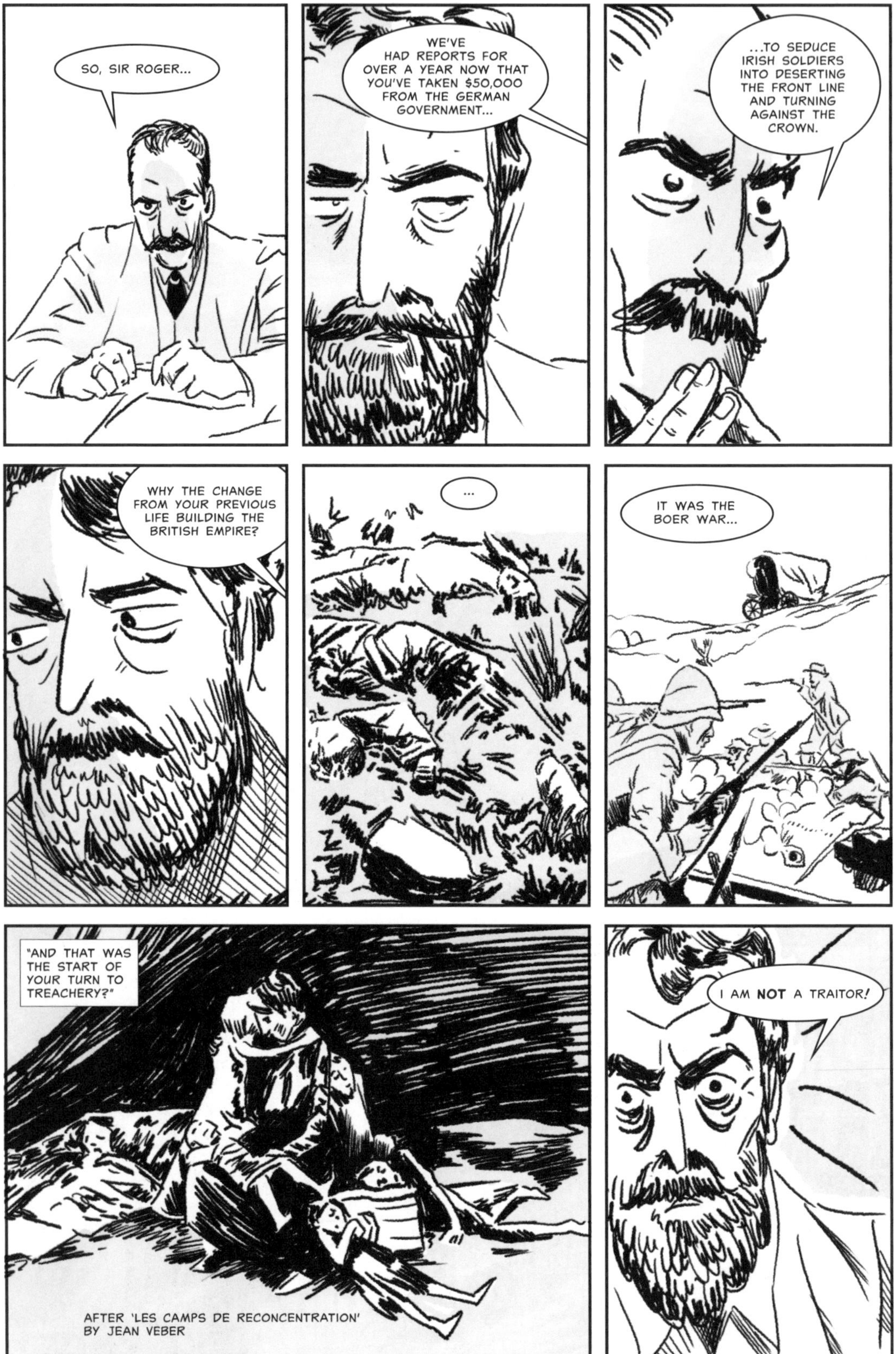
SO, SIR ROGER...
WE'VE HAD REPORTS FOR OVER A YEAR NOW THAT YOU'VE TAKEN $50,000 FROM THE GERMAN GOVERNMENT...
...TO SEDUCE IRISH SOLDIERS INTO DESERTING THE FRONT LINE AND TURNING AGAINST THE CROWN.
WHY THE CHANGE FROM YOUR PREVIOUS LIFE BUILDING THE BRITISH EMPIRE?
...
IT WAS THE BOER WAR...
"AND THAT WAS THE START OF YOUR TURN TO TREACHERY?"
AFTER 'LES CAMPS DE RECONCENTRATION' BY JEAN VEBER
I AM **NOT** A TRAITOR!

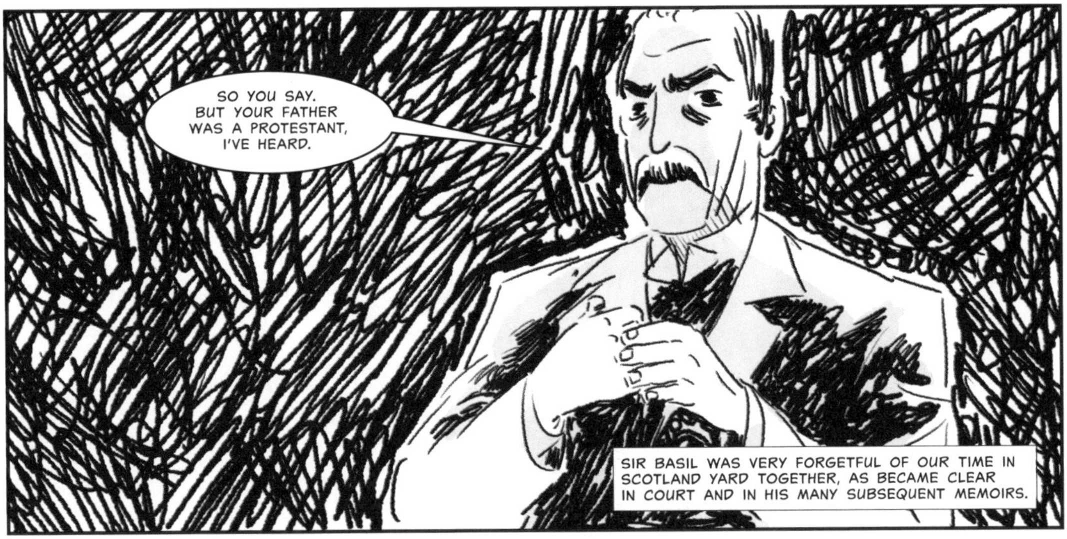
SO YOU SAY. BUT YOUR FATHER WAS A PROTESTANT, I'VE HEARD.
SIR BASIL WAS VERY FORGETFUL OF OUR TIME IN SCOTLAND YARD TOGETHER, AS BECAME CLEAR IN COURT AND IN HIS MANY SUBSEQUENT MEMOIRS.

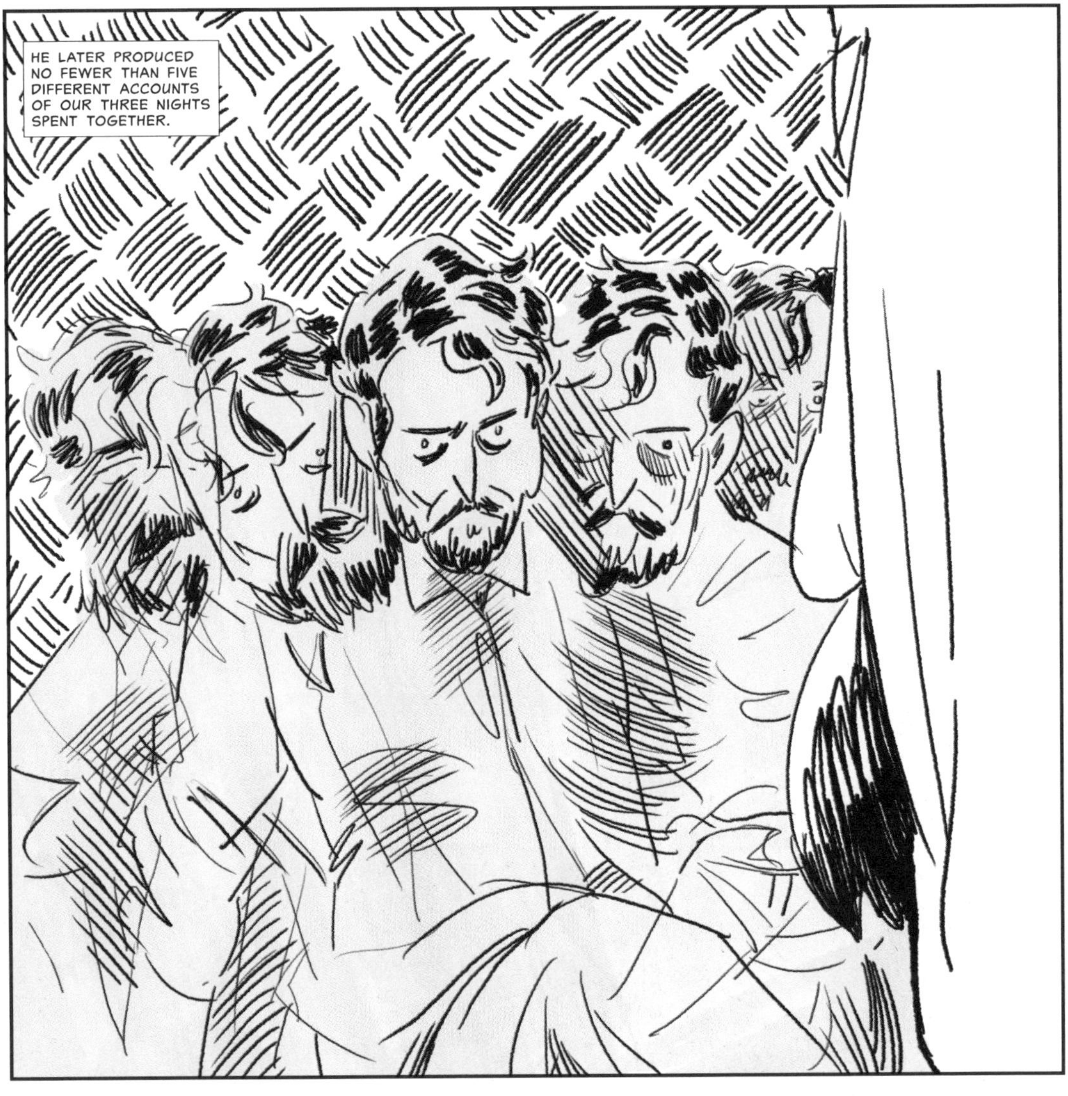
HE LATER PRODUCED NO FEWER THAN FIVE DIFFERENT ACCOUNTS OF OUR THREE NIGHTS SPENT TOGETHER.

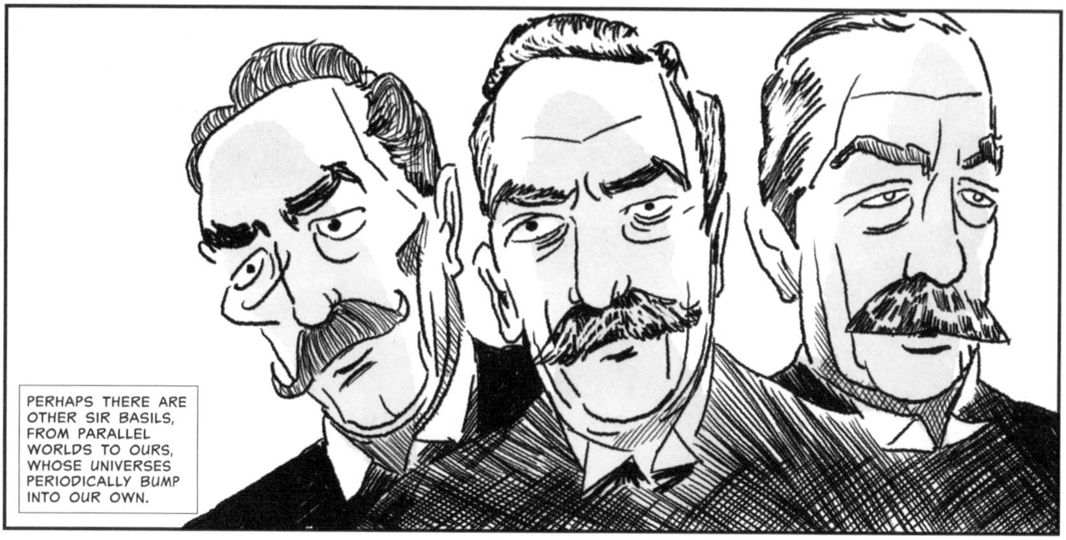
PERHAPS THERE ARE OTHER SIR BASILS, FROM PARALLEL WORLDS TO OURS, WHOSE UNIVERSES PERIODICALLY BUMP INTO OUR OWN.

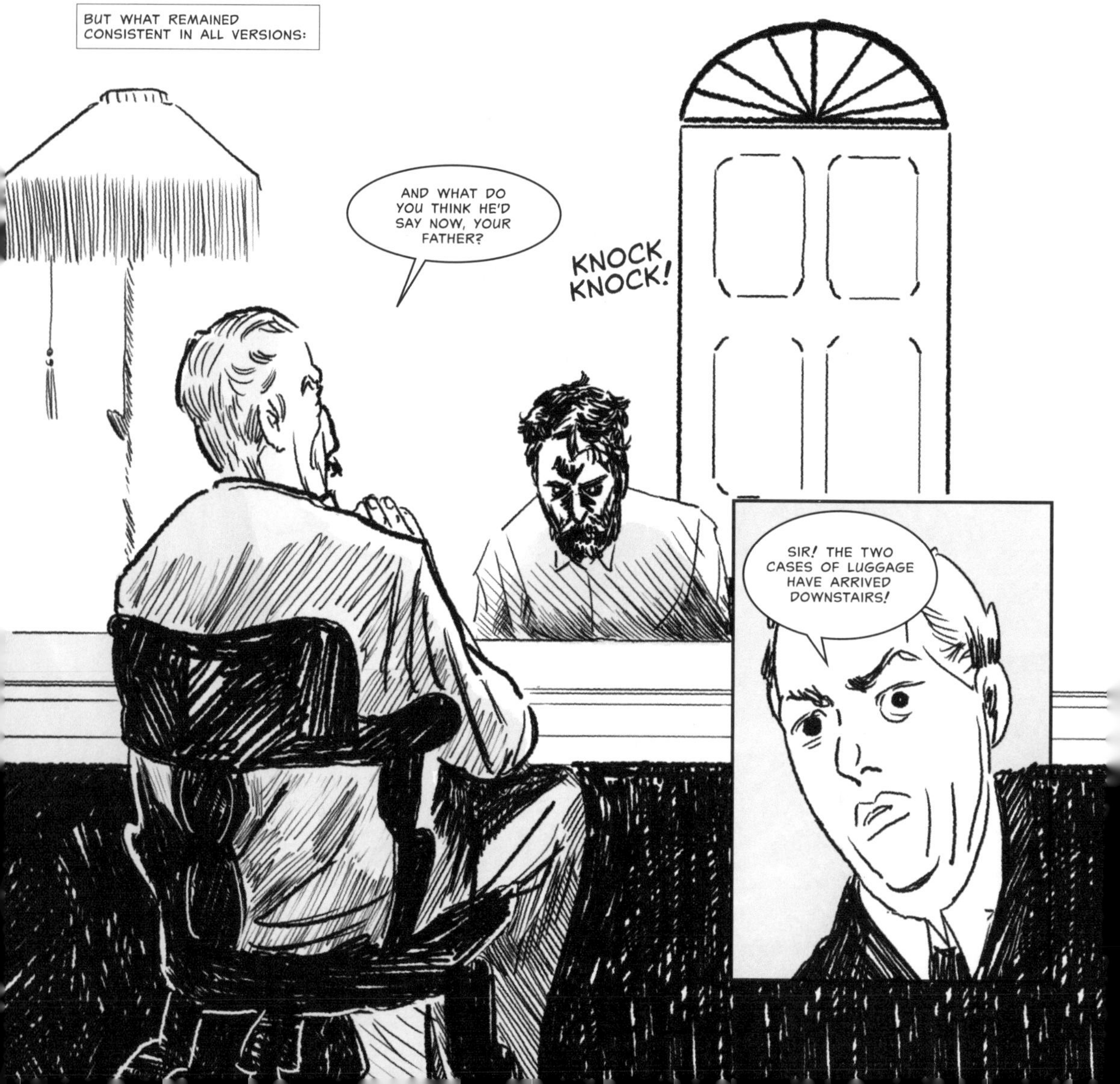
BUT WHAT REMAINED CONSISTENT IN ALL VERSIONS:
AND WHAT DO YOU THINK HE'D SAY NOW, YOUR FATHER?
KNOCK KNOCK!
SIR! THE TWO CASES OF LUGGAGE HAVE ARRIVED DOWNSTAIRS!

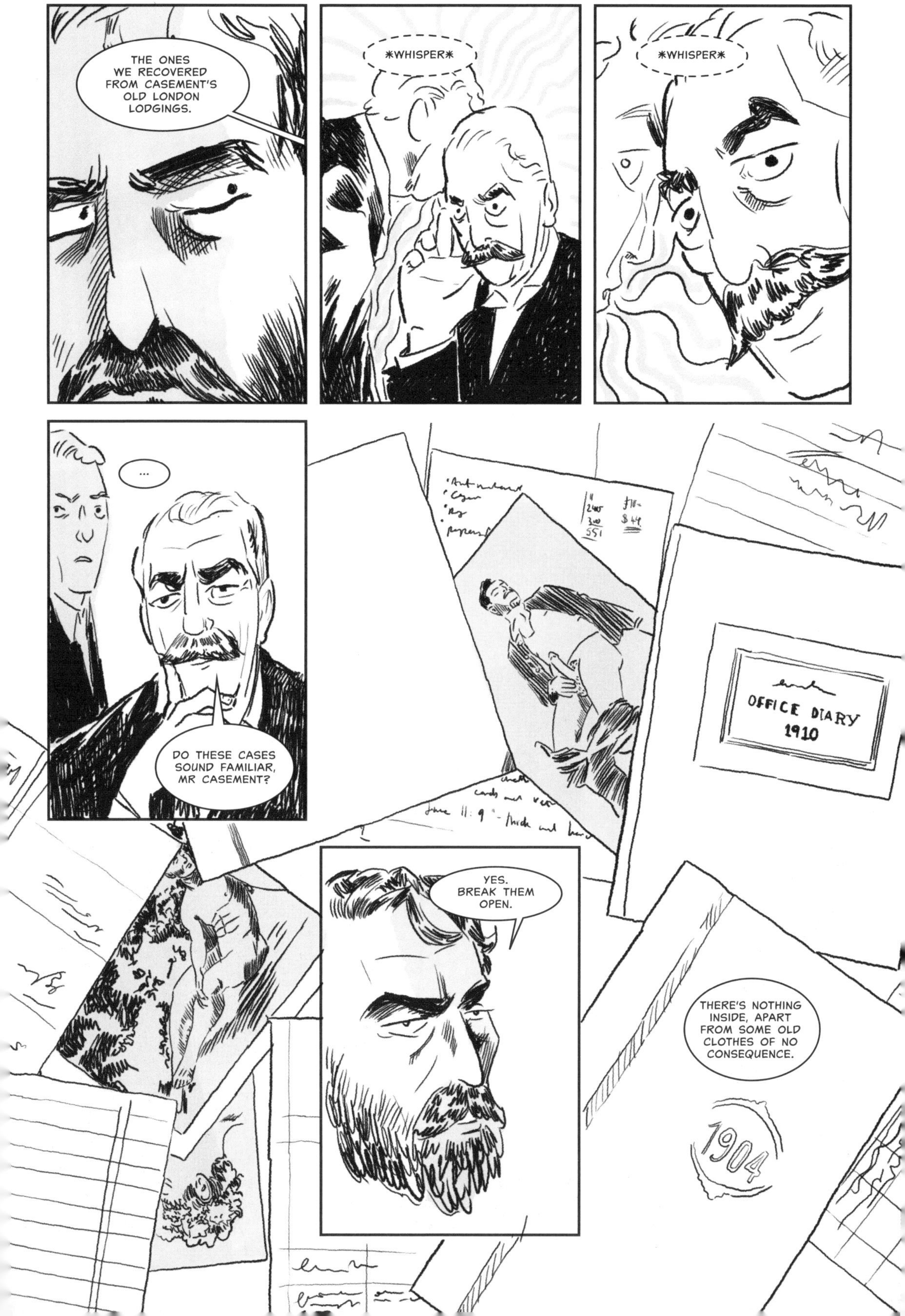
THE ONES WE RECOVERED FROM CASEMENT'S OLD LONDON LODGINGS.
WHISPER
WHISPER
...
DO THESE CASES SOUND FAMILIAR, MR CASEMENT?
OFFICE DIARY 1910
YES. BREAK THEM OPEN.
THERE'S NOTHING INSIDE, APART FROM SOME OLD CLOTHES OF NO CONSEQUENCE.
1904

...OF NO CONSEQUENCE, EH?
SIR. THE EVIDENCE YOU REQUESTED.
NONE AT ALL.
I THINK WE'VE TALKED ENOUGH, CASEMENT...

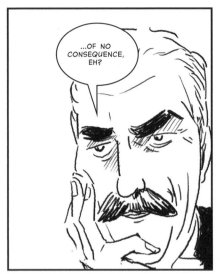

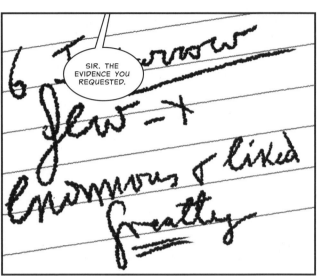

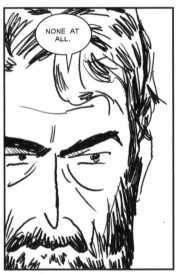

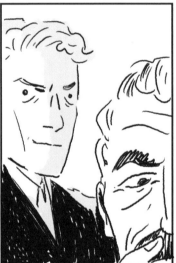

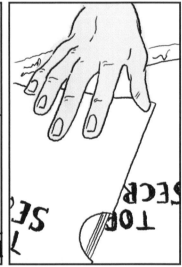

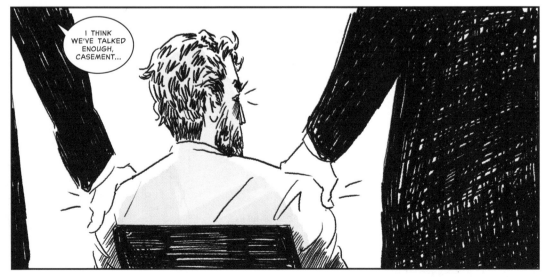

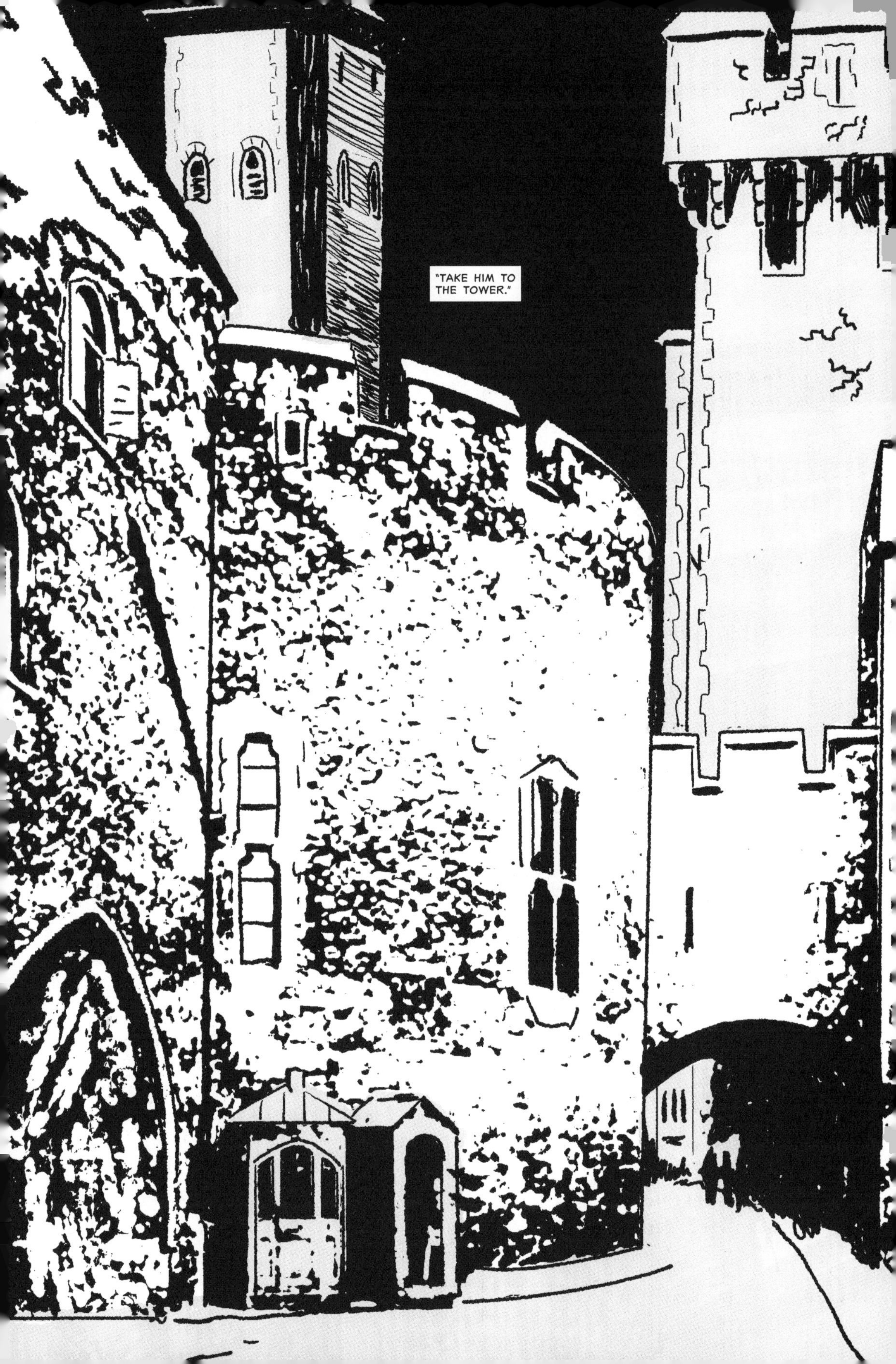
"TAKE HIM TO THE TOWER."

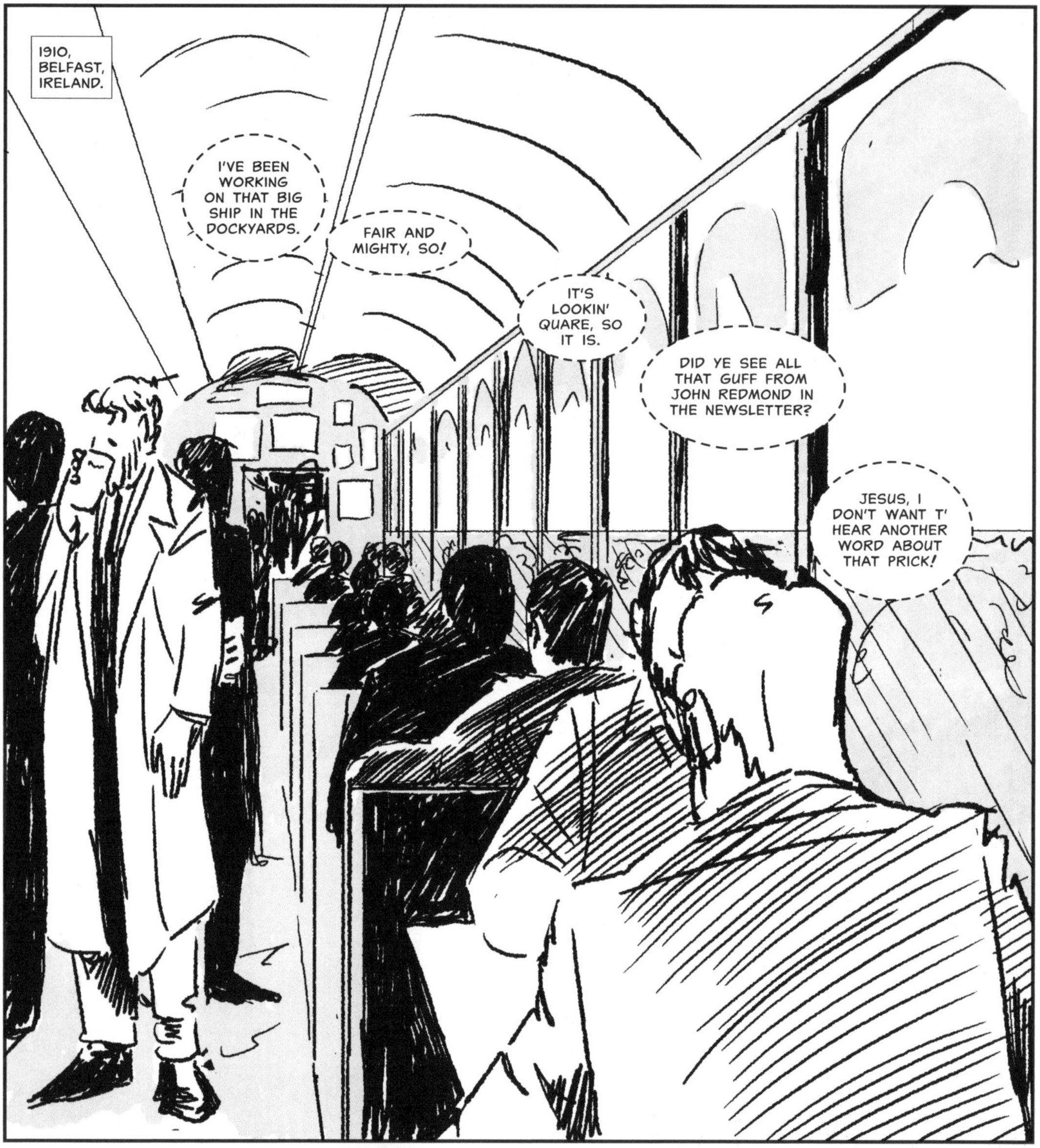
1910, BELFAST, IRELAND.
I'VE BEEN WORKING ON THAT BIG SHIP IN THE DOCKYARDS.
FAIR AND MIGHTY, SO!
IT'S LOOKIN' QUARE, SO IT IS.
DID YE SEE ALL THAT GUFF FROM JOHN REDMOND IN THE NEWSLETTER?
JESUS, I DON'T WANT T' HEAR ANOTHER WORD ABOUT THAT PRICK!

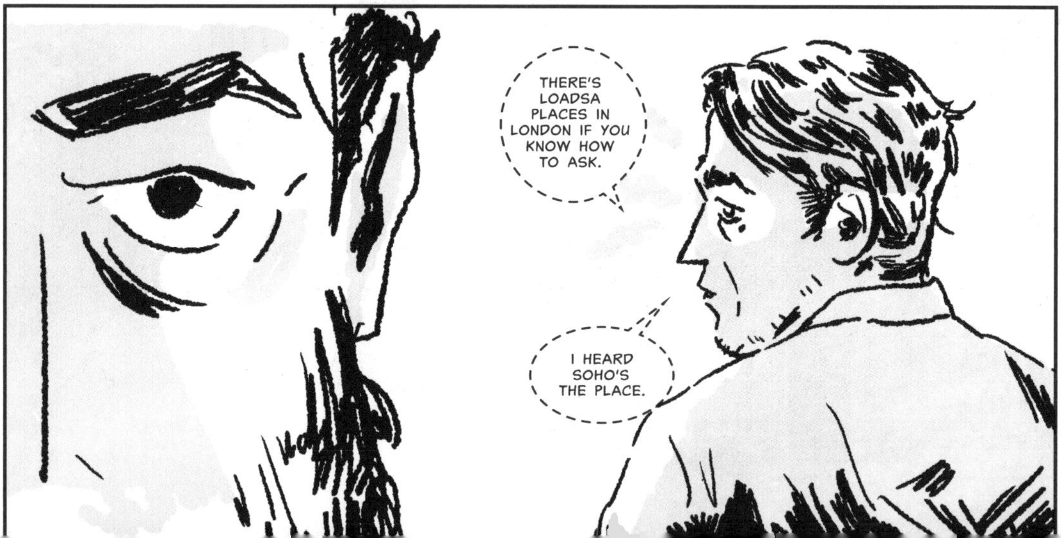
THERE'S LOADSA PLACES IN LONDON IF YOU KNOW HOW TO ASK.
I HEARD SOHO'S THE PLACE.

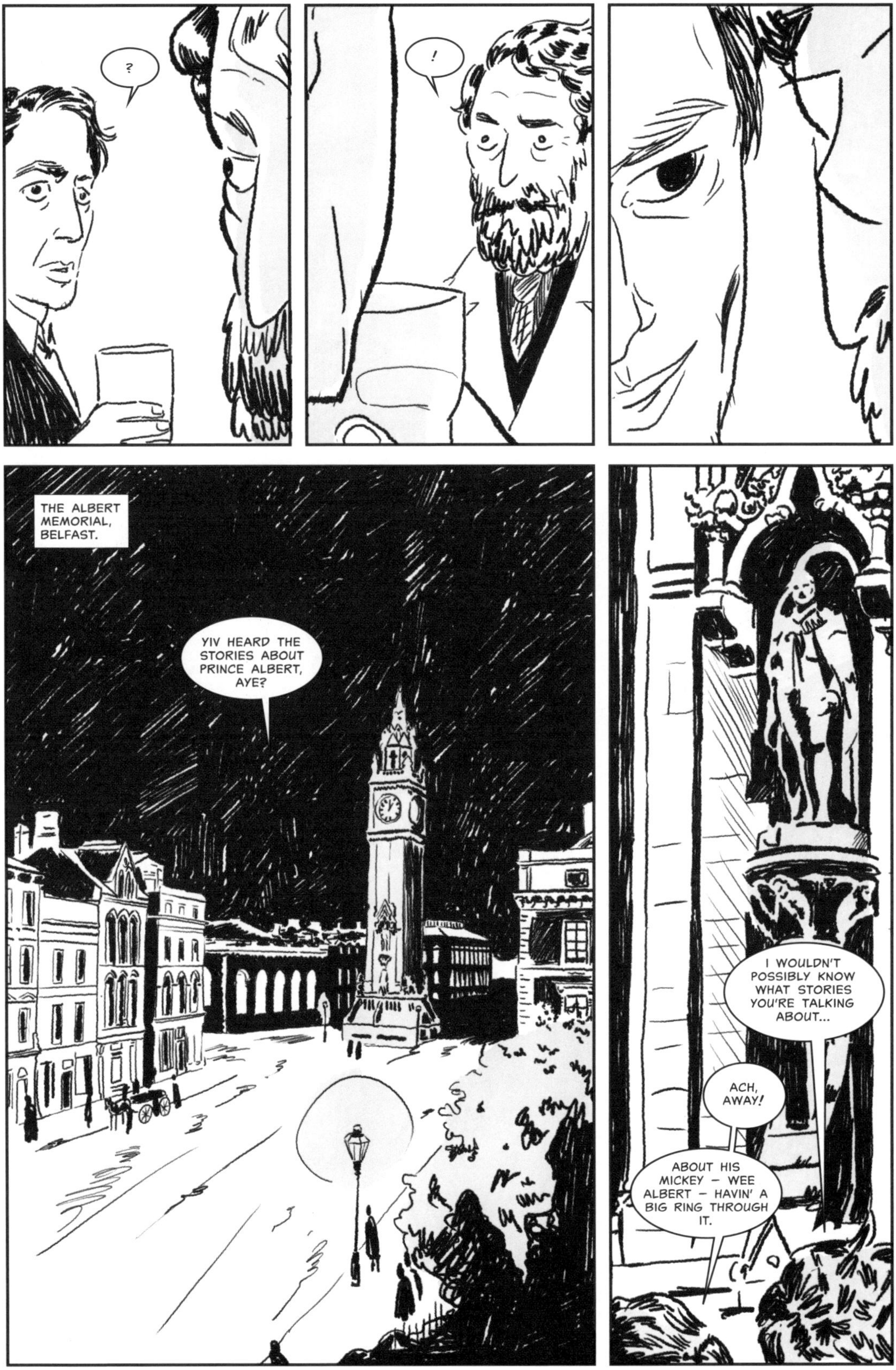
?
!
THE ALBERT MEMORIAL, BELFAST.
YIV HEARD THE STORIES ABOUT PRINCE ALBERT, AYE?
I WOULDN'T POSSIBLY KNOW WHAT STORIES YOU'RE TALKING ABOUT...
ACH, AWAY!
ABOUT HIS MICKEY - WEE ALBERT - HAVIN' A BIG RING THROUGH IT.

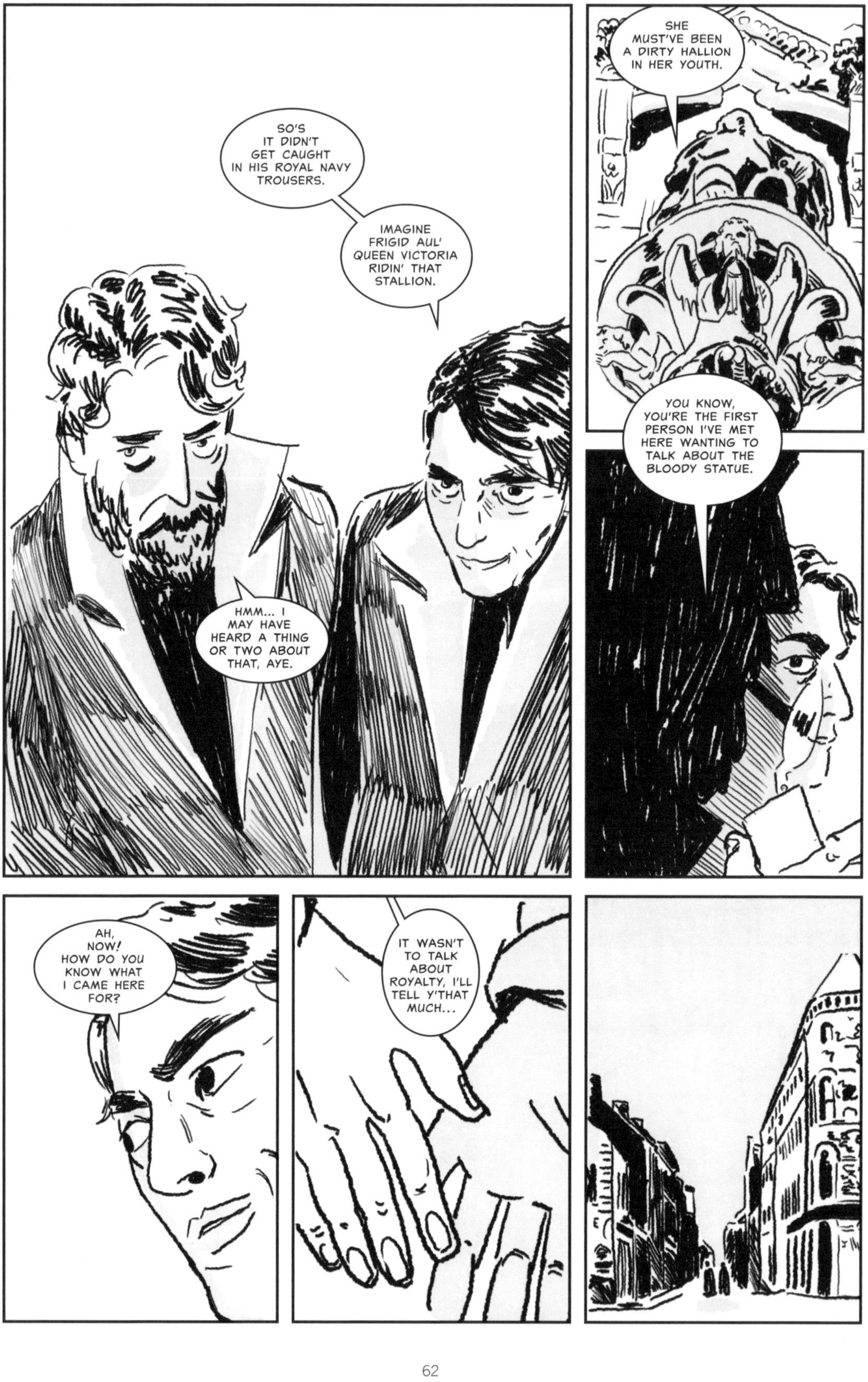
SO'S IT DIDN'T GET CAUGHT IN HIS ROYAL NAVY TROUSERS.
IMAGINE FRIGID AUL' QUEEN VICTORIA RIDIN' THAT STALLION.
HMM... I MAY HAVE HEARD A THING OR TWO ABOUT THAT, AYE.
SHE MUST'VE BEEN A DIRTY HALLION IN HER YOUTH.
YOU KNOW, YOU'RE THE FIRST PERSON I'VE MET HERE WANTING TO TALK ABOUT THE BLOODY STATUE.
AH, NOW! HOW DO YOU KNOW WHAT I CAME HERE FOR?
IT WASN'T TO TALK ABOUT ROYALTY, I'LL TELL Y'THAT MUCH...

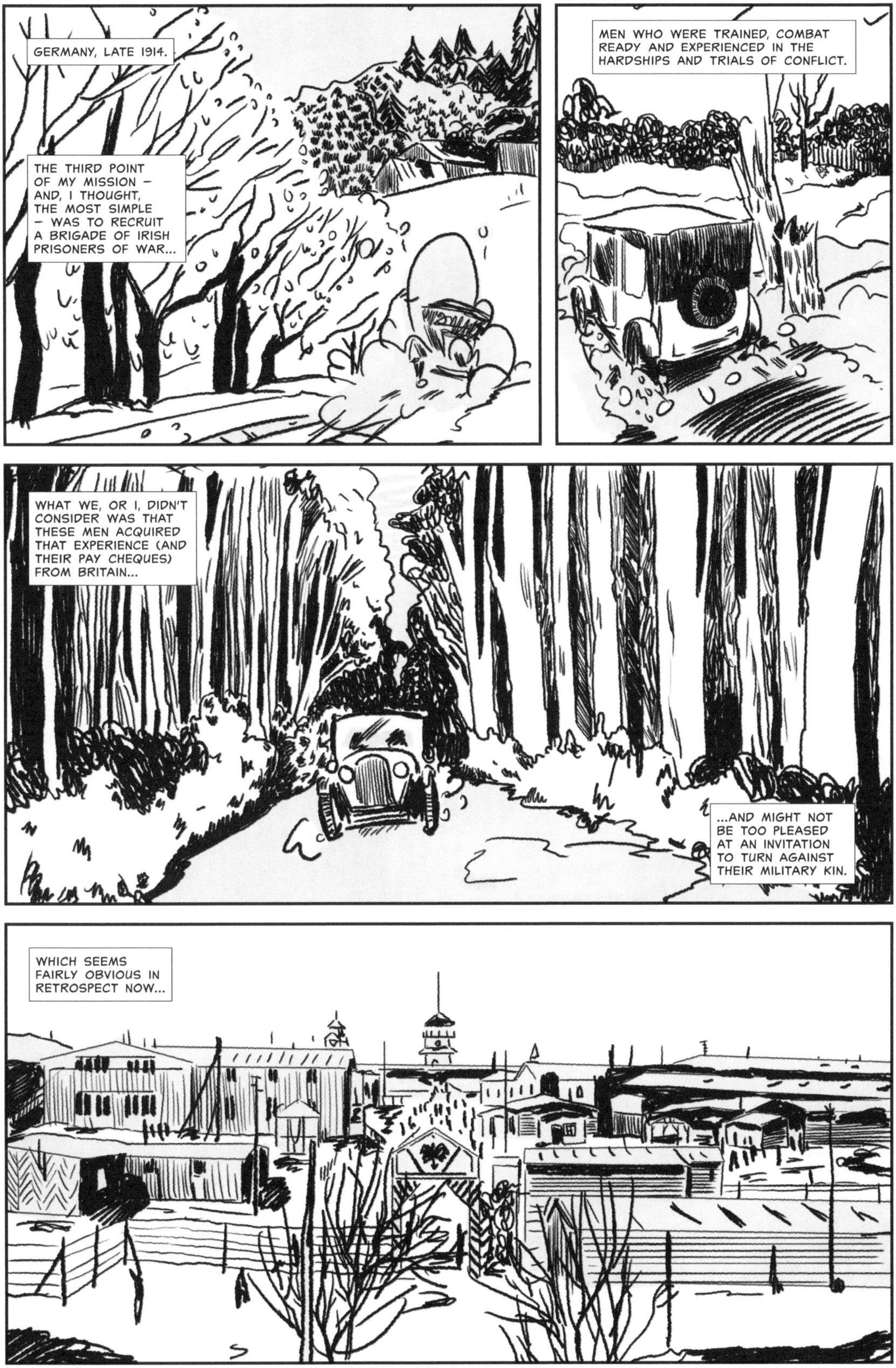
GERMANY, LATE 1914.
THE THIRD POINT OF MY MISSION – AND, I THOUGHT, THE MOST SIMPLE – WAS TO RECRUIT A BRIGADE OF IRISH PRISONERS OF WAR...
MEN WHO WERE TRAINED, COMBAT READY AND EXPERIENCED IN THE HARDSHIPS AND TRIALS OF CONFLICT.
WHAT WE, OR I, DIDN'T CONSIDER WAS THAT THESE MEN ACQUIRED THAT EXPERIENCE (AND THEIR PAY CHEQUES) FROM BRITAIN...
...AND MIGHT NOT BE TOO PLEASED AT AN INVITATION TO TURN AGAINST THEIR MILITARY KIN.
WHICH SEEMS FAIRLY OBVIOUS IN RETROSPECT NOW...

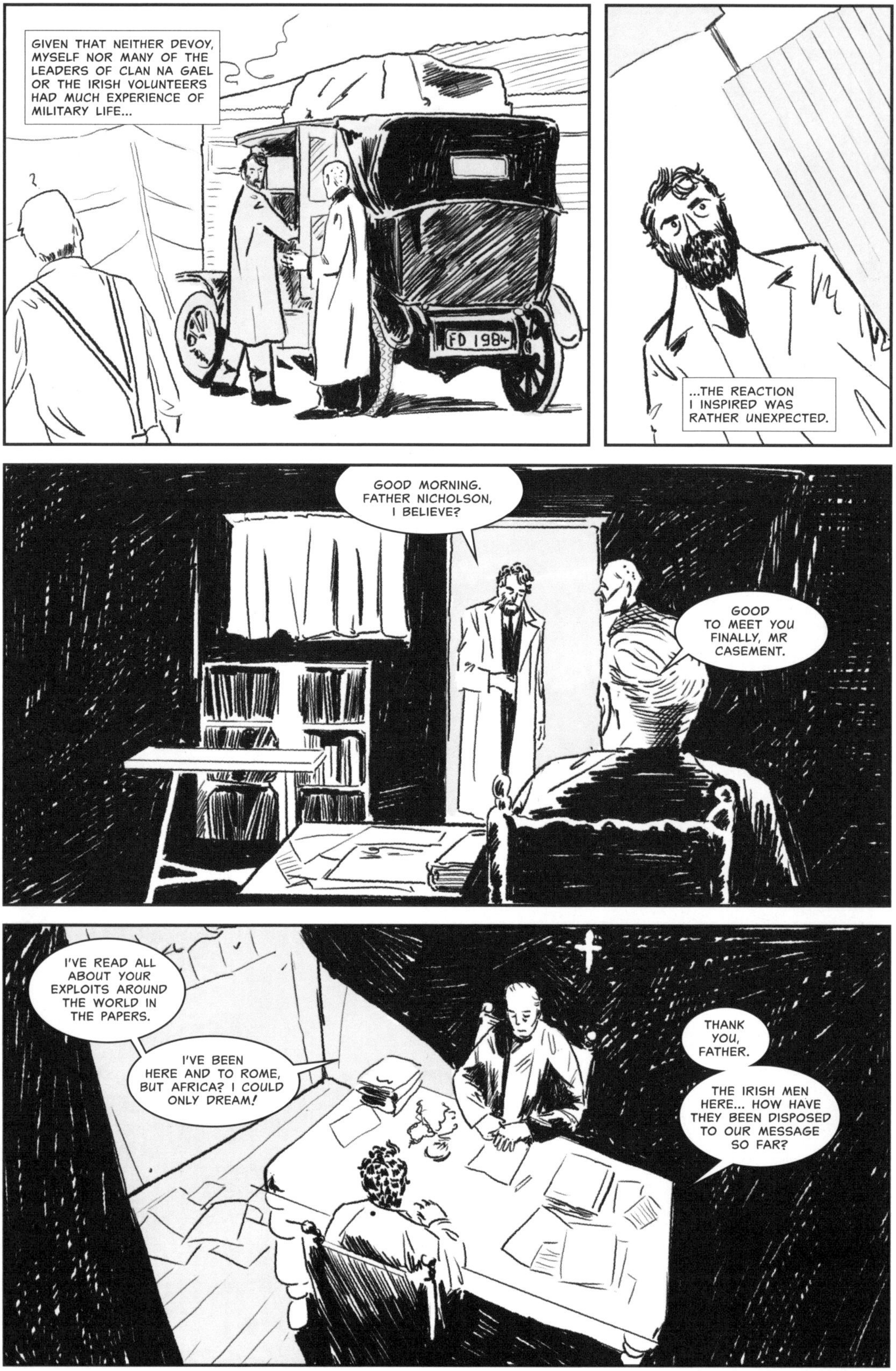
GIVEN THAT NEITHER DEVOY, MYSELF NOR MANY OF THE LEADERS OF CLAN NA GAEL OR THE IRISH VOLUNTEERS HAD MUCH EXPERIENCE OF MILITARY LIFE...
FD 1984
...THE REACTION I INSPIRED WAS RATHER UNEXPECTED.
GOOD MORNING. FATHER NICHOLSON, I BELIEVE?
GOOD TO MEET YOU FINALLY, MR CASEMENT.
I'VE READ ALL ABOUT YOUR EXPLOITS AROUND THE WORLD IN THE PAPERS.
I'VE BEEN HERE AND TO ROME, BUT AFRICA? I COULD ONLY DREAM!
THANK YOU, FATHER.
THE IRISH MEN HERE... HOW HAVE THEY BEEN DISPOSED TO OUR MESSAGE SO FAR?

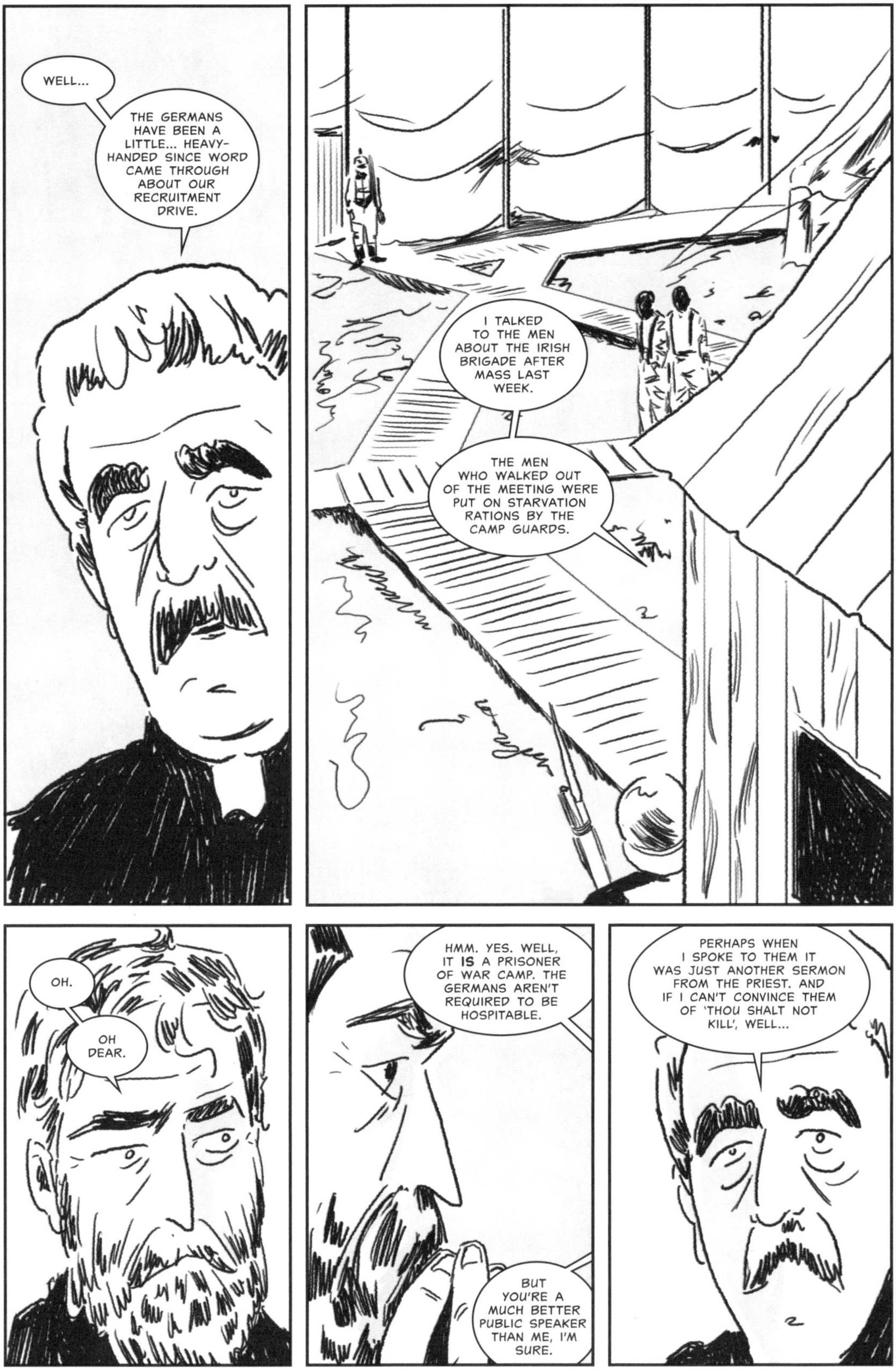
WELL...
THE GERMANS HAVE BEEN A LITTLE... HEAVY-HANDED SINCE WORD CAME THROUGH ABOUT OUR RECRUITMENT DRIVE.
I TALKED TO THE MEN ABOUT THE IRISH BRIGADE AFTER MASS LAST WEEK.
THE MEN WHO WALKED OUT OF THE MEETING WERE PUT ON STARVATION RATIONS BY THE CAMP GUARDS.
OH.
OH DEAR.
HMM. YES. WELL, IT **IS** A PRISONER OF WAR CAMP. THE GERMANS AREN'T REQUIRED TO BE HOSPITABLE.
BUT YOU'RE A MUCH BETTER PUBLIC SPEAKER THAN ME, I'M SURE.
PERHAPS WHEN I SPOKE TO THEM IT WAS JUST ANOTHER SERMON FROM THE PRIEST. AND IF I CAN'T CONVINCE THEM OF 'THOU SHALT NOT KILL', WELL...

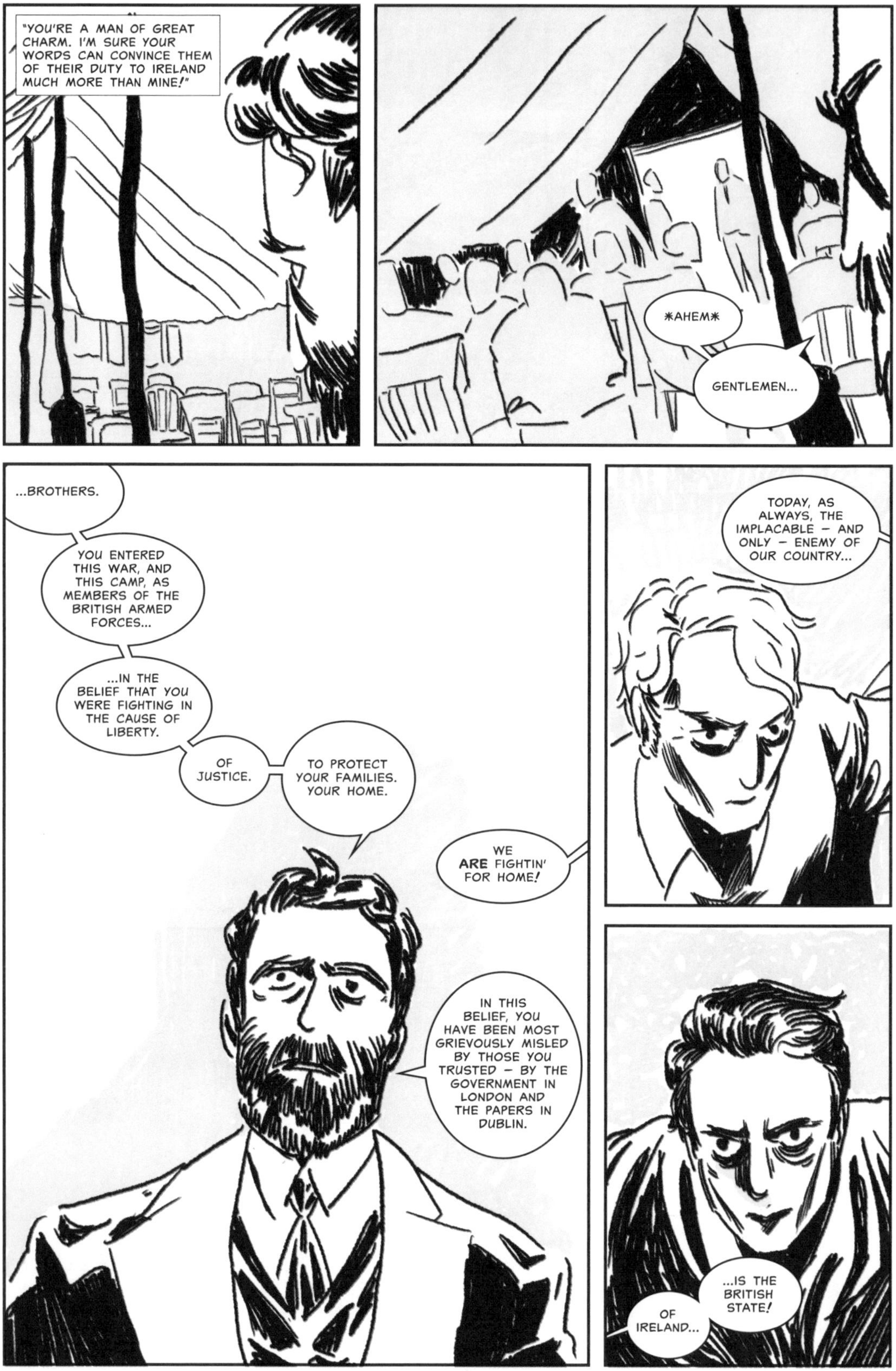
"YOU'RE A MAN OF GREAT CHARM. I'M SURE YOUR WORDS CAN CONVINCE THEM OF THEIR DUTY TO IRELAND MUCH MORE THAN MINE!"
AHEM
GENTLEMEN...
...BROTHERS.
YOU ENTERED THIS WAR, AND THIS CAMP, AS MEMBERS OF THE BRITISH ARMED FORCES...
...IN THE BELIEF THAT YOU WERE FIGHTING IN THE CAUSE OF LIBERTY.
OF JUSTICE.
TO PROTECT YOUR FAMILIES. YOUR HOME.
WE **ARE** FIGHTIN' FOR HOME!
IN THIS BELIEF, YOU HAVE BEEN MOST GRIEVOUSLY MISLED BY THOSE YOU TRUSTED – BY THE GOVERNMENT IN LONDON AND THE PAPERS IN DUBLIN.
TODAY, AS ALWAYS, THE IMPLACABLE – AND ONLY – ENEMY OF OUR COUNTRY...
OF IRELAND...
...IS THE BRITISH STATE!

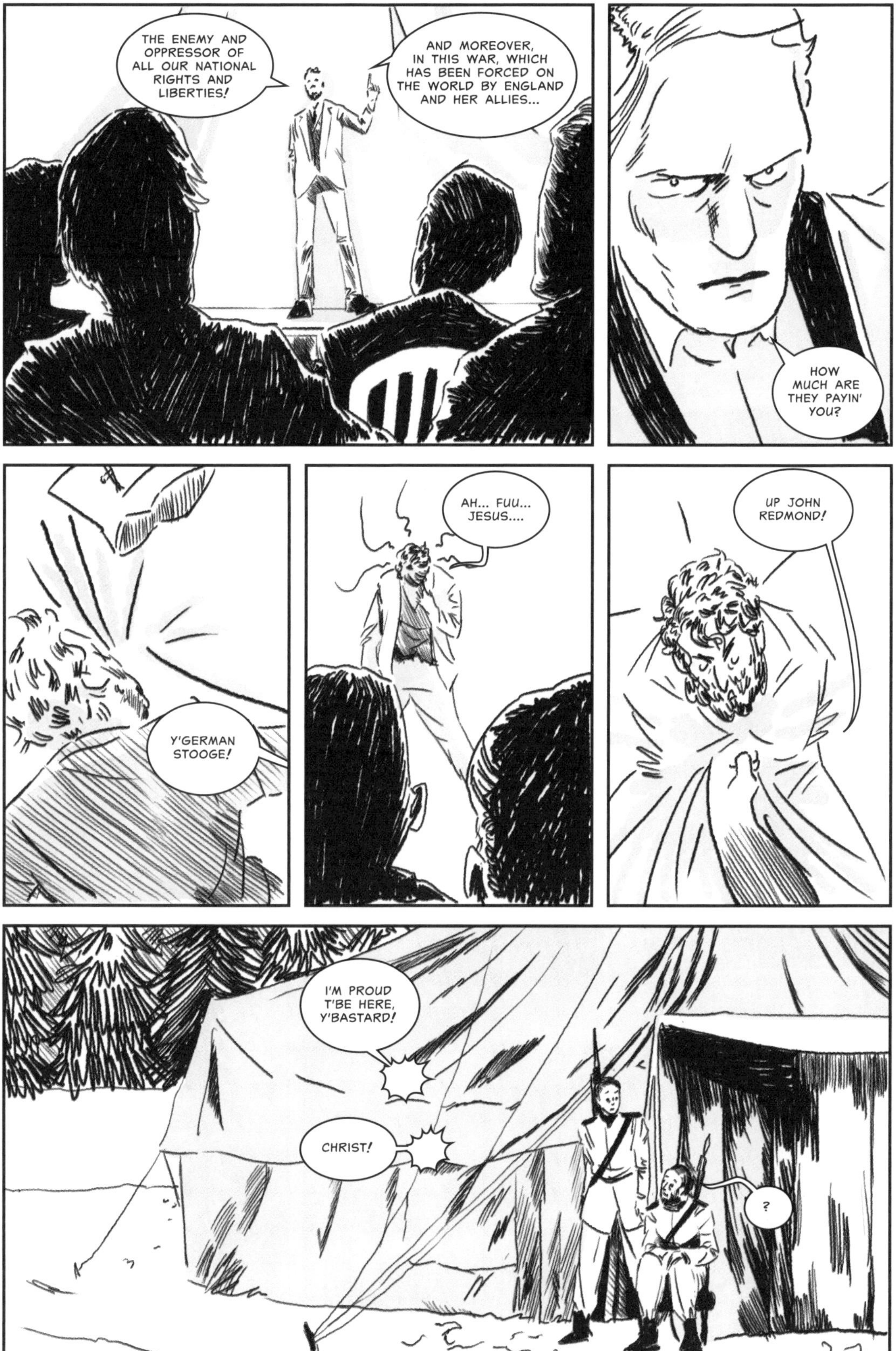
THE ENEMY AND OPPRESSOR OF ALL OUR NATIONAL RIGHTS AND LIBERTIES!
AND MOREOVER, IN THIS WAR, WHICH HAS BEEN FORCED ON THE WORLD BY ENGLAND AND HER ALLIES...
HOW MUCH ARE THEY PAYIN' YOU?
Y'GERMAN STOOGE!
AH... FUU... JESUS....
UP JOHN REDMOND!
I'M PROUD T'BE HERE, Y'BASTARD!
CHRIST!
?

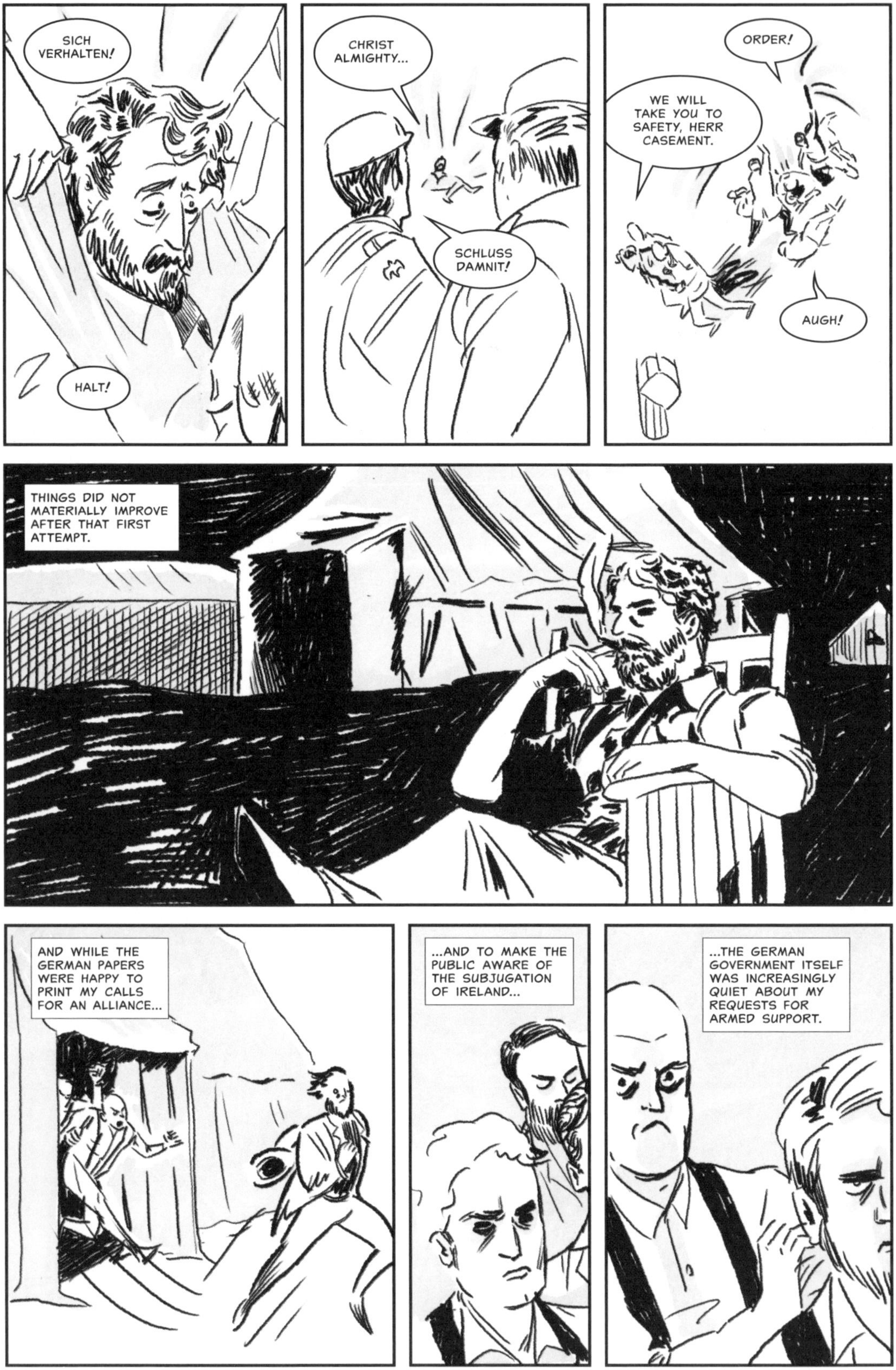
SICH VERHALTEN!
HALT!
CHRIST ALMIGHTY...
SCHLUSS DAMNIT!
ORDER!
WE WILL TAKE YOU TO SAFETY, HERR CASEMENT.
AUGH!
THINGS DID NOT MATERIALLY IMPROVE AFTER THAT FIRST ATTEMPT.
AND WHILE THE GERMAN PAPERS WERE HAPPY TO PRINT MY CALLS FOR AN ALLIANCE...
...AND TO MAKE THE PUBLIC AWARE OF THE SUBJUGATION OF IRELAND...
...THE GERMAN GOVERNMENT ITSELF WAS INCREASINGLY QUIET ABOUT MY REQUESTS FOR ARMED SUPPORT.

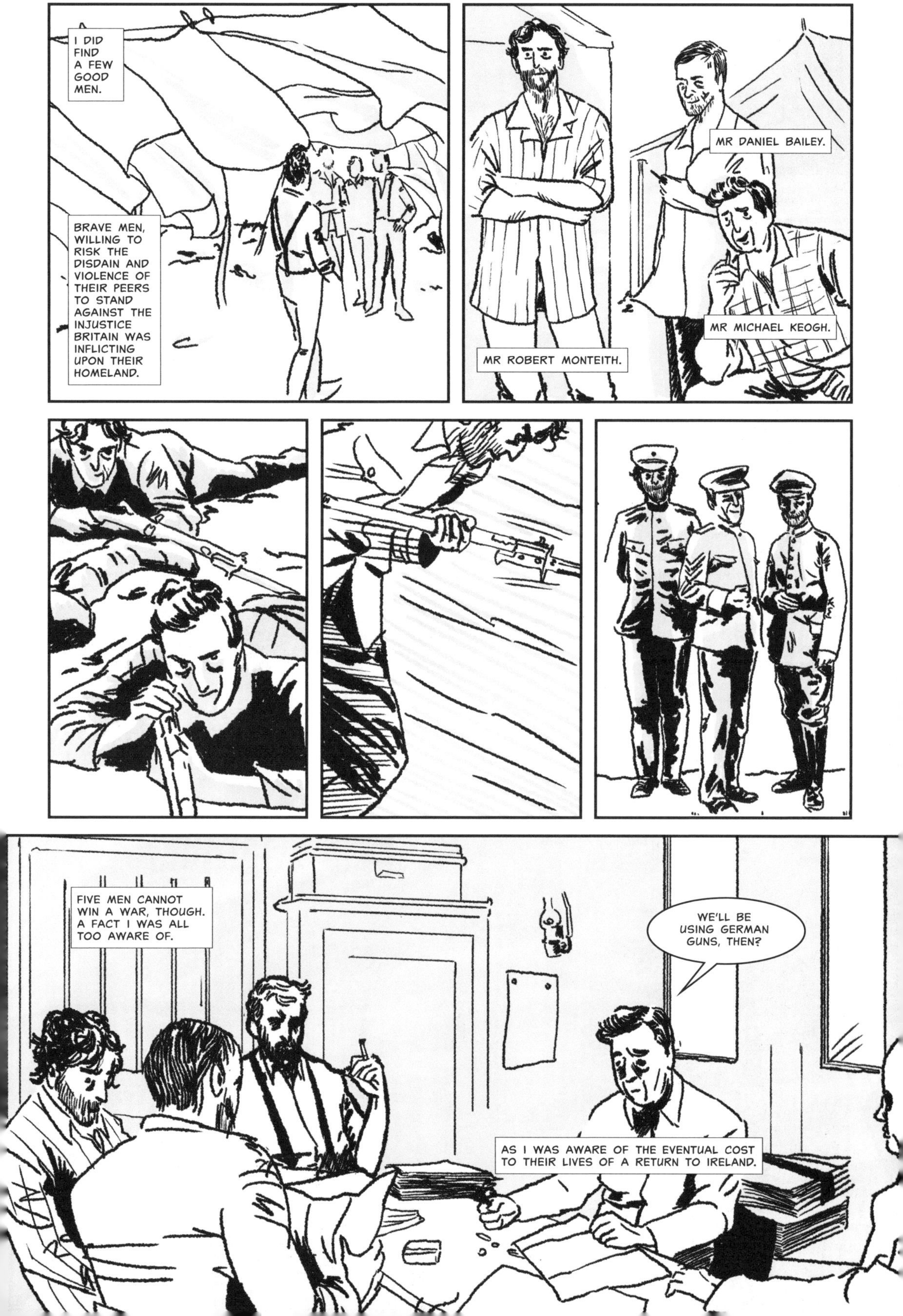
I DID FIND A FEW GOOD MEN.
BRAVE MEN, WILLING TO RISK THE DISDAIN AND VIOLENCE OF THEIR PEERS TO STAND AGAINST THE INJUSTICE BRITAIN WAS INFLICTING UPON THEIR HOMELAND.
MR DANIEL BAILEY.
MR MICHAEL KEOGH.
MR ROBERT MONTEITH.
FIVE MEN CANNOT WIN A WAR, THOUGH. A FACT I WAS ALL TOO AWARE OF.
WE'LL BE USING GERMAN GUNS, THEN?
AS I WAS AWARE OF THE EVENTUAL COST TO THEIR LIVES OF A RETURN TO IRELAND.

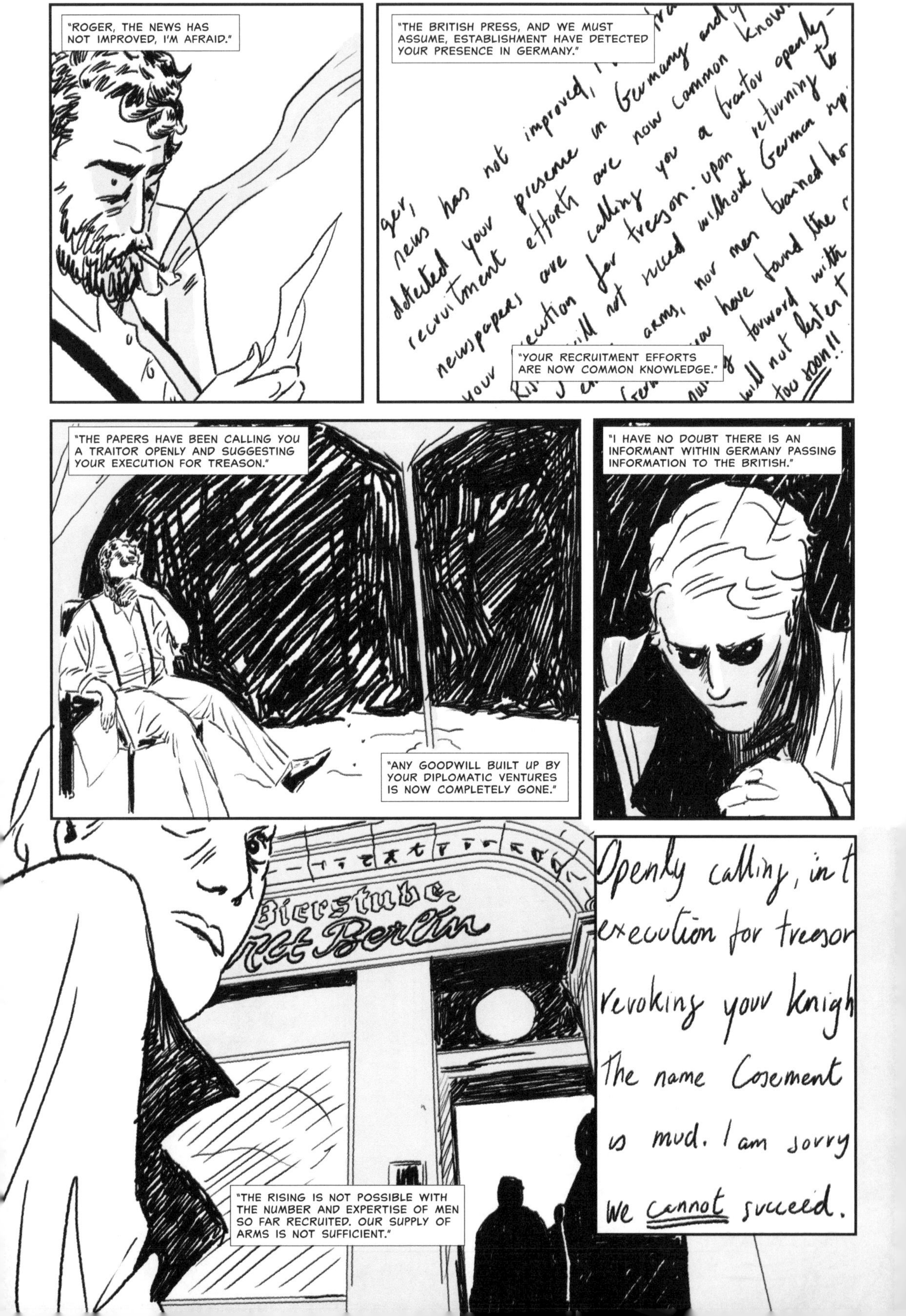
"ROGER, THE NEWS HAS NOT IMPROVED, I'M AFRAID."
"THE BRITISH PRESS, AND WE MUST ASSUME, ESTABLISHMENT HAVE DETECTED YOUR PRESENCE IN GERMANY."
"YOUR RECRUITMENT EFFORTS ARE NOW COMMON KNOWLEDGE."
"THE PAPERS HAVE BEEN CALLING YOU A TRAITOR OPENLY AND SUGGESTING YOUR EXECUTION FOR TREASON."
"ANY GOODWILL BUILT UP BY YOUR DIPLOMATIC VENTURES IS NOW COMPLETELY GONE."
"I HAVE NO DOUBT THERE IS AN INFORMANT WITHIN GERMANY PASSING INFORMATION TO THE BRITISH."
Bierstube
"THE RISING IS NOT POSSIBLE WITH THE NUMBER AND EXPERTISE OF MEN SO FAR RECRUITED. OUR SUPPLY OF ARMS IS NOT SUFFICIENT."
Openly calling, in t
execution for treason
revoking your knigh
The name Casement
is mud. I am sorry
we cannot succeed.

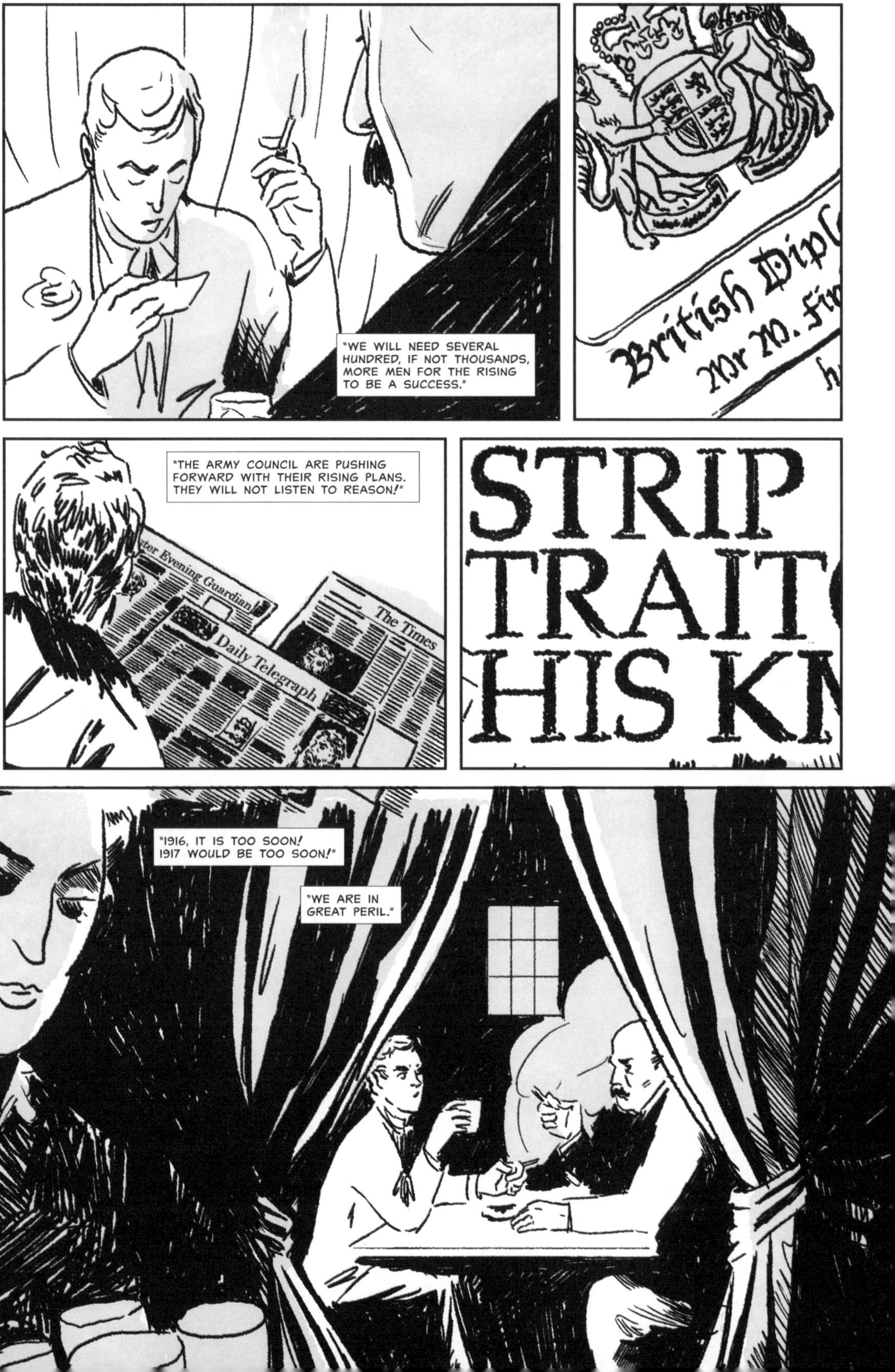
"WE WILL NEED SEVERAL HUNDRED, IF NOT THOUSANDS, MORE MEN FOR THE RISING TO BE A SUCCESS."
British
"THE ARMY COUNCIL ARE PUSHING FORWARD WITH THEIR RISING PLANS. THEY WILL NOT LISTEN TO REASON!"
Evening Guardian
The Times
Daily Telegraph
STRIP
"1916, IT IS TOO SOON! 1917 WOULD BE TOO SOON!"
"WE ARE IN GREAT PERIL."

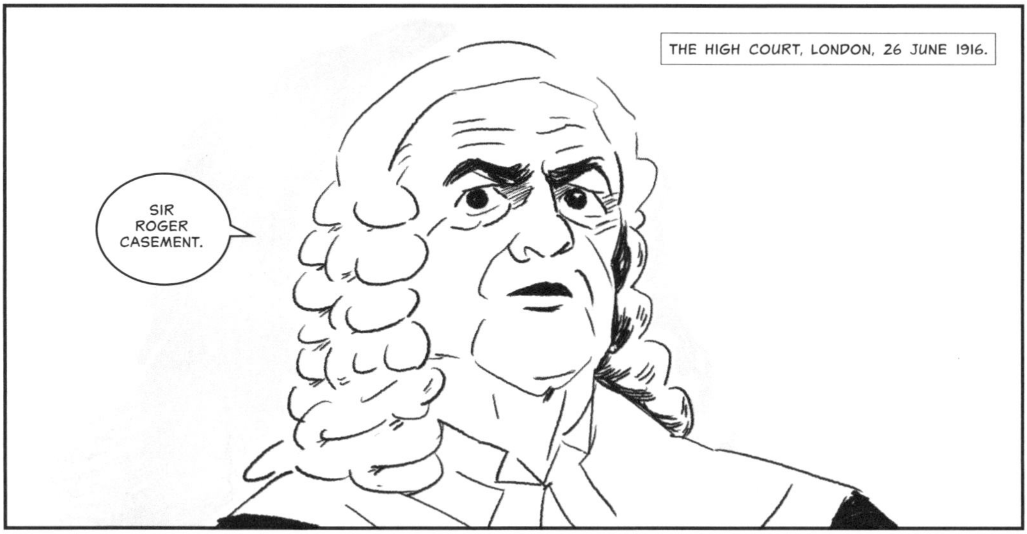
THE HIGH COURT, LONDON, 26 JUNE 1916.
SIR ROGER CASEMENT.

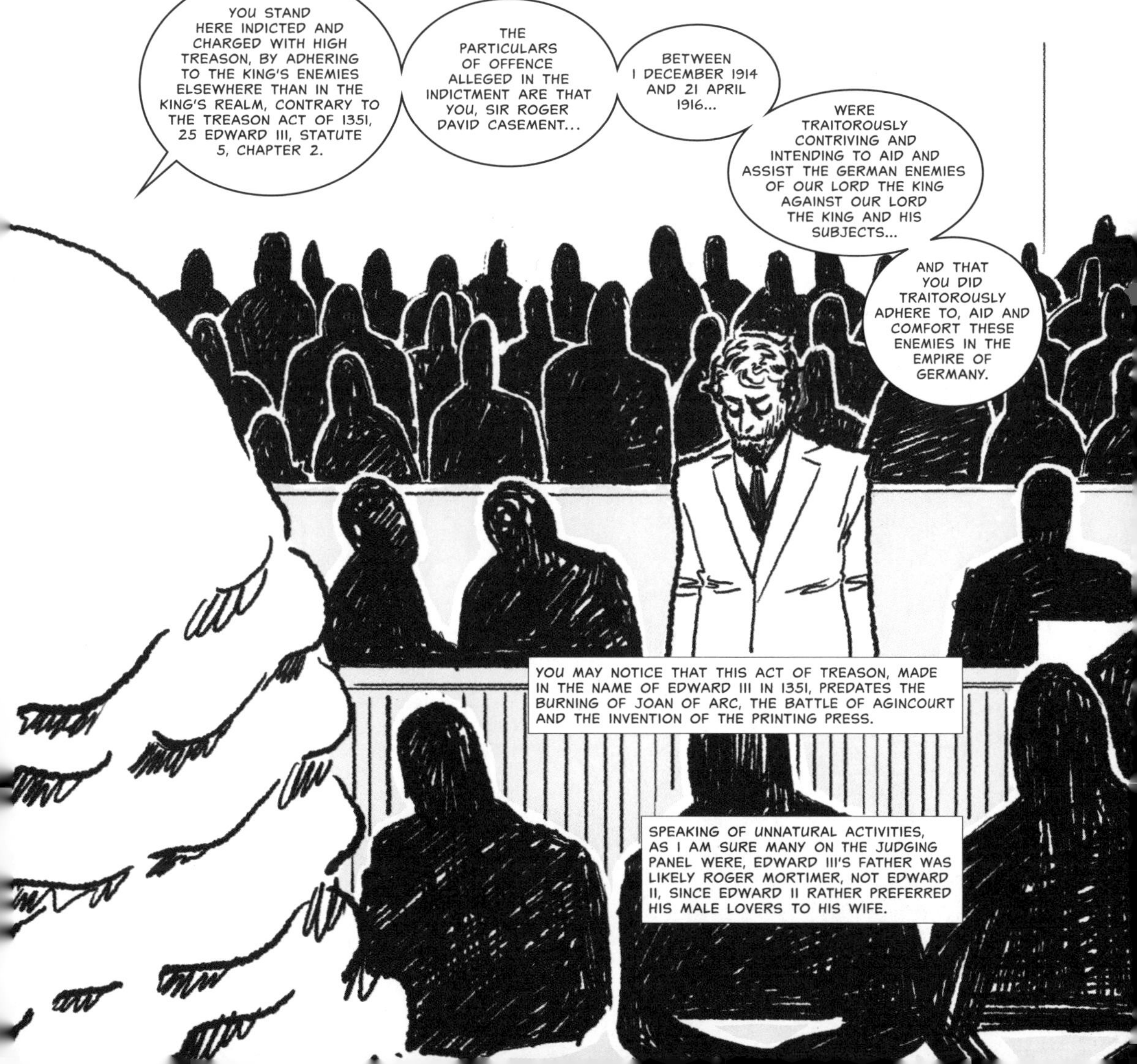
YOU STAND HERE INDICTED AND CHARGED WITH HIGH TREASON, BY ADHERING TO THE KING'S ENEMIES ELSEWHERE THAN IN THE KING'S REALM, CONTRARY TO THE TREASON ACT OF 1351, 25 EDWARD III, STATUTE 5, CHAPTER 2.
THE PARTICULARS OF OFFENCE ALLEGED IN THE INDICTMENT ARE THAT YOU, SIR ROGER DAVID CASEMENT...
BETWEEN 1 DECEMBER 1914 AND 21 APRIL 1916...
WERE TRAITOROUSLY CONTRIVING AND INTENDING TO AID AND ASSIST THE GERMAN ENEMIES OF OUR LORD THE KING AGAINST OUR LORD THE KING AND HIS SUBJECTS...
AND THAT YOU DID TRAITOROUSLY ADHERE TO, AID AND COMFORT THESE ENEMIES IN THE EMPIRE OF GERMANY.
YOU MAY NOTICE THAT THIS ACT OF TREASON, MADE IN THE NAME OF EDWARD III IN 1351, PREDATES THE BURNING OF JOAN OF ARC, THE BATTLE OF AGINCOURT AND THE INVENTION OF THE PRINTING PRESS.
SPEAKING OF UNNATURAL ACTIVITIES, AS I AM SURE MANY ON THE JUDGING PANEL WERE, EDWARD III'S FATHER WAS LIKELY ROGER MORTIMER, NOT EDWARD II, SINCE EDWARD II RATHER PREFERRED HIS MALE LOVERS TO HIS WIFE.

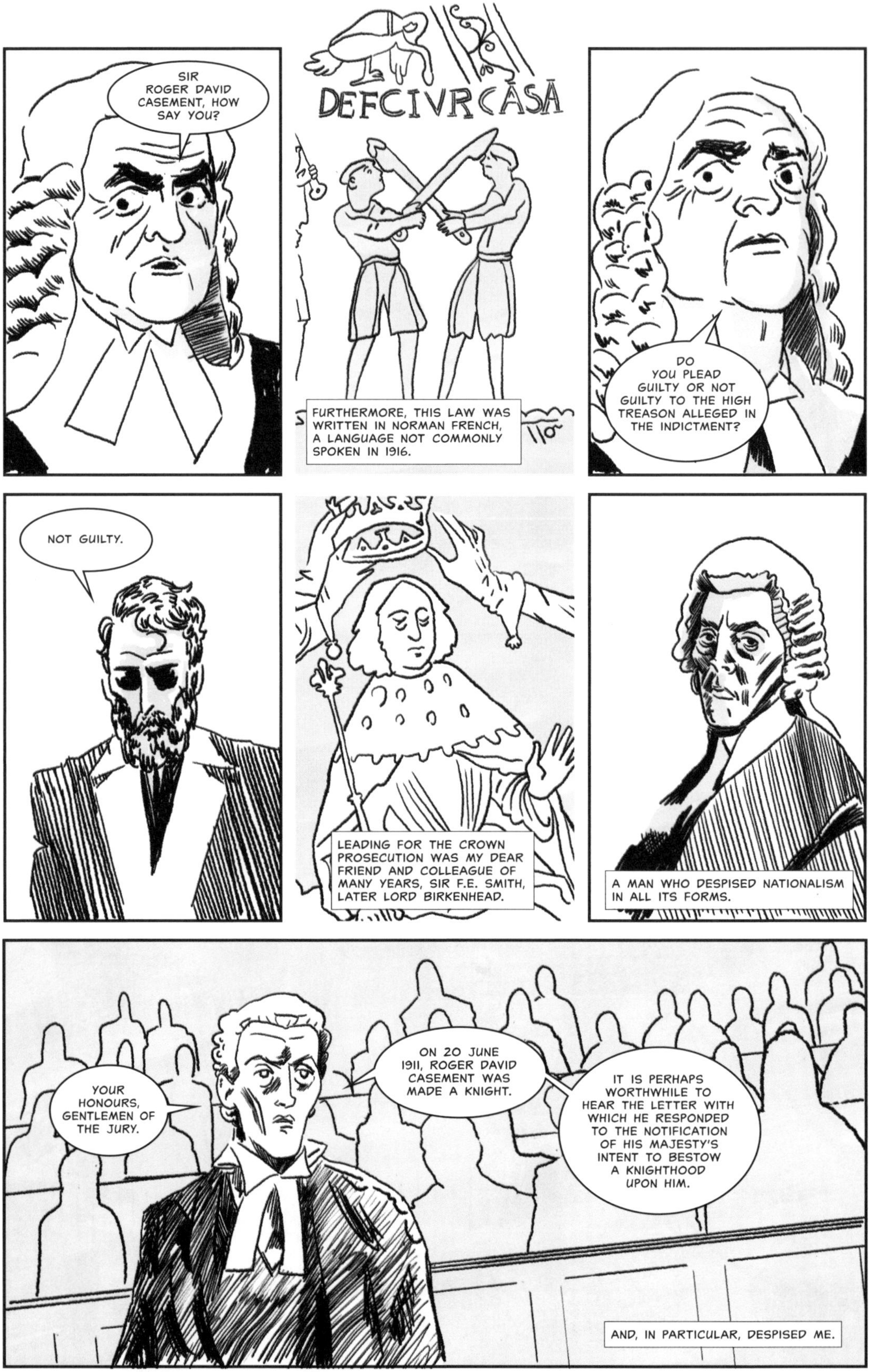
SIR ROGER DAVID CASEMENT, HOW SAY YOU?
DEFCIVRCĀSĀ
FURTHERMORE, THIS LAW WAS WRITTEN IN NORMAN FRENCH, A LANGUAGE NOT COMMONLY SPOKEN IN 1916.
DO YOU PLEAD GUILTY OR NOT GUILTY TO THE HIGH TREASON ALLEGED IN THE INDICTMENT?
NOT GUILTY.
LEADING FOR THE CROWN PROSECUTION WAS MY DEAR FRIEND AND COLLEAGUE OF MANY YEARS, SIR F.E. SMITH, LATER LORD BIRKENHEAD.
A MAN WHO DESPISED NATIONALISM IN ALL ITS FORMS.
YOUR HONOURS, GENTLEMEN OF THE JURY.
ON 20 JUNE 1911, ROGER DAVID CASEMENT WAS MADE A KNIGHT.
IT IS PERHAPS WORTHWHILE TO HEAR THE LETTER WITH WHICH HE RESPONDED TO THE NOTIFICATION OF HIS MAJESTY'S INTENT TO BESTOW A KNIGHTHOOD UPON HIM.
AND, IN PARTICULAR, DESPISED ME.

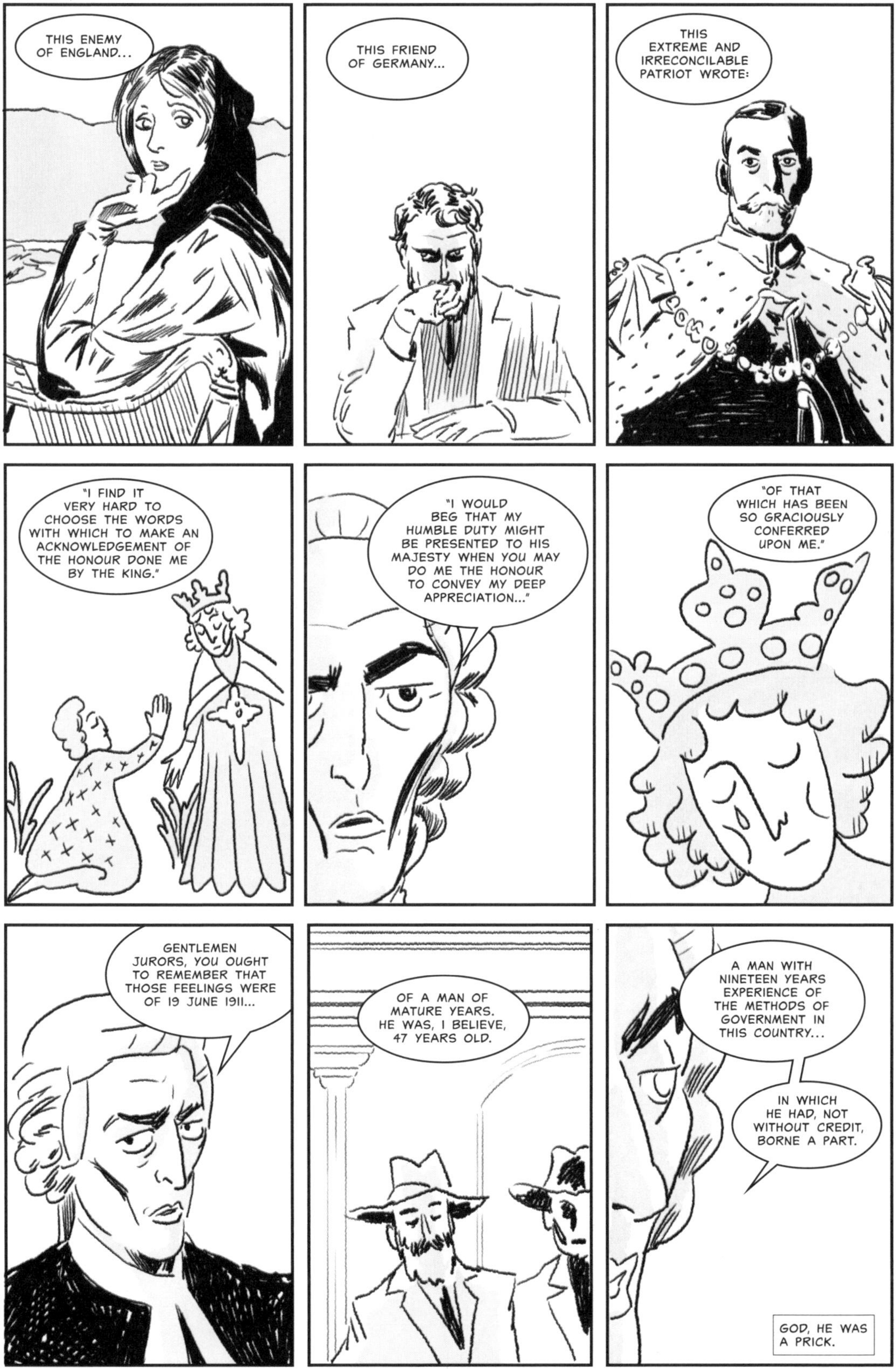
THIS ENEMY OF ENGLAND...
THIS FRIEND OF GERMANY...
THIS EXTREME AND IRRECONCILABLE PATRIOT WROTE:
"I FIND IT VERY HARD TO CHOOSE THE WORDS WITH WHICH TO MAKE AN ACKNOWLEDGEMENT OF THE HONOUR DONE ME BY THE KING."
"I WOULD BEG THAT MY HUMBLE DUTY MIGHT BE PRESENTED TO HIS MAJESTY WHEN YOU MAY DO ME THE HONOUR TO CONVEY MY DEEP APPRECIATION..."
"OF THAT WHICH HAS BEEN SO GRACIOUSLY CONFERRED UPON ME."
GENTLEMEN JURORS, YOU OUGHT TO REMEMBER THAT THOSE FEELINGS WERE OF 19 JUNE 1911...
OF A MAN OF MATURE YEARS. HE WAS, I BELIEVE, 47 YEARS OLD.
A MAN WITH NINETEEN YEARS EXPERIENCE OF THE METHODS OF GOVERNMENT IN THIS COUNTRY...
IN WHICH HE HAD, NOT WITHOUT CREDIT, BORNE A PART.
GOD, HE WAS A PRICK.

SUCH A MAN WRITES IN TERMS OF GRATITUDE, UNUSUAL, PERHAPS, IN THEIR WARMTH.

IN THE LANGUAGE ALMOST OF A COURTIER, HE EXPRESSES HIS PLEASURE AT THE TITLE BESTOWED UPON HIM.

THE HISTORY OF THE RELATIONS BETWEEN ENGLAND AND IRELAND WERE AS WELL KNOWN THOSE FIVE YEARS AGO AS THEY ARE NOW.

THE CONTROVERSIES BITTER.

THE POLITICISM OFTEN TRAGIC.

AND WELL UNDERSTANDING THOSE CONTROVERSIES...

...FULLY VERSED IN THE WRONGS OF WHICH IRISHMEN WERE FRUITFUL IN COMPLAINT...

...KNOWING ENGLAND'S IDEALS OF GOVERNMENT WELL, FOR AT THOSE OUTPOSTS OF EMPIRE HE CARRIED THEM OUT PERSONALLY...

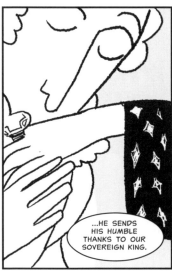

...HE SENDS HIS HUMBLE THANKS TO OUR SOVEREIGN KING.

WHAT OCCURRED BETWEEN 1911 AND 1914 TO PERVERT AND CORRUPT THE PRISONER'S MIND...

...I CANNOT TELL, FOR I DO NOT KNOW.

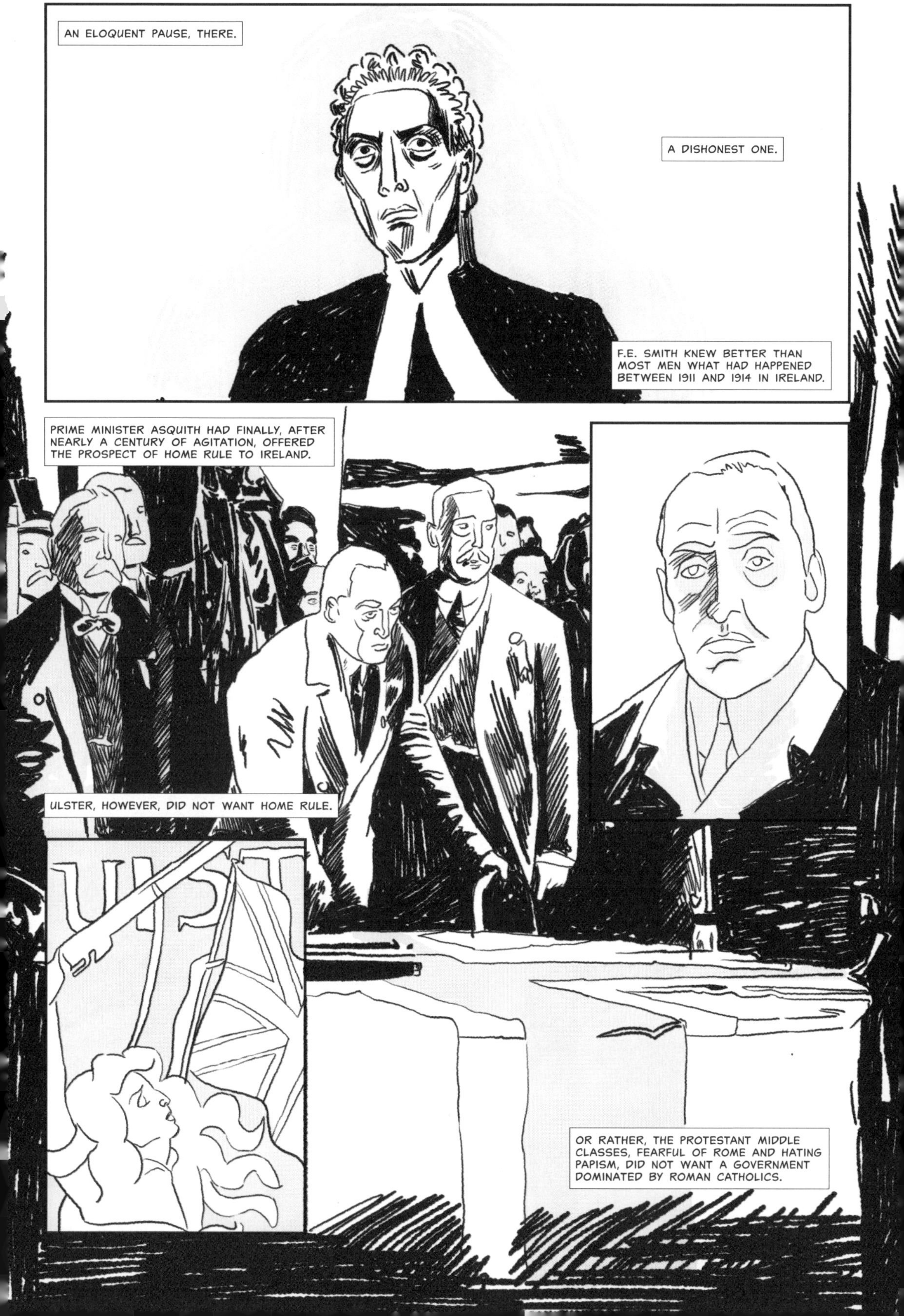
AN ELOQUENT PAUSE, THERE.
A DISHONEST ONE.
F.E. SMITH KNEW BETTER THAN MOST MEN WHAT HAD HAPPENED BETWEEN 1911 AND 1914 IN IRELAND.
PRIME MINISTER ASQUITH HAD FINALLY, AFTER NEARLY A CENTURY OF AGITATION, OFFERED THE PROSPECT OF HOME RULE TO IRELAND.
ULSTER, HOWEVER, DID NOT WANT HOME RULE.
OR RATHER, THE PROTESTANT MIDDLE CLASSES, FEARFUL OF ROME AND HATING PAPISM, DID NOT WANT A GOVERNMENT DOMINATED BY ROMAN CATHOLICS.

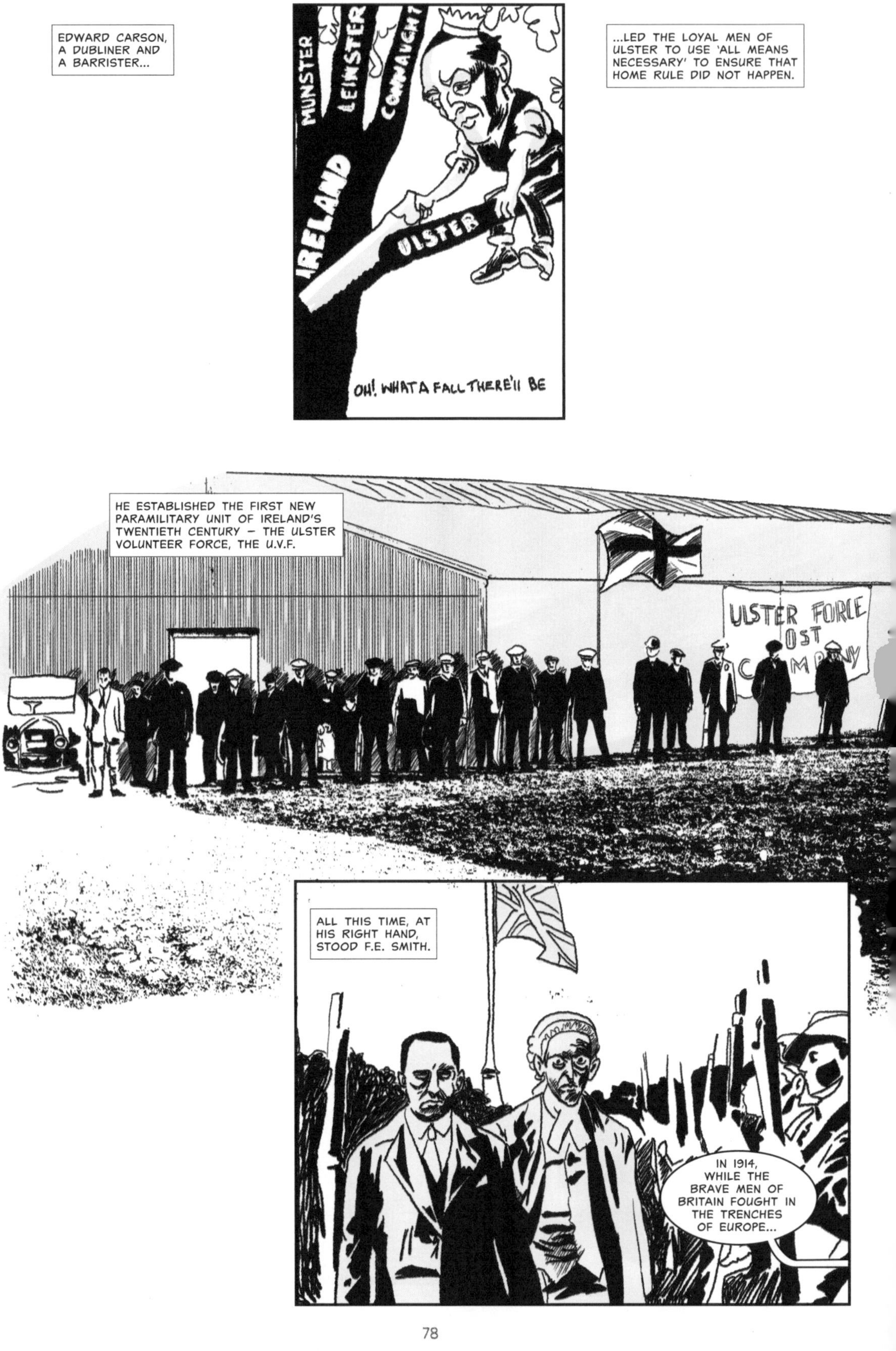
EDWARD CARSON, A DUBLINER AND A BARRISTER...
MUNSTER
LEINSTER
CONNAUGHT
IRELAND
ULSTER
OH! WHAT A FALL THERE'll BE
...LED THE LOYAL MEN OF ULSTER TO USE 'ALL MEANS NECESSARY' TO ENSURE THAT HOME RULE DID NOT HAPPEN.
HE ESTABLISHED THE FIRST NEW PARAMILITARY UNIT OF IRELAND'S TWENTIETH CENTURY – THE ULSTER VOLUNTEER FORCE, THE U.V.F.
ULSTER FORCE
ALL THIS TIME, AT HIS RIGHT HAND, STOOD F.E. SMITH.
IN 1914, WHILE THE BRAVE MEN OF BRITAIN FOUGHT IN THE TRENCHES OF EUROPE...

THE PRISONER MOVED WITH FREEDOM IN GERMANY, APPARENTLY AN HONOURED GUEST OF THE GERMAN NATION.

THERE, HE PLAYED THE PART OF A VILLAIN, SEDUCING THESE BRAVE MEN FROM THEIR ALLEGIANCES TO THE KING, THEIR SOVEREIGN...

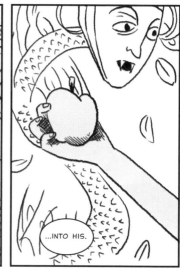

...INTO HIS.

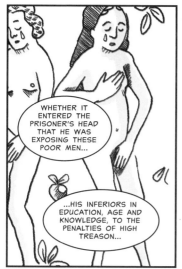

WHETHER IT ENTERED THE PRISONER'S HEAD THAT HE WAS EXPOSING THESE POOR MEN...

...HIS INFERIORS IN EDUCATION, AGE AND KNOWLEDGE, TO THE PENALTIES OF HIGH TREASON...

...I CANNOT TELL YOU.

ON 21 APRIL 1916, GOOD FRIDAY, THE AUD, A GERMAN VESSEL WHICH HAD TAKEN EVERY MEANS OF DISGUISING HER GERMAN CHARACTER...

...WAS SIGHTED APPROACHING THE SHORES OF IRELAND IN THE NEIGHBOURHOOD OF TRALEE BY HIS MAJESTY'S SLOOP, THE BLUEBELL.

THE BLUEBELL ESCORTED THE AUD TO HARBOUR, BUT SHE WAS SCUTTLED BY HER CREW OFF THE DAUNT ROCK LIGHTSHIP.

DIVERS HAVE SINCE ASCERTAINED THAT HER CARGO CONSISTED OF RIFLES.

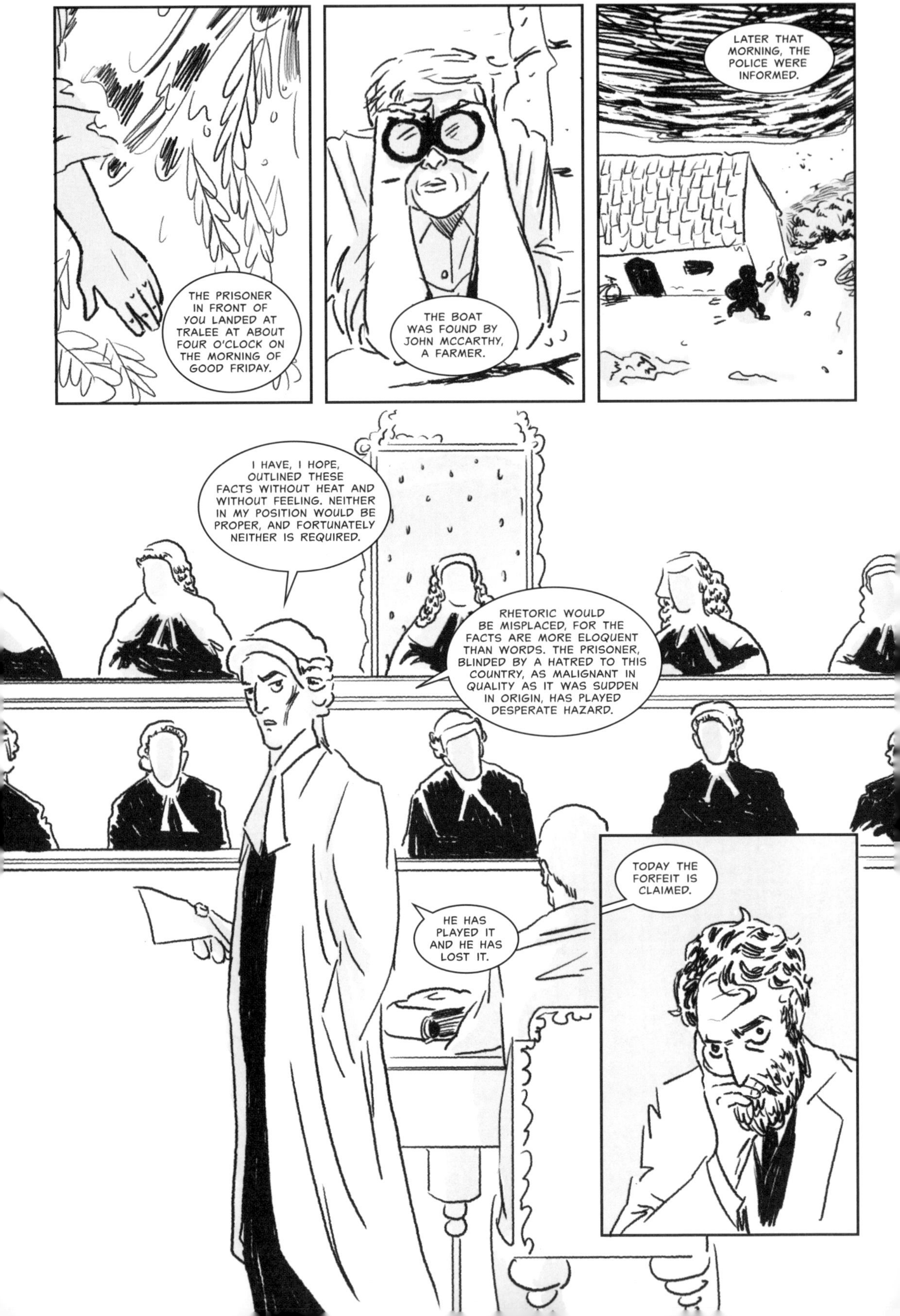
THE PRISONER IN FRONT OF YOU LANDED AT TRALEE AT ABOUT FOUR O'CLOCK ON THE MORNING OF GOOD FRIDAY.
THE BOAT WAS FOUND BY JOHN MCCARTHY, A FARMER.
LATER THAT MORNING, THE POLICE WERE INFORMED.
I HAVE, I HOPE, OUTLINED THESE FACTS WITHOUT HEAT AND WITHOUT FEELING. NEITHER IN MY POSITION WOULD BE PROPER, AND FORTUNATELY NEITHER IS REQUIRED.
RHETORIC WOULD BE MISPLACED, FOR THE FACTS ARE MORE ELOQUENT THAN WORDS. THE PRISONER, BLINDED BY A HATRED TO THIS COUNTRY, AS MALIGNANT IN QUALITY AS IT WAS SUDDEN IN ORIGIN, HAS PLAYED DESPERATE HAZARD.
HE HAS PLAYED IT AND HE HAS LOST IT.
TODAY THE FORFEIT IS CLAIMED.

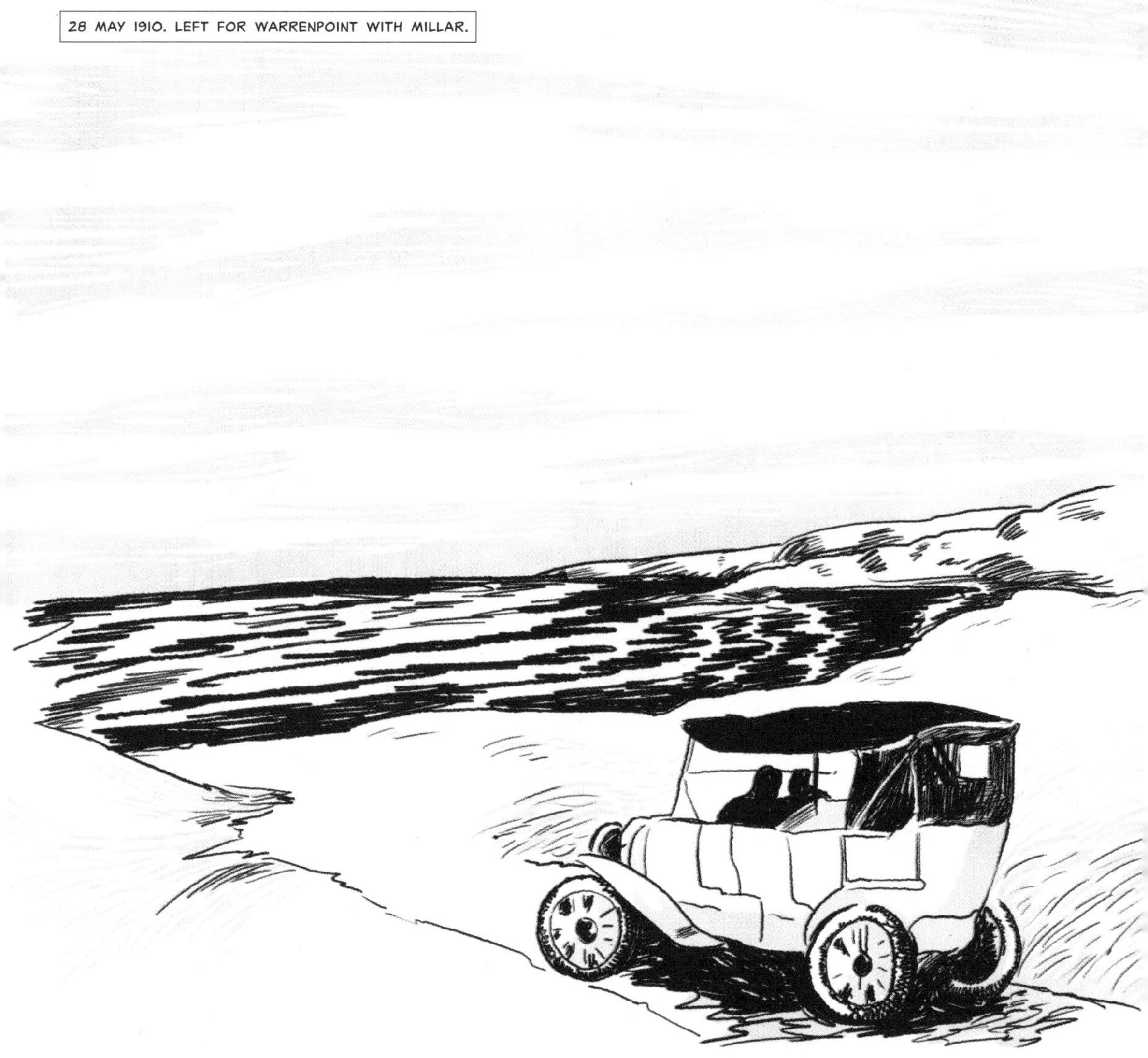
28 MAY 1910. LEFT FOR WARRENPOINT WITH MILLAR.

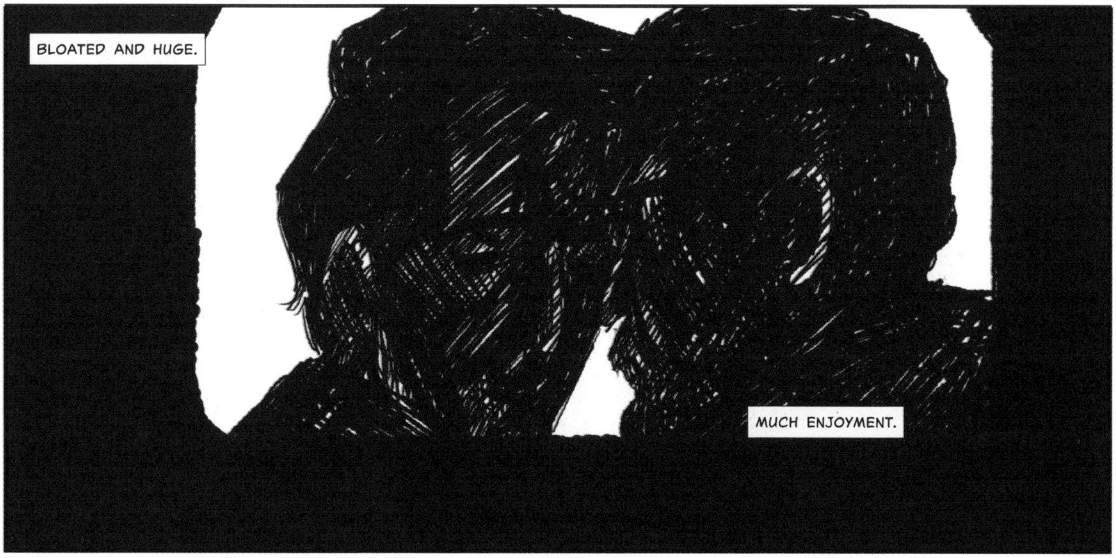
BLOATED AND HUGE.
MUCH ENJOYMENT.

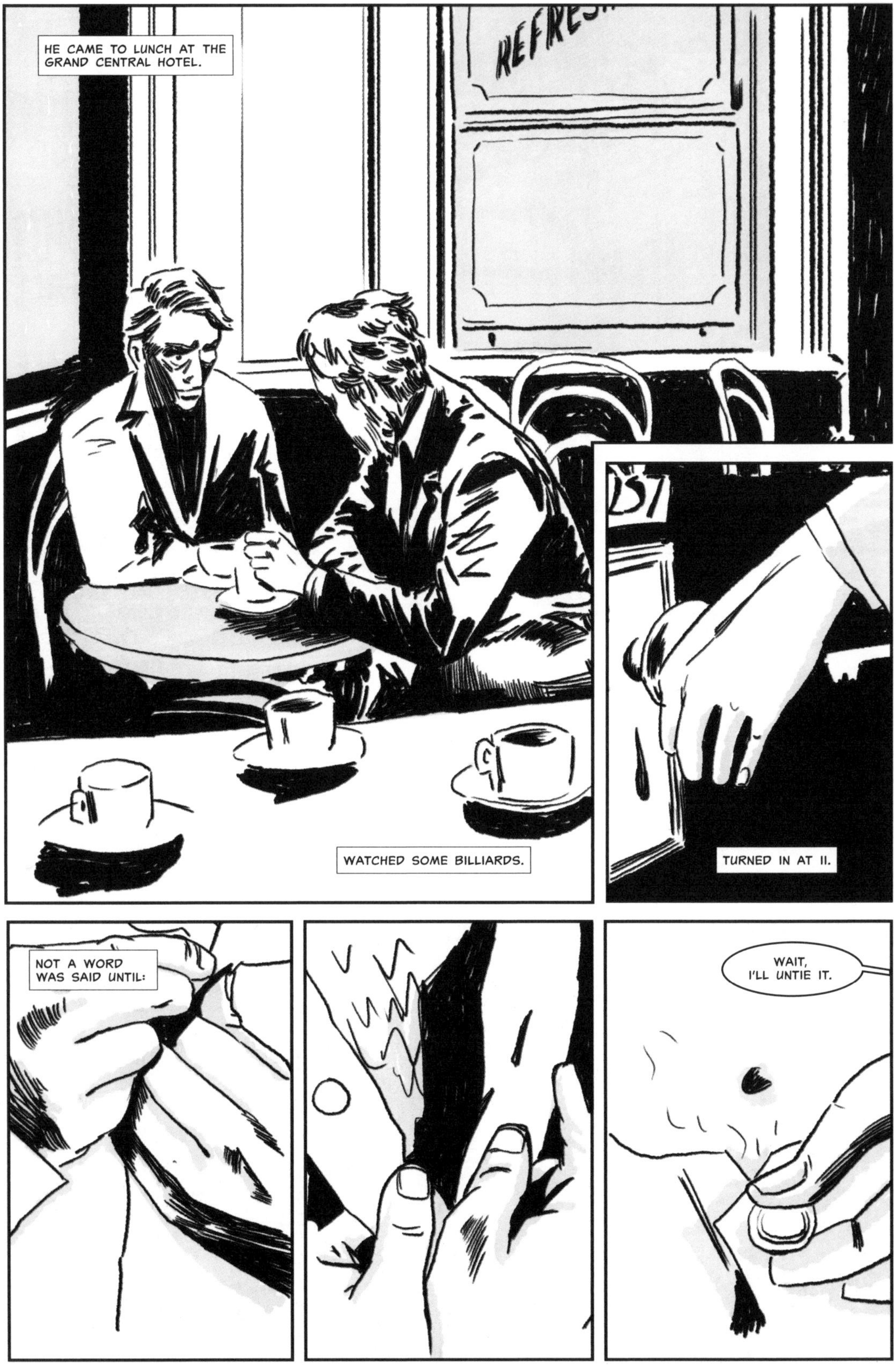

HE CAME TO LUNCH AT THE GRAND CENTRAL HOTEL.
WATCHED SOME BILLIARDS.
TURNED IN AT 11.
NOT A WORD WAS SAID UNTIL:
WAIT, I'LL UNTIE IT.

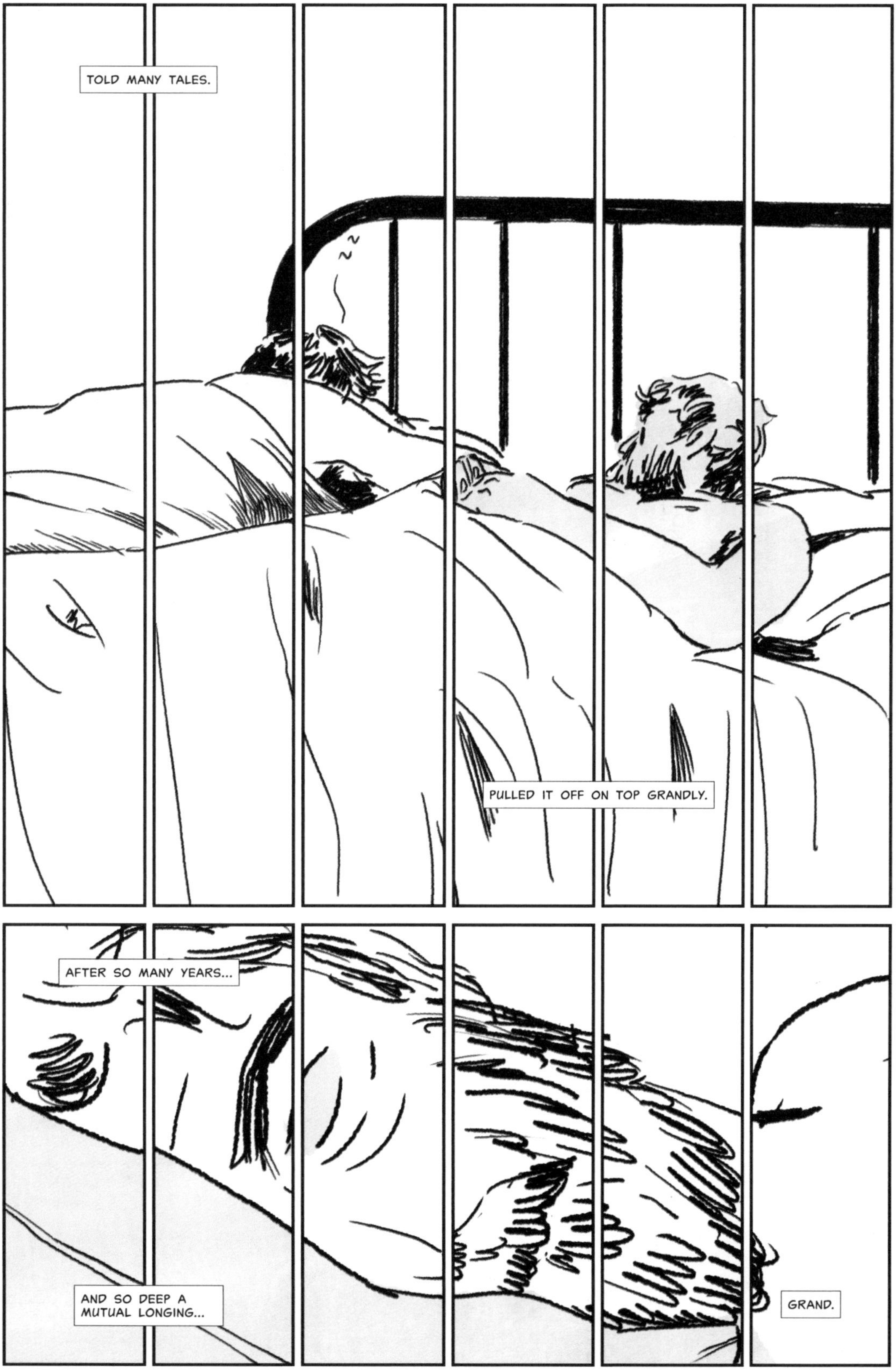
TOLD MANY TALES.
PULLED IT OFF ON TOP GRANDLY.
AFTER SO MANY YEARS...
AND SO DEEP A MUTUAL LONGING...
GRAND.

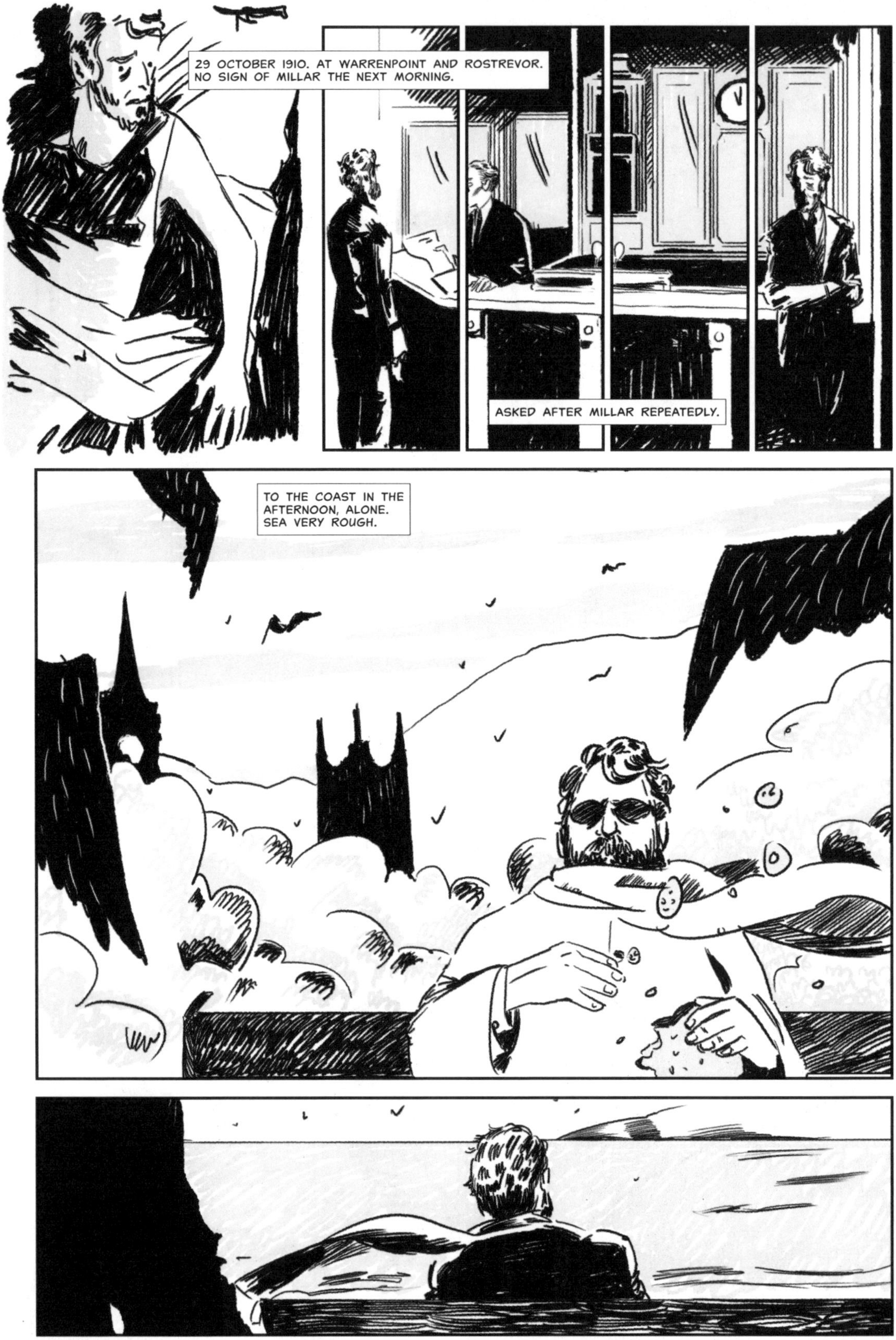
29 OCTOBER 1910. AT WARRENPOINT AND ROSTREVOR.
NO SIGN OF MILLAR THE NEXT MORNING.
ASKED AFTER MILLAR REPEATEDLY.
TO THE COAST IN THE AFTERNOON, ALONE. SEA VERY ROUGH.

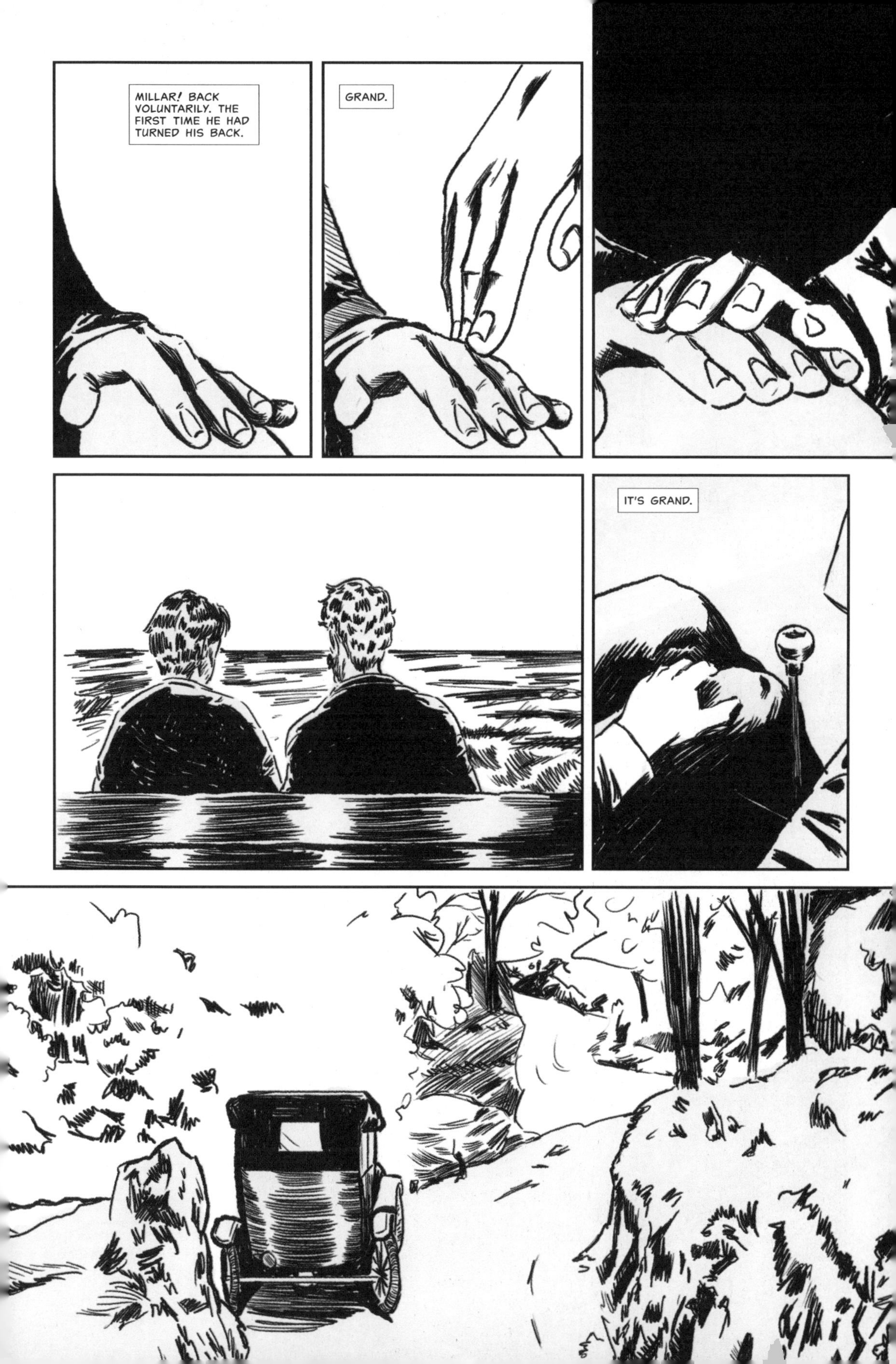
MILLAR! BACK VOLUNTARILY. THE FIRST TIME HE HAD TURNED HIS BACK.
GRAND.
IT'S GRAND.

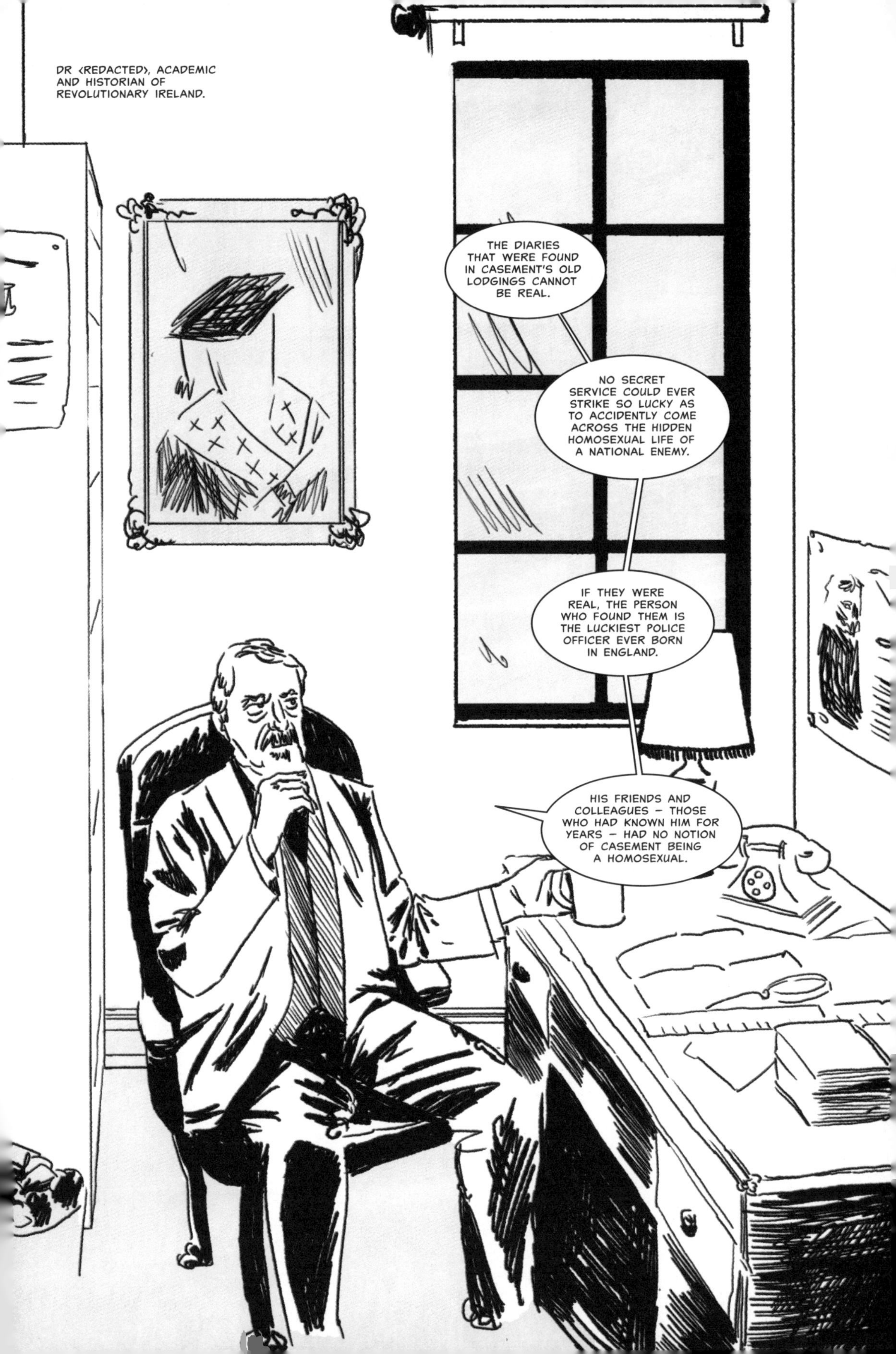
DR <REDACTED>, ACADEMIC AND HISTORIAN OF REVOLUTIONARY IRELAND.
THE DIARIES THAT WERE FOUND IN CASEMENT'S OLD LODGINGS CANNOT BE REAL.
NO SECRET SERVICE COULD EVER STRIKE SO LUCKY AS TO ACCIDENTLY COME ACROSS THE HIDDEN HOMOSEXUAL LIFE OF A NATIONAL ENEMY.
IF THEY WERE REAL, THE PERSON WHO FOUND THEM IS THE LUCKIEST POLICE OFFICER EVER BORN IN ENGLAND.
HIS FRIENDS AND COLLEAGUES – THOSE WHO HAD KNOWN HIM FOR YEARS – HAD NO NOTION OF CASEMENT BEING A HOMOSEXUAL.

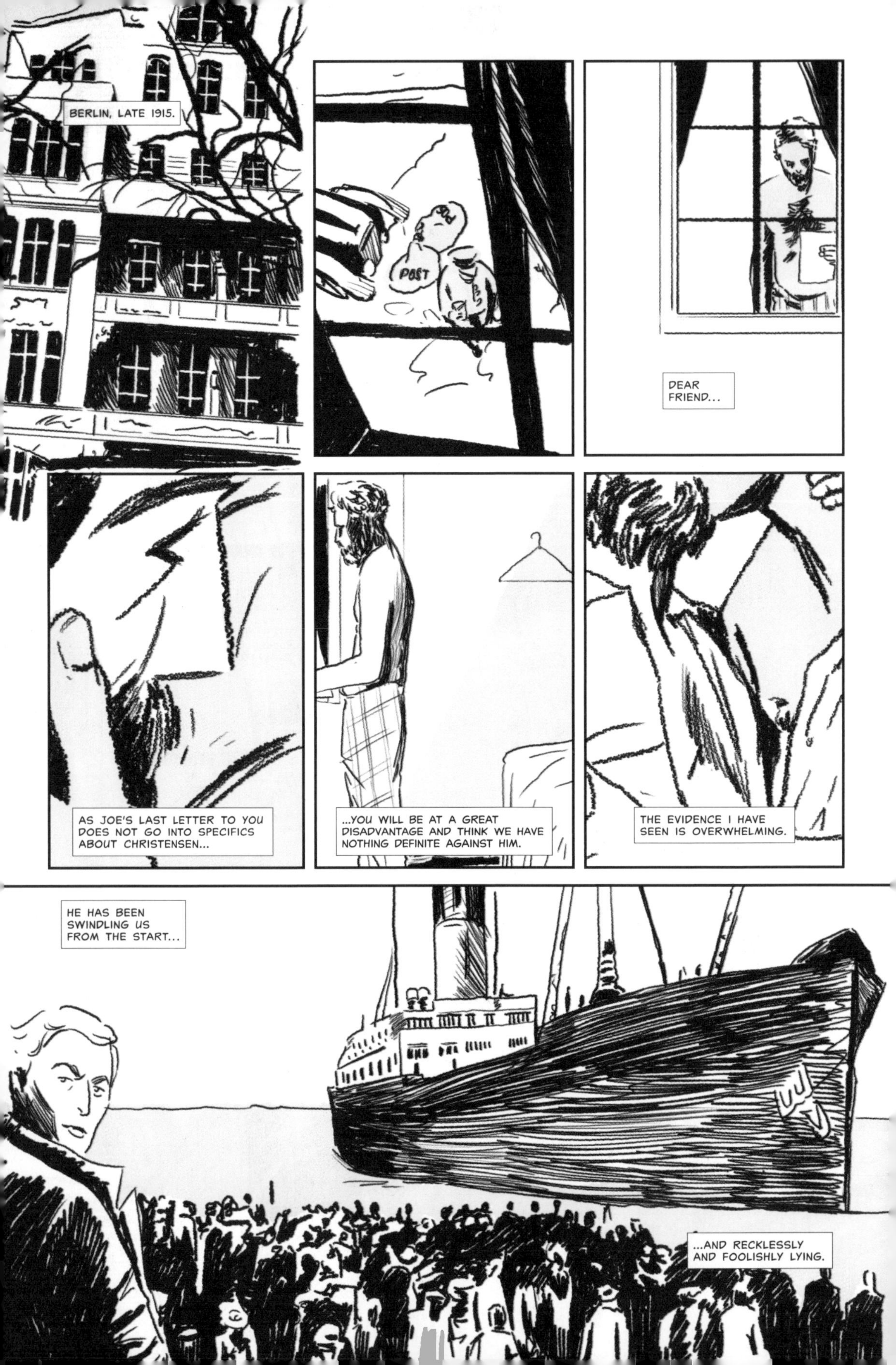
BERLIN, LATE 1915.
POST
POST
DEAR FRIEND...
AS JOE'S LAST LETTER TO YOU DOES NOT GO INTO SPECIFICS ABOUT CHRISTENSEN...
...YOU WILL BE AT A GREAT DISADVANTAGE AND THINK WE HAVE NOTHING DEFINITE AGAINST HIM.
THE EVIDENCE I HAVE SEEN IS OVERWHELMING.
HE HAS BEEN SWINDLING US FROM THE START...
...AND RECKLESSLY AND FOOLISHLY LYING.

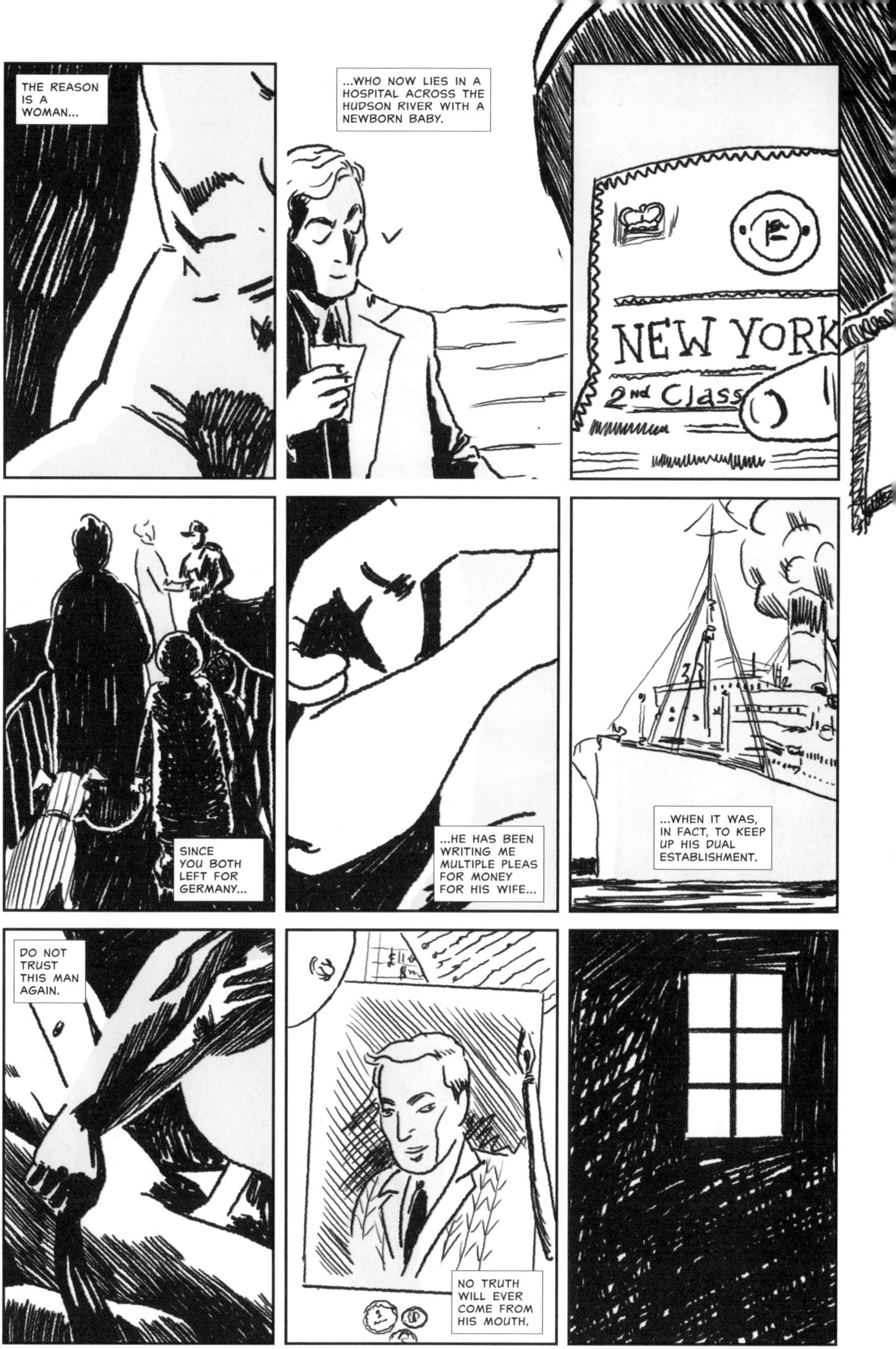
THE REASON IS A WOMAN...
...WHO NOW LIES IN A HOSPITAL ACROSS THE HUDSON RIVER WITH A NEWBORN BABY.
NEW YORK
2nd Class
SINCE YOU BOTH LEFT FOR GERMANY...
...HE HAS BEEN WRITING ME MULTIPLE PLEAS FOR MONEY FOR HIS WIFE...
...WHEN IT WAS, IN FACT, TO KEEP UP HIS DUAL ESTABLISHMENT.
DO NOT TRUST THIS MAN AGAIN.
NO TRUTH WILL EVER COME FROM HIS MOUTH.

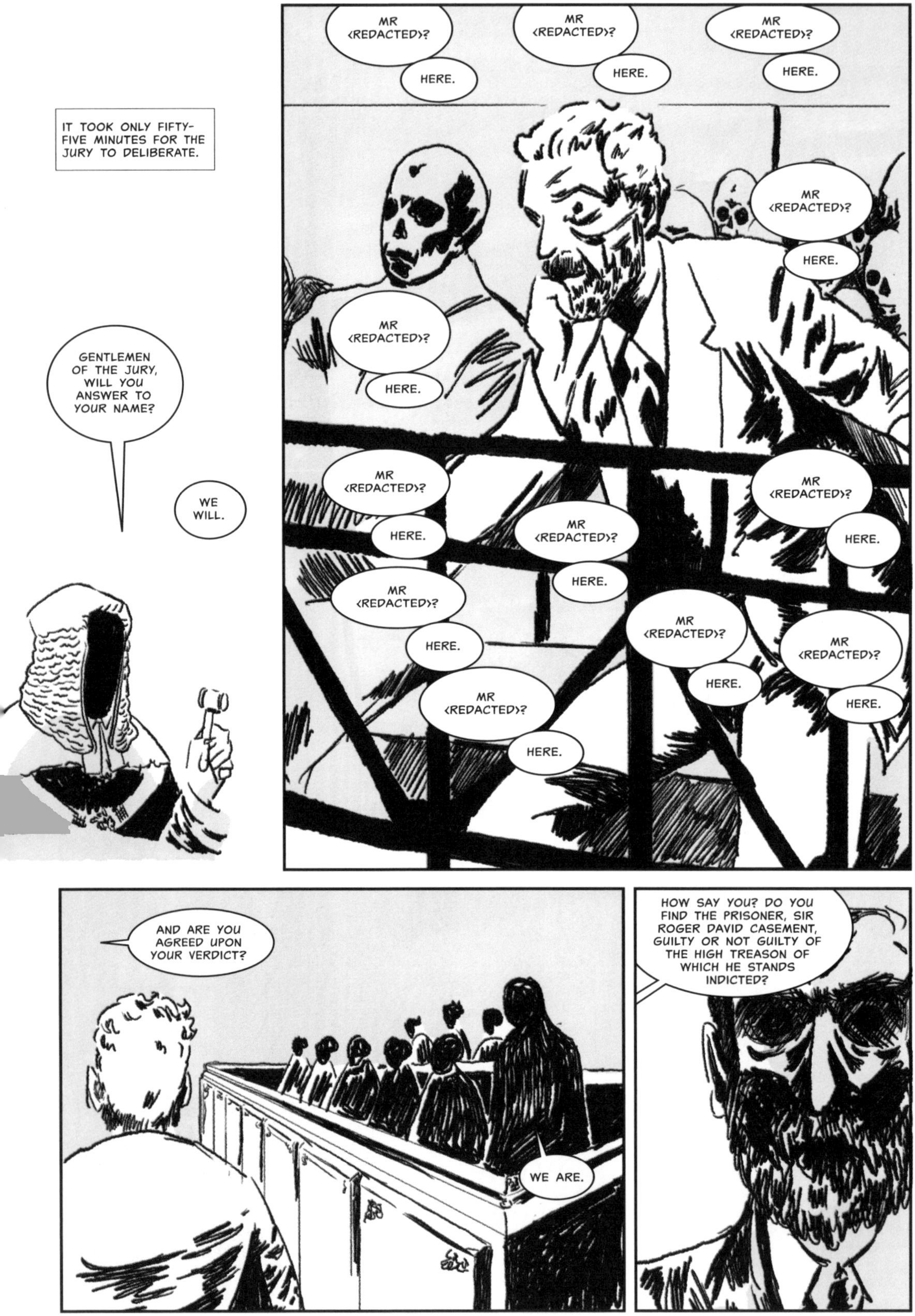
IT TOOK ONLY FIFTY-FIVE MINUTES FOR THE JURY TO DELIBERATE.
GENTLEMEN OF THE JURY, WILL YOU ANSWER TO YOUR NAME?
WE WILL.
MR <REDACTED>?
HERE.
MR <REDACTED>?
HERE.
MR <REDACTED>?
HERE.
MR <REDACTED>?
HERE.
MR <REDACTED>?
HERE.
MR <REDACTED>?
HERE.
MR <REDACTED>?
HERE.
MR <REDACTED>?
HERE.
MR <REDACTED>?
HERE.
MR <REDACTED>?
HERE.
MR <REDACTED>?
HERE.
MR <REDACTED>?
HERE.
AND ARE YOU AGREED UPON YOUR VERDICT?
WE ARE.
HOW SAY YOU? DO YOU FIND THE PRISONER, SIR ROGER DAVID CASEMENT, GUILTY OR NOT GUILTY OF THE HIGH TREASON OF WHICH HE STANDS INDICTED?

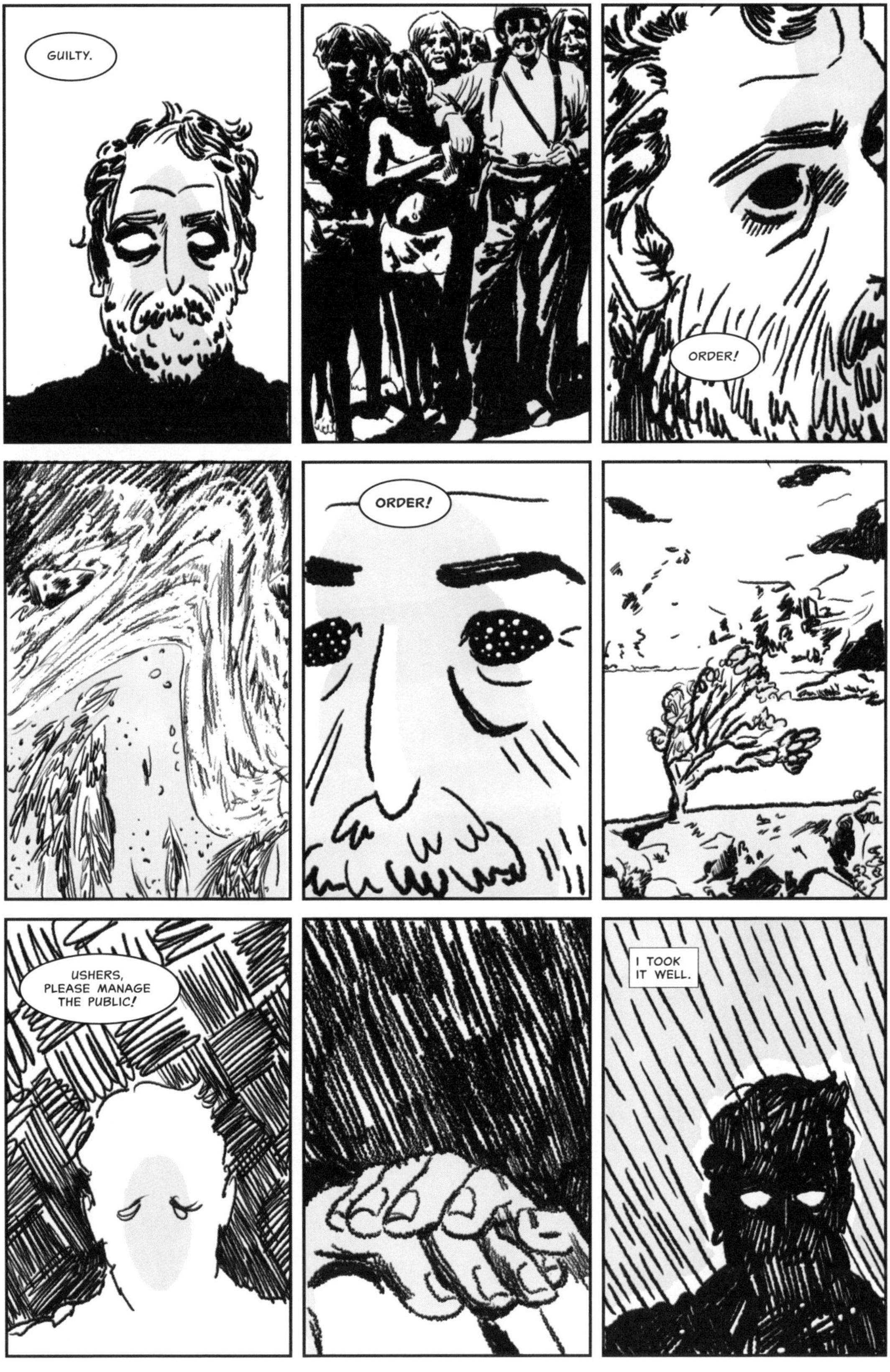
GUILTY.
ORDER!
ORDER!
USHERS, PLEASE MANAGE THE PUBLIC!
I TOOK IT WELL.

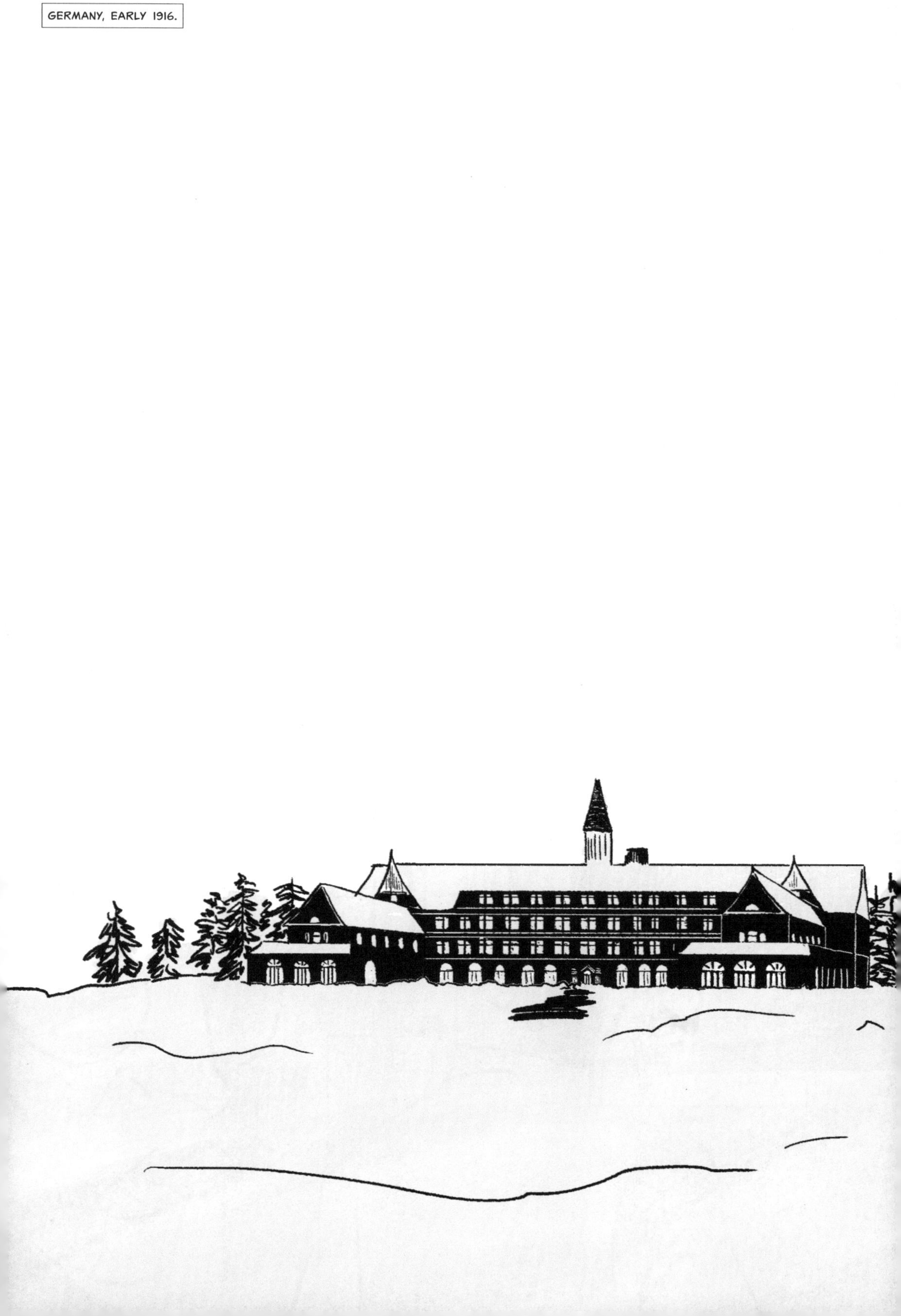
GERMANY, EARLY 1916.

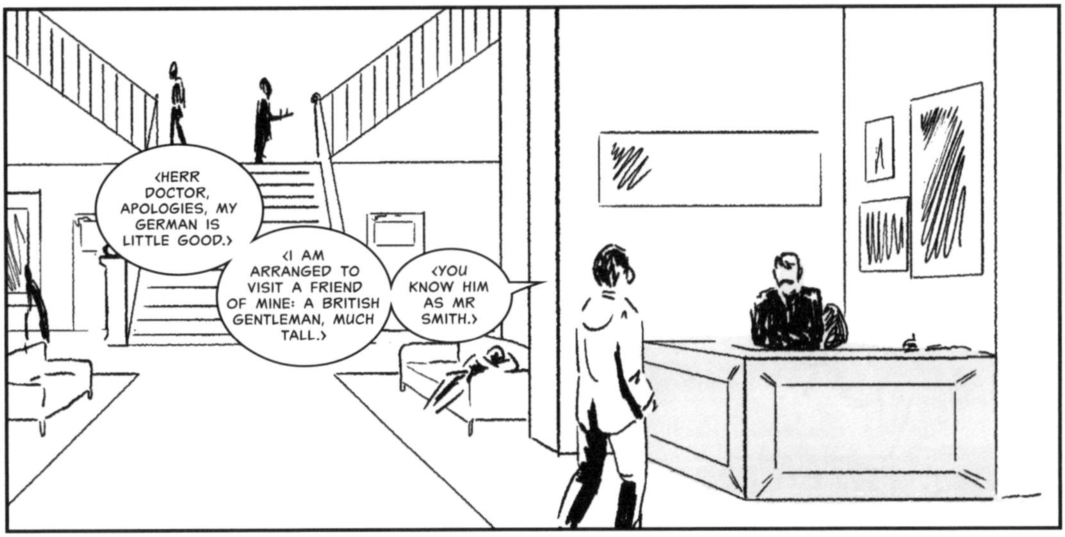
<HERR DOCTOR, APOLOGIES, MY GERMAN IS LITTLE GOOD.>
<I AM ARRANGED TO VISIT A FRIEND OF MINE: A BRITISH GENTLEMAN, MUCH TALL.>
<YOU KNOW HIM AS MR SMITH.>

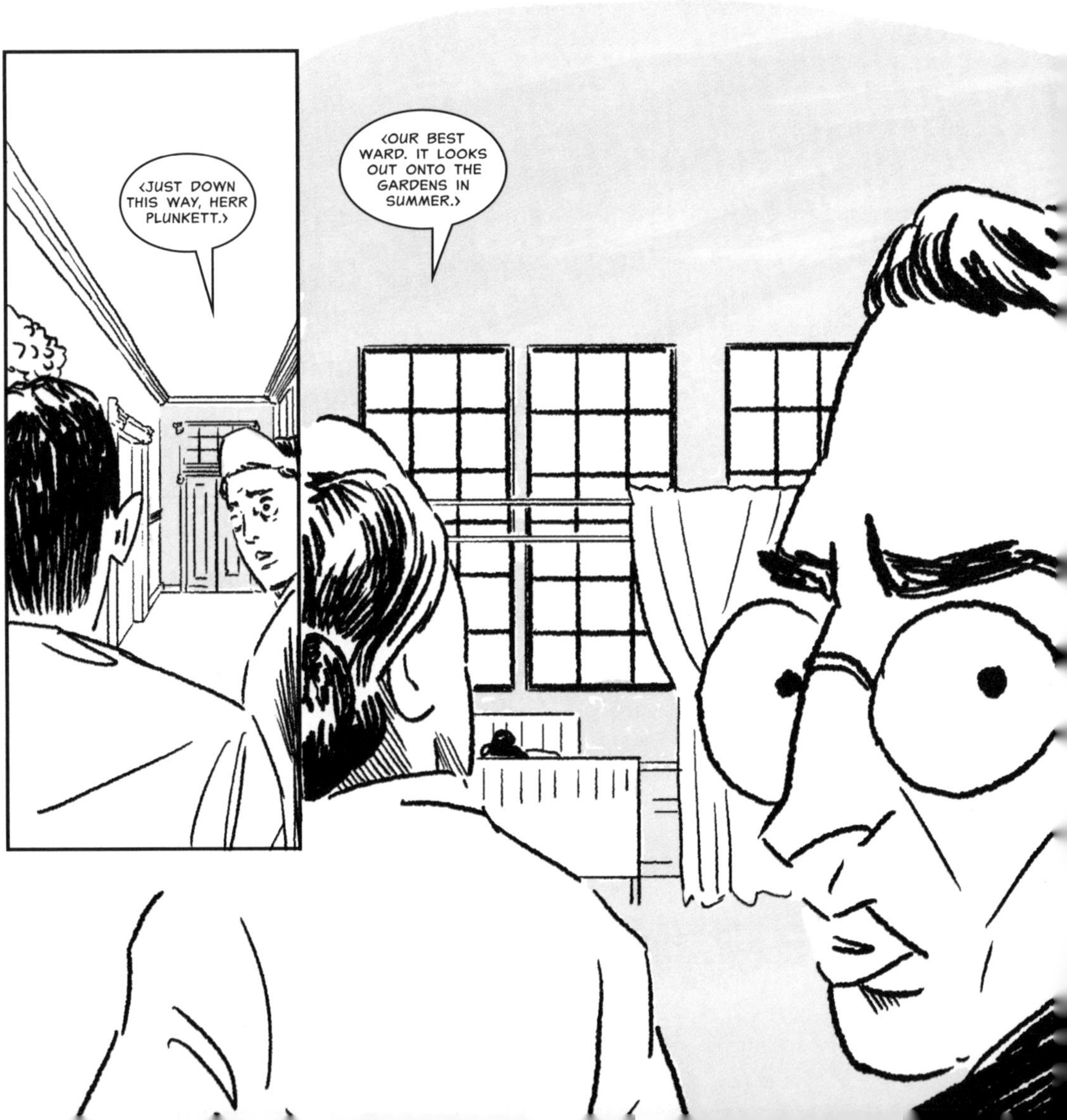
<JUST DOWN THIS WAY, HERR PLUNKETT.>
<OUR BEST WARD. IT LOOKS OUT ONTO THE GARDENS IN SUMMER.>

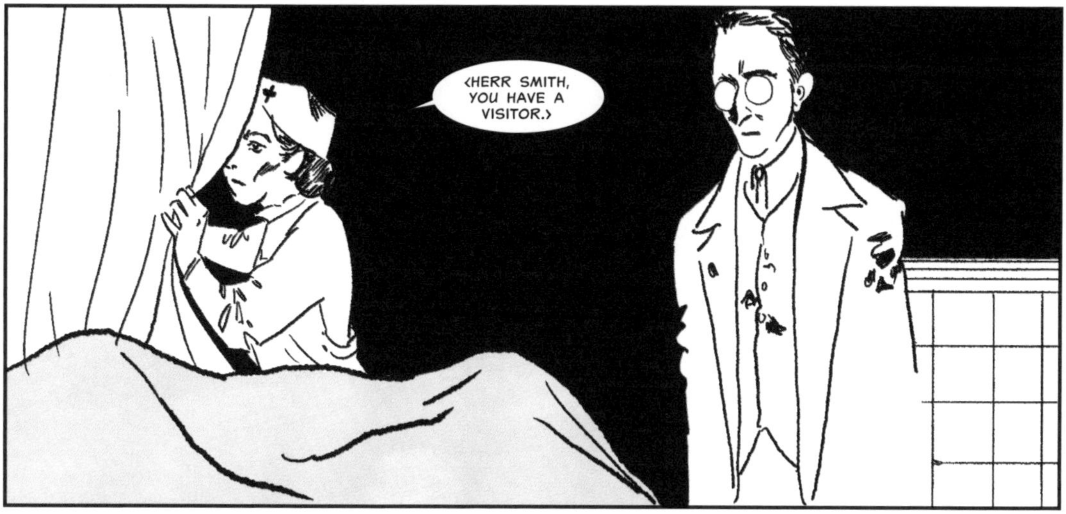
‹HERR SMITH, YOU HAVE A VISITOR.›

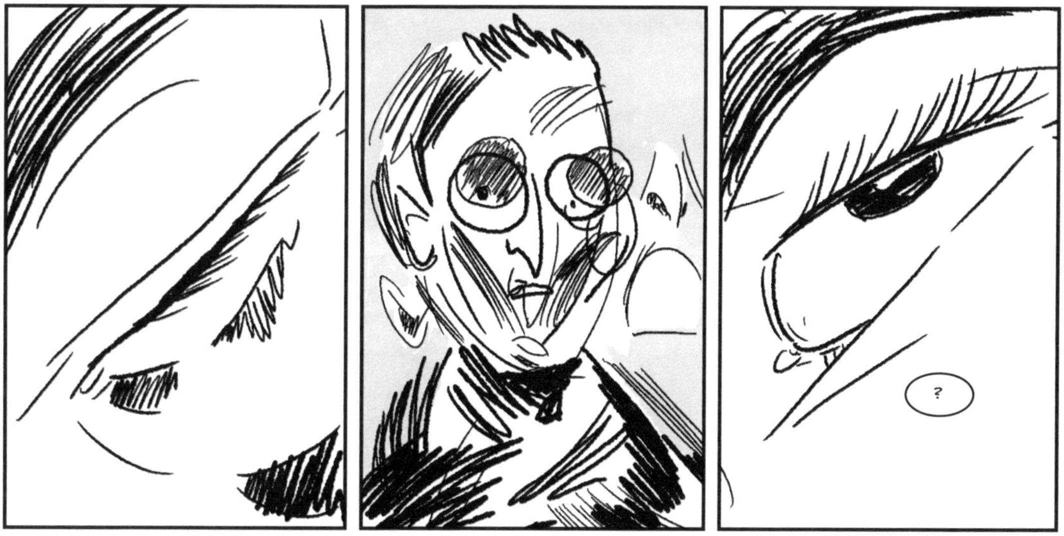
?

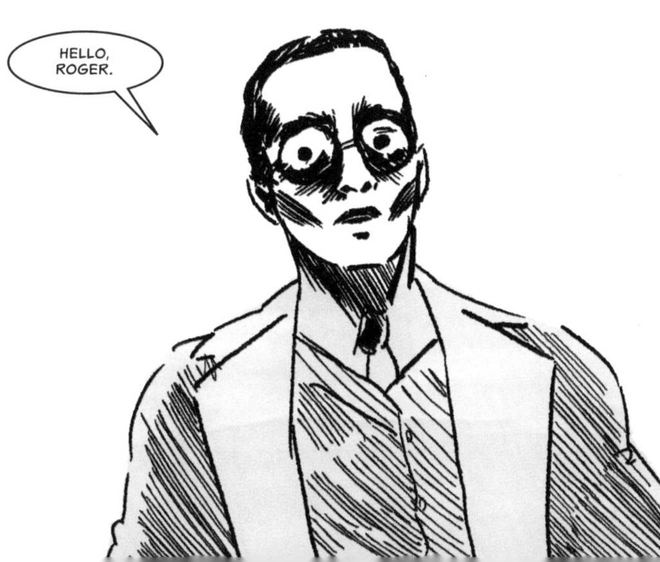
HELLO, ROGER.

...PLUNKETT?

PLUNKETT, HOW ON EARTH DID YOU GET INTO GERMANY...?

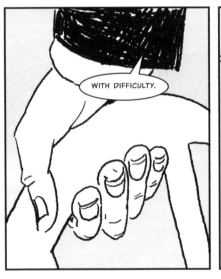

WITH DIFFICULTY.

NO MATTER. THAT'S NOT IMPORTANT NOW.

OUR LETTERS ARE BEING INTERCEPTED. THIS IS THE ONLY SECURE METHOD OF COMMUNICATION NOW.

AS I WROTE TO YOU MANY WEEKS AGO, THE I.R.B. COUNCIL AGREES WITH YOU — THE GERMANS HAVE NO REAL INTENTIONS OF HELPING US AGAINST THE BRITISH.

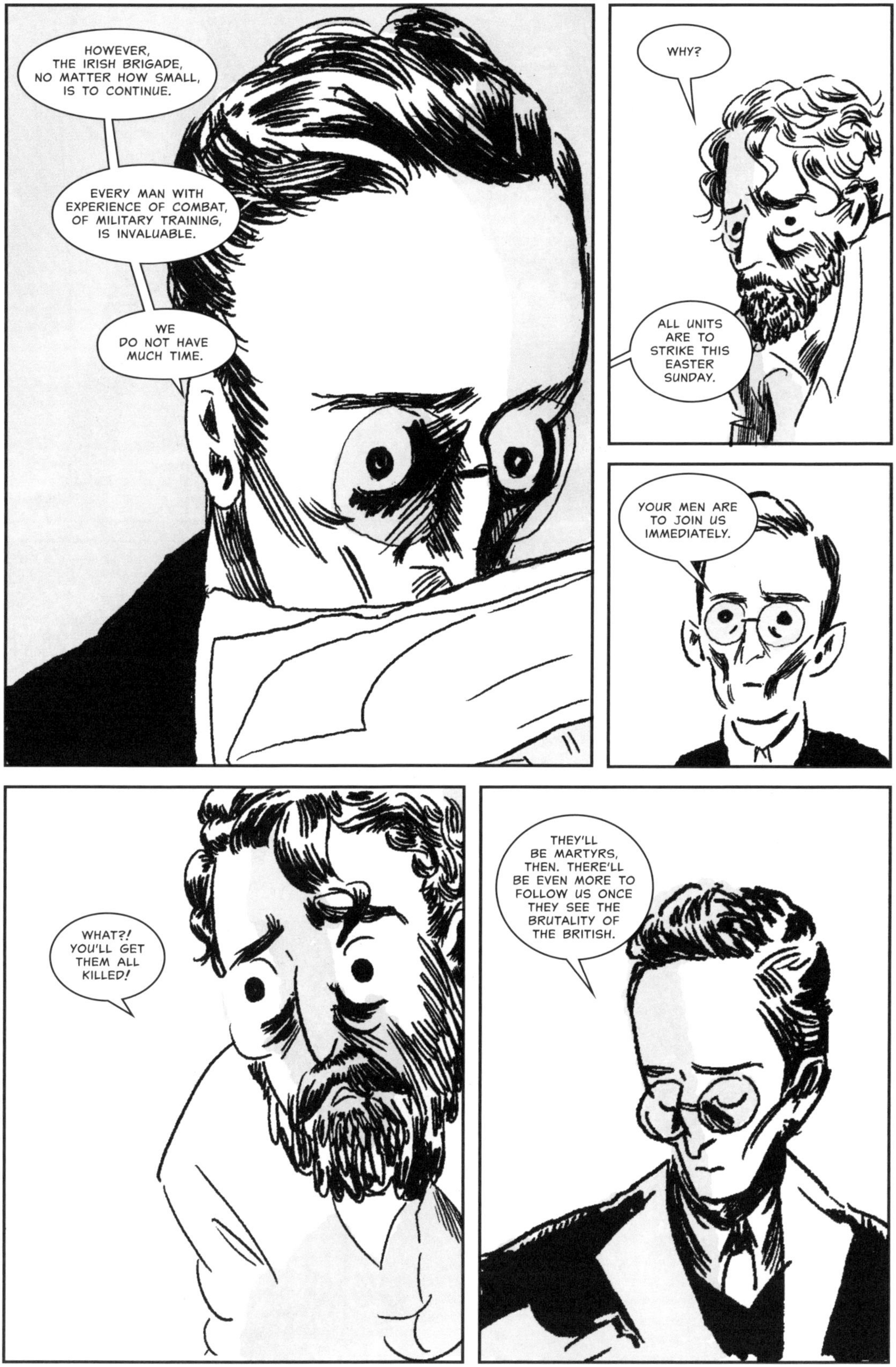

HOWEVER, THE IRISH BRIGADE, NO MATTER HOW SMALL, IS TO CONTINUE.
EVERY MAN WITH EXPERIENCE OF COMBAT, OF MILITARY TRAINING, IS INVALUABLE.
WE DO NOT HAVE MUCH TIME.
WHY?
ALL UNITS ARE TO STRIKE THIS EASTER SUNDAY.
YOUR MEN ARE TO JOIN US IMMEDIATELY.
WHAT?! YOU'LL GET THEM ALL KILLED!
THEY'LL BE MARTYRS, THEN. THERE'LL BE EVEN MORE TO FOLLOW US ONCE THEY SEE THE BRUTALITY OF THE BRITISH.

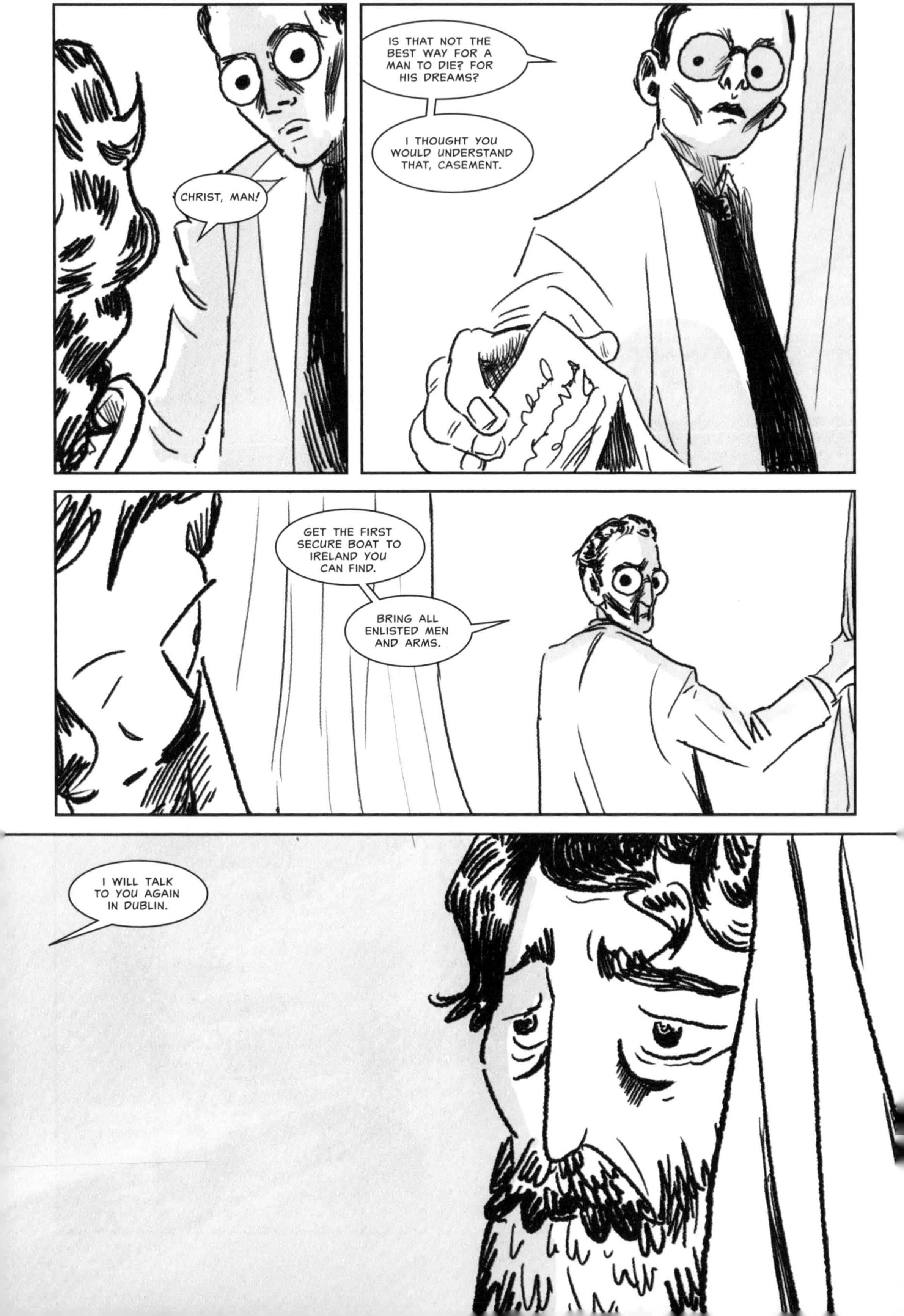
CHRIST, MAN!
IS THAT NOT THE BEST WAY FOR A MAN TO DIE? FOR HIS DREAMS?
I THOUGHT YOU WOULD UNDERSTAND THAT, CASEMENT.
GET THE FIRST SECURE BOAT TO IRELAND YOU CAN FIND.
BRING ALL ENLISTED MEN AND ARMS.
I WILL TALK TO YOU AGAIN IN DUBLIN.

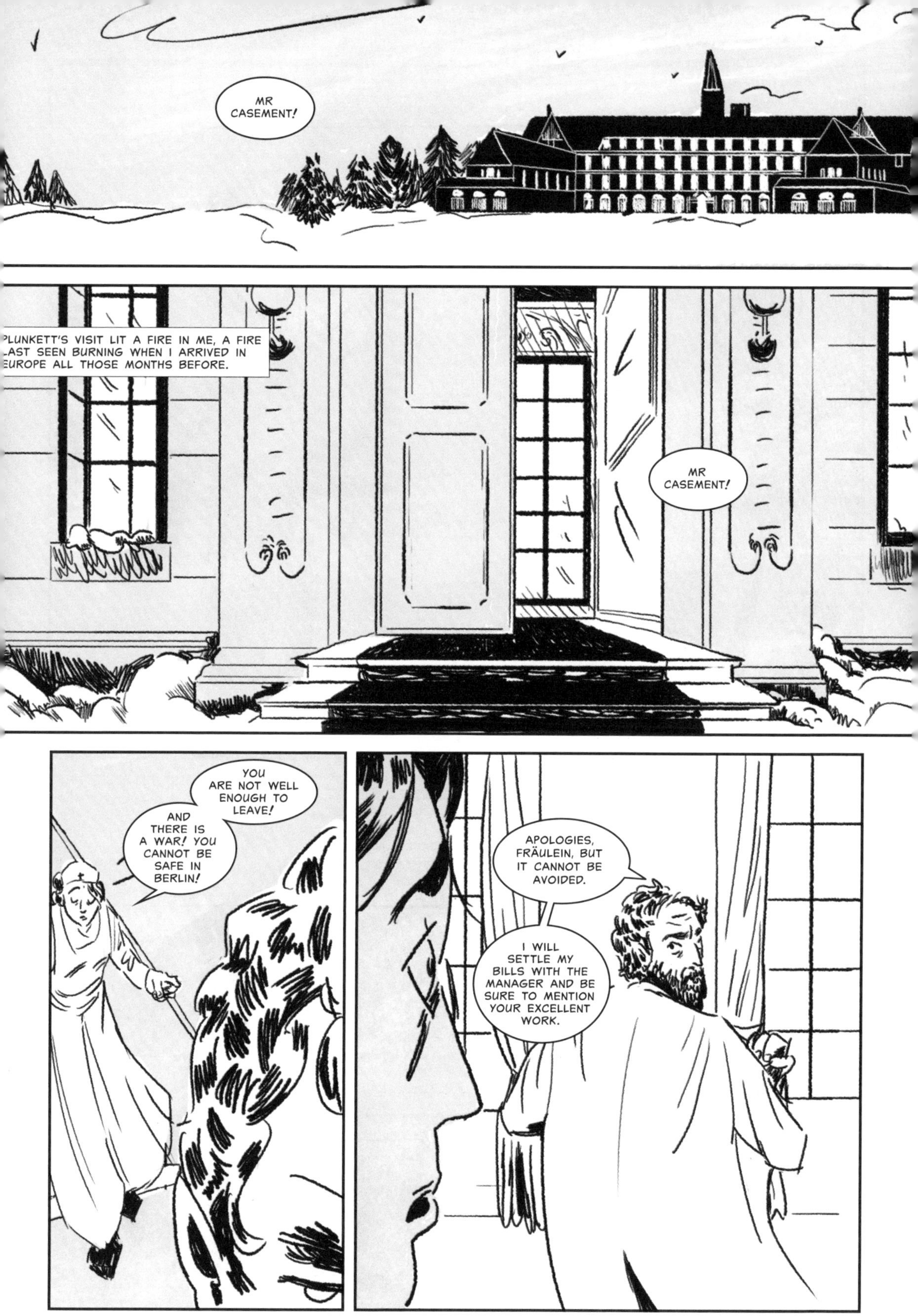
MR CASEMENT!
PLUNKETT'S VISIT LIT A FIRE IN ME, A FIRE LAST SEEN BURNING WHEN I ARRIVED IN EUROPE ALL THOSE MONTHS BEFORE.
MR CASEMENT!
YOU ARE NOT WELL ENOUGH TO LEAVE!
AND THERE IS A WAR! YOU CANNOT BE SAFE IN BERLIN!
APOLOGIES, FRÄULEIN, BUT IT CANNOT BE AVOIDED.
I WILL SETTLE MY BILLS WITH THE MANAGER AND BE SURE TO MENTION YOUR EXCELLENT WORK.

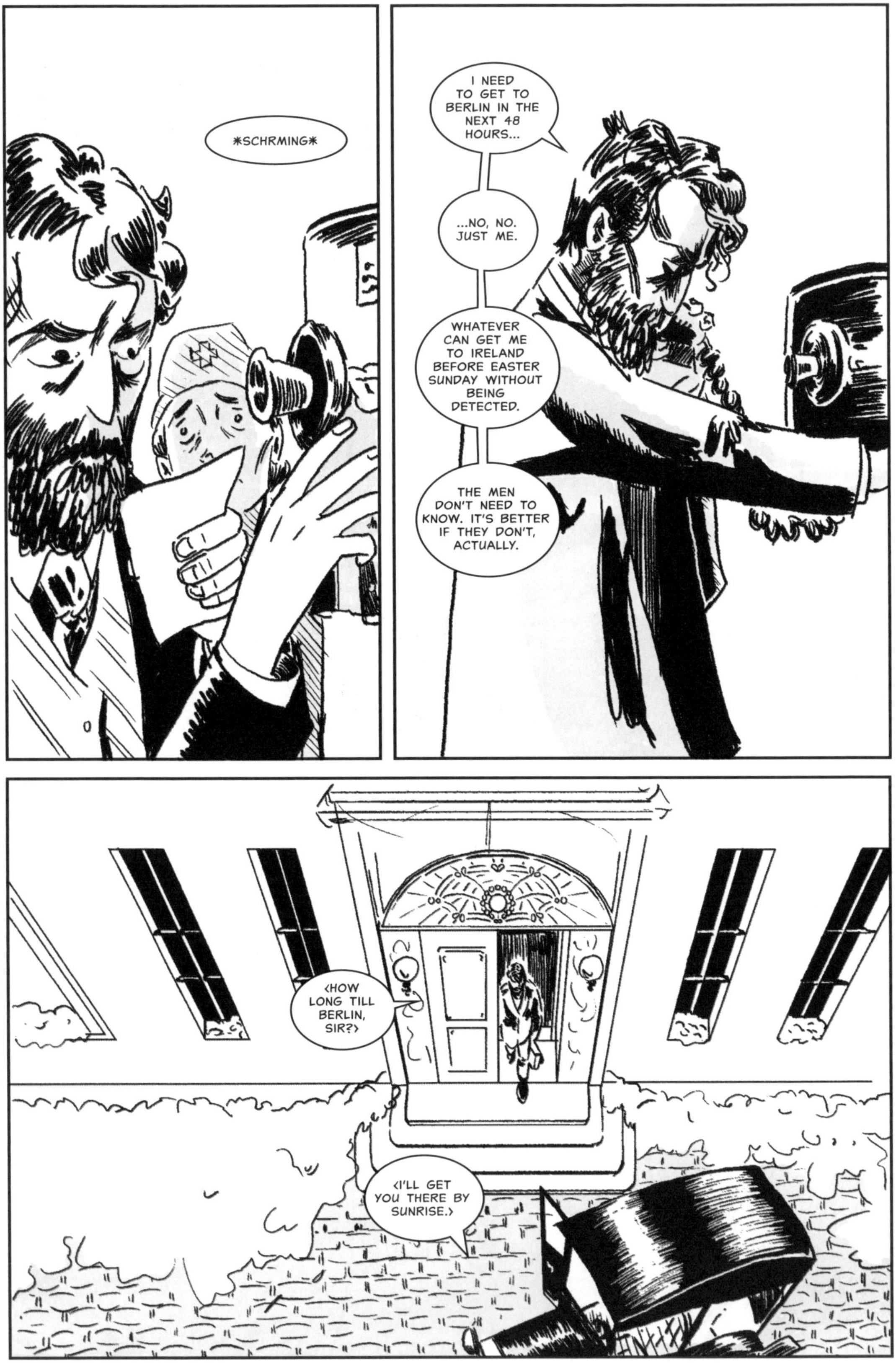
SCHRMING
I NEED TO GET TO BERLIN IN THE NEXT 48 HOURS...
...NO, NO. JUST ME.
WHATEVER CAN GET ME TO IRELAND BEFORE EASTER SUNDAY WITHOUT BEING DETECTED.
THE MEN DON'T NEED TO KNOW. IT'S BETTER IF THEY DON'T, ACTUALLY.
‹HOW LONG TILL BERLIN, SIR?›
‹I'LL GET YOU THERE BY SUNRISE.›

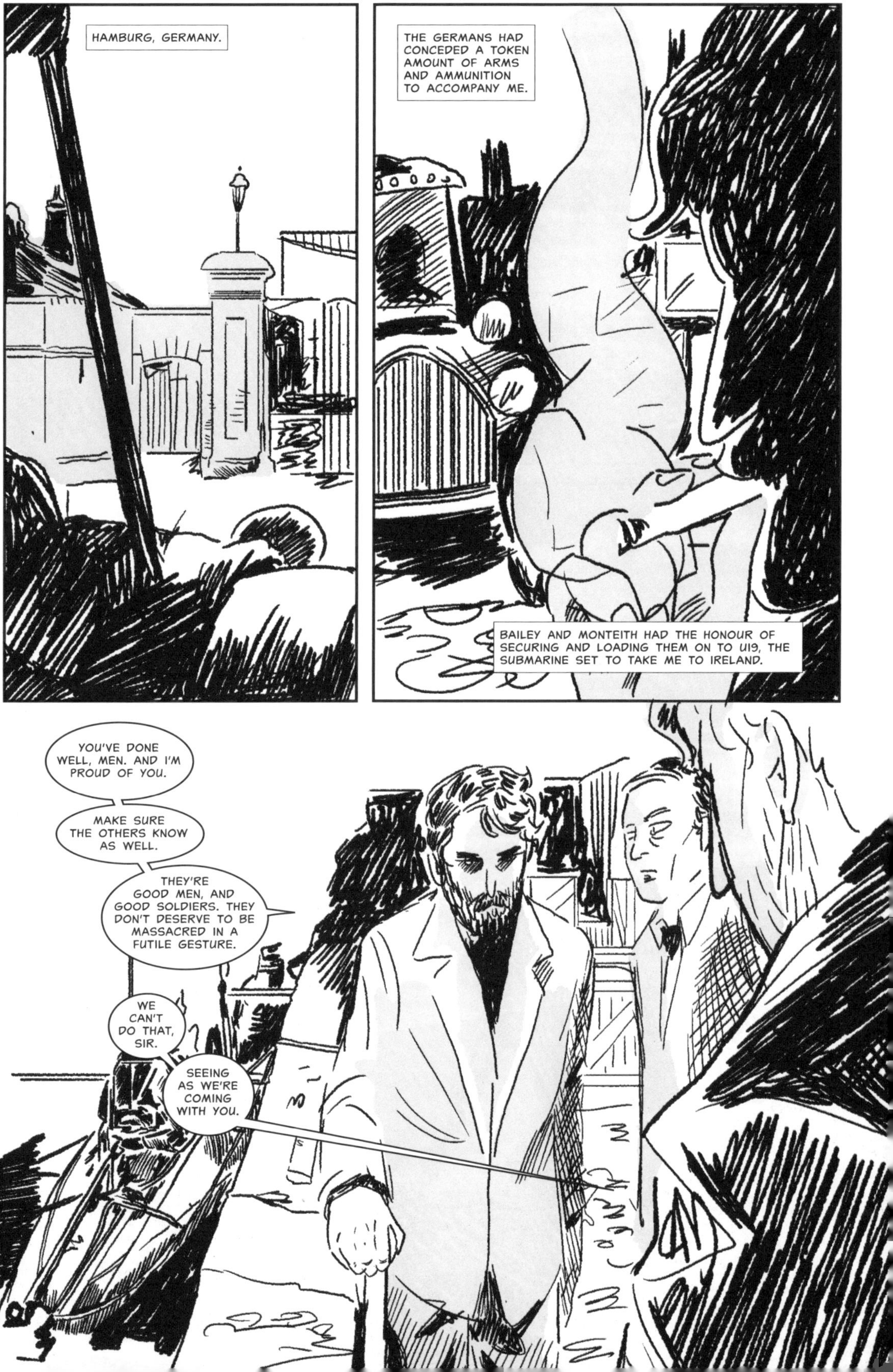
HAMBURG, GERMANY.
THE GERMANS HAD CONCEDED A TOKEN AMOUNT OF ARMS AND AMMUNITION TO ACCOMPANY ME.
BAILEY AND MONTEITH HAD THE HONOUR OF SECURING AND LOADING THEM ON TO U19, THE SUBMARINE SET TO TAKE ME TO IRELAND.
YOU'VE DONE WELL, MEN. AND I'M PROUD OF YOU.
MAKE SURE THE OTHERS KNOW AS WELL.
THEY'RE GOOD MEN, AND GOOD SOLDIERS. THEY DON'T DESERVE TO BE MASSACRED IN A FUTILE GESTURE.
WE CAN'T DO THAT, SIR.
SEEING AS WE'RE COMING WITH YOU.

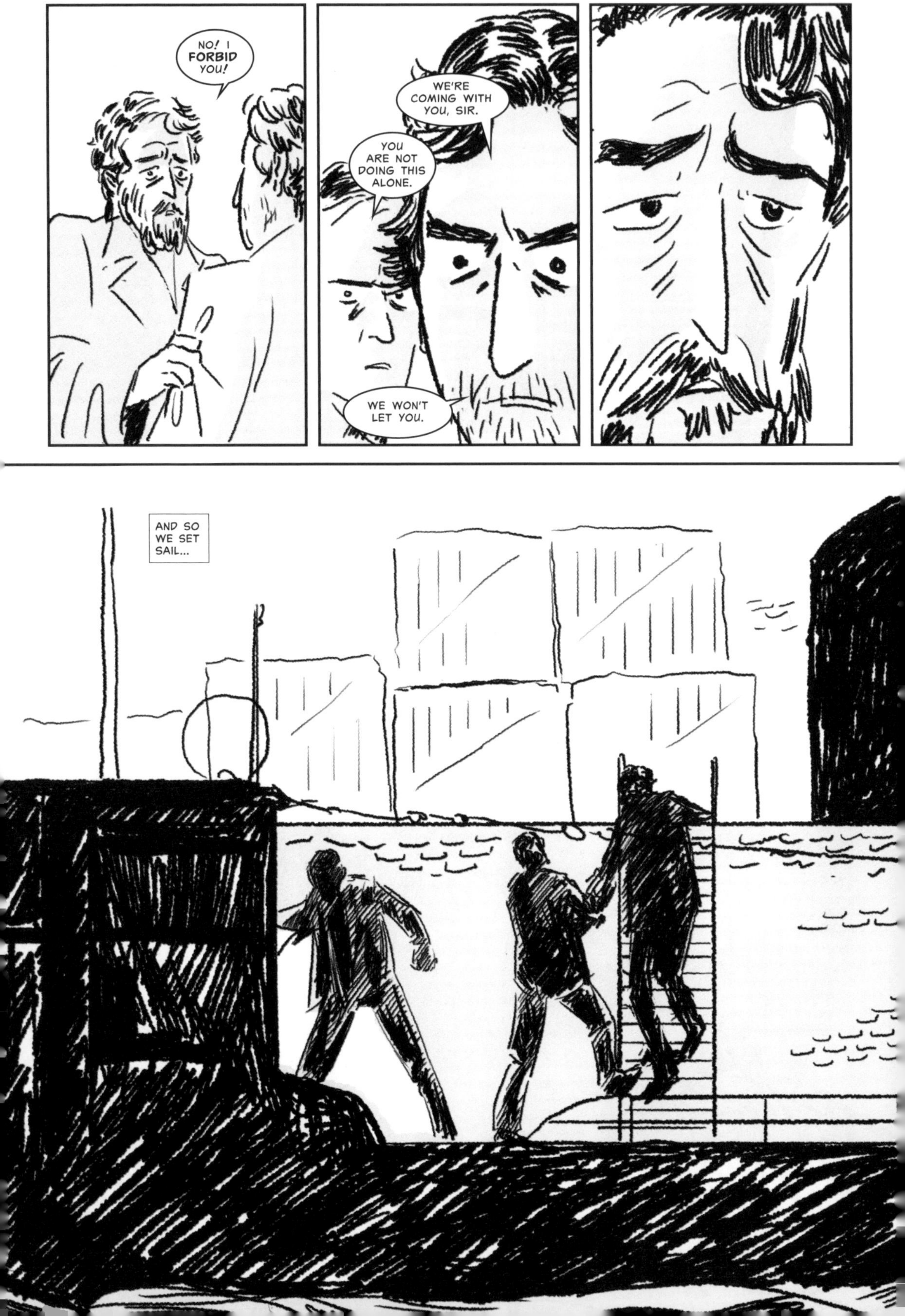
NO! I FORBID YOU!
WE'RE COMING WITH YOU, SIR.
YOU ARE NOT DOING THIS ALONE.
WE WON'T LET YOU.
AND SO WE SET SAIL...

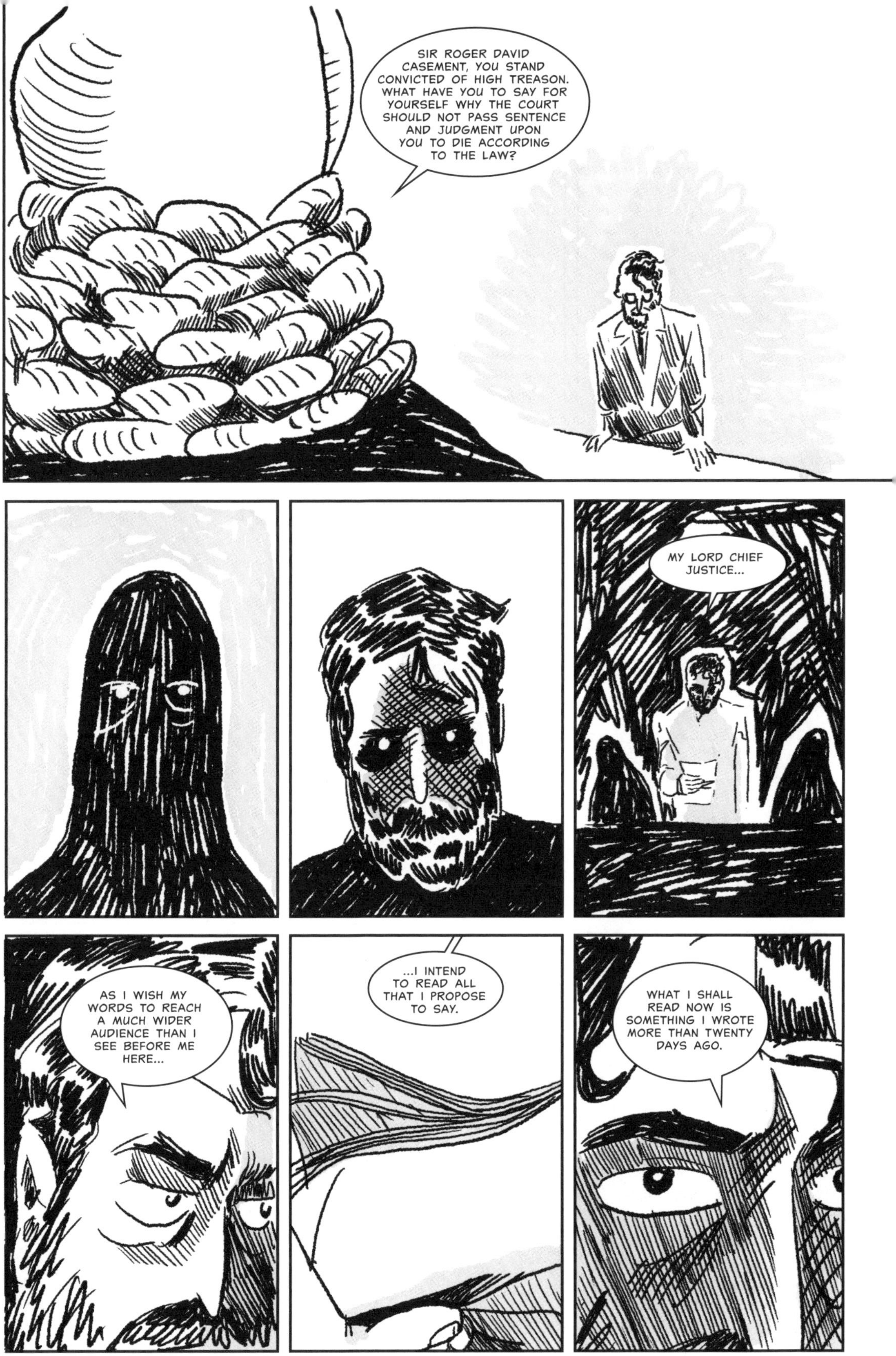
SIR ROGER DAVID CASEMENT, YOU STAND CONVICTED OF HIGH TREASON. WHAT HAVE YOU TO SAY FOR YOURSELF WHY THE COURT SHOULD NOT PASS SENTENCE AND JUDGMENT UPON YOU TO DIE ACCORDING TO THE LAW?
MY LORD CHIEF JUSTICE...
AS I WISH MY WORDS TO REACH A MUCH WIDER AUDIENCE THAN I SEE BEFORE ME HERE...
...I INTEND TO READ ALL THAT I PROPOSE TO SAY.
WHAT I SHALL READ NOW IS SOMETHING I WROTE MORE THAN TWENTY DAYS AGO.

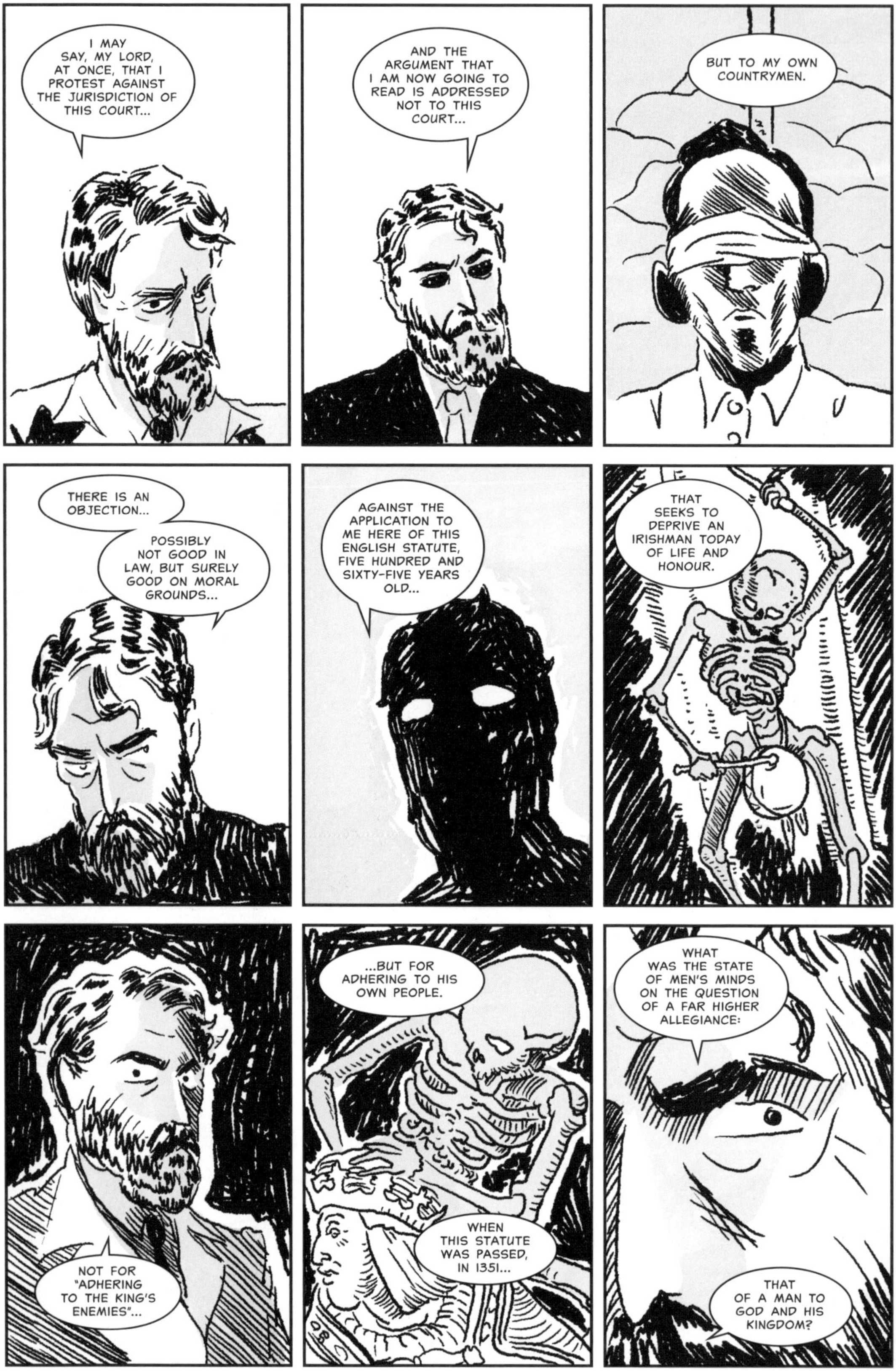
I MAY SAY, MY LORD, AT ONCE, THAT I PROTEST AGAINST THE JURISDICTION OF THIS COURT...
AND THE ARGUMENT THAT I AM NOW GOING TO READ IS ADDRESSED NOT TO THIS COURT...
BUT TO MY OWN COUNTRYMEN.
THERE IS AN OBJECTION...
POSSIBLY NOT GOOD IN LAW, BUT SURELY GOOD ON MORAL GROUNDS...
AGAINST THE APPLICATION TO ME HERE OF THIS ENGLISH STATUTE, FIVE HUNDRED AND SIXTY-FIVE YEARS OLD...
THAT SEEKS TO DEPRIVE AN IRISHMAN TODAY OF LIFE AND HONOUR.
NOT FOR "ADHERING TO THE KING'S ENEMIES"...
...BUT FOR ADHERING TO HIS OWN PEOPLE.
WHEN THIS STATUTE WAS PASSED, IN 1351...
WHAT WAS THE STATE OF MEN'S MINDS ON THE QUESTION OF A FAR HIGHER ALLEGIANCE:
THAT OF A MAN TO GOD AND HIS KINGDOM?

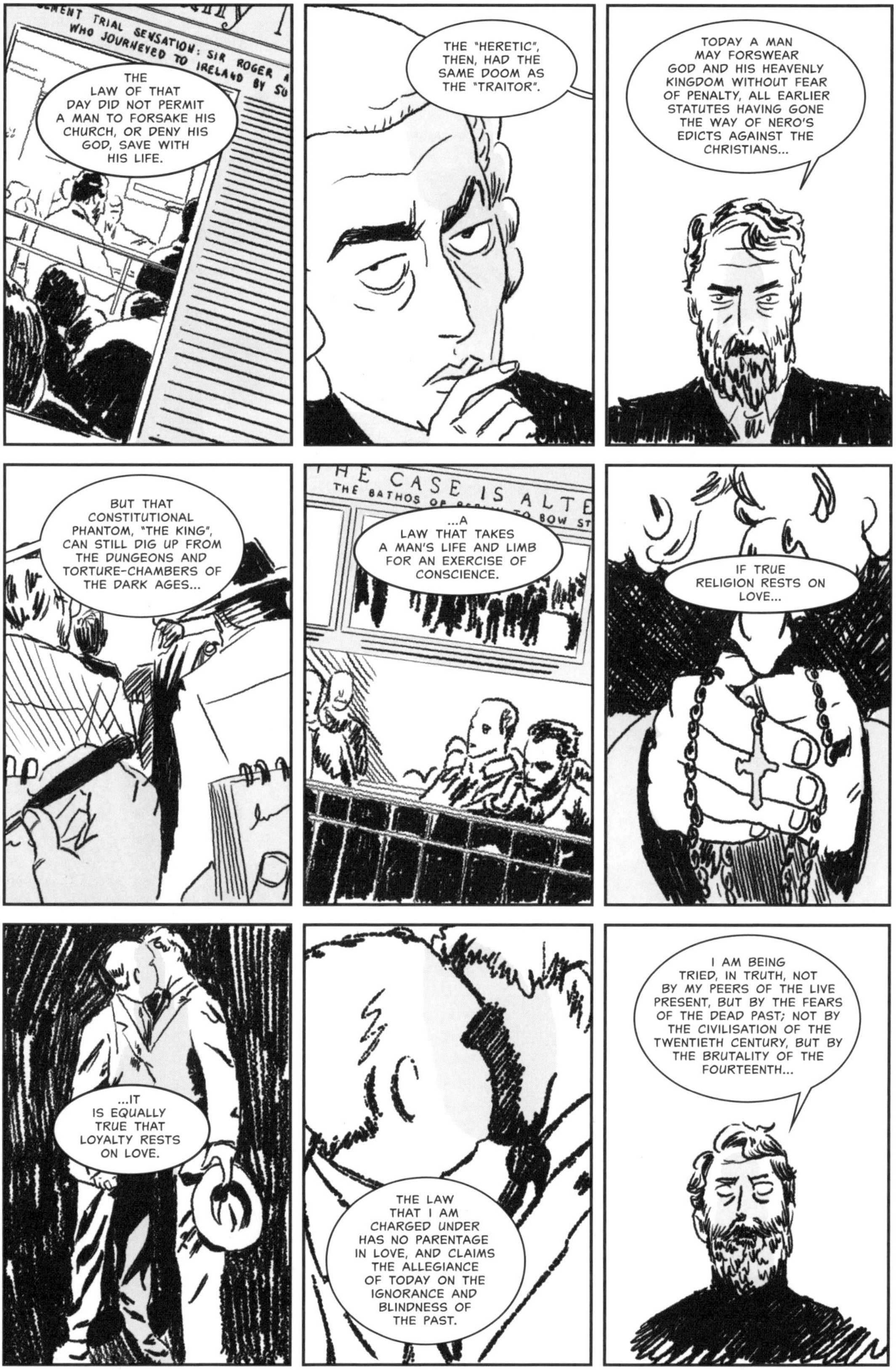
TRIAL SENSATION: SIR ROGER
WHO JOURNEYED TO IRELAND BY
THE LAW OF THAT DAY DID NOT PERMIT A MAN TO FORSAKE HIS CHURCH, OR DENY HIS GOD, SAVE WITH HIS LIFE.
THE "HERETIC", THEN, HAD THE SAME DOOM AS THE "TRAITOR".
TODAY A MAN MAY FORSWEAR GOD AND HIS HEAVENLY KINGDOM WITHOUT FEAR OF PENALTY, ALL EARLIER STATUTES HAVING GONE THE WAY OF NERO'S EDICTS AGAINST THE CHRISTIANS...
BUT THAT CONSTITUTIONAL PHANTOM, "THE KING", CAN STILL DIG UP FROM THE DUNGEONS AND TORTURE-CHAMBERS OF THE DARK AGES...
CASE IS
THE BATHOS OF
...A LAW THAT TAKES A MAN'S LIFE AND LIMB FOR AN EXERCISE OF CONSCIENCE.
IF TRUE RELIGION RESTS ON LOVE...
...IT IS EQUALLY TRUE THAT LOYALTY RESTS ON LOVE.
THE LAW THAT I AM CHARGED UNDER HAS NO PARENTAGE IN LOVE, AND CLAIMS THE ALLEGIANCE OF TODAY ON THE IGNORANCE AND BLINDNESS OF THE PAST.
I AM BEING TRIED, IN TRUTH, NOT BY MY PEERS OF THE LIVE PRESENT, BUT BY THE FEARS OF THE DEAD PAST; NOT BY THE CIVILISATION OF THE TWENTIETH CENTURY, BUT BY THE BRUTALITY OF THE FOURTEENTH...

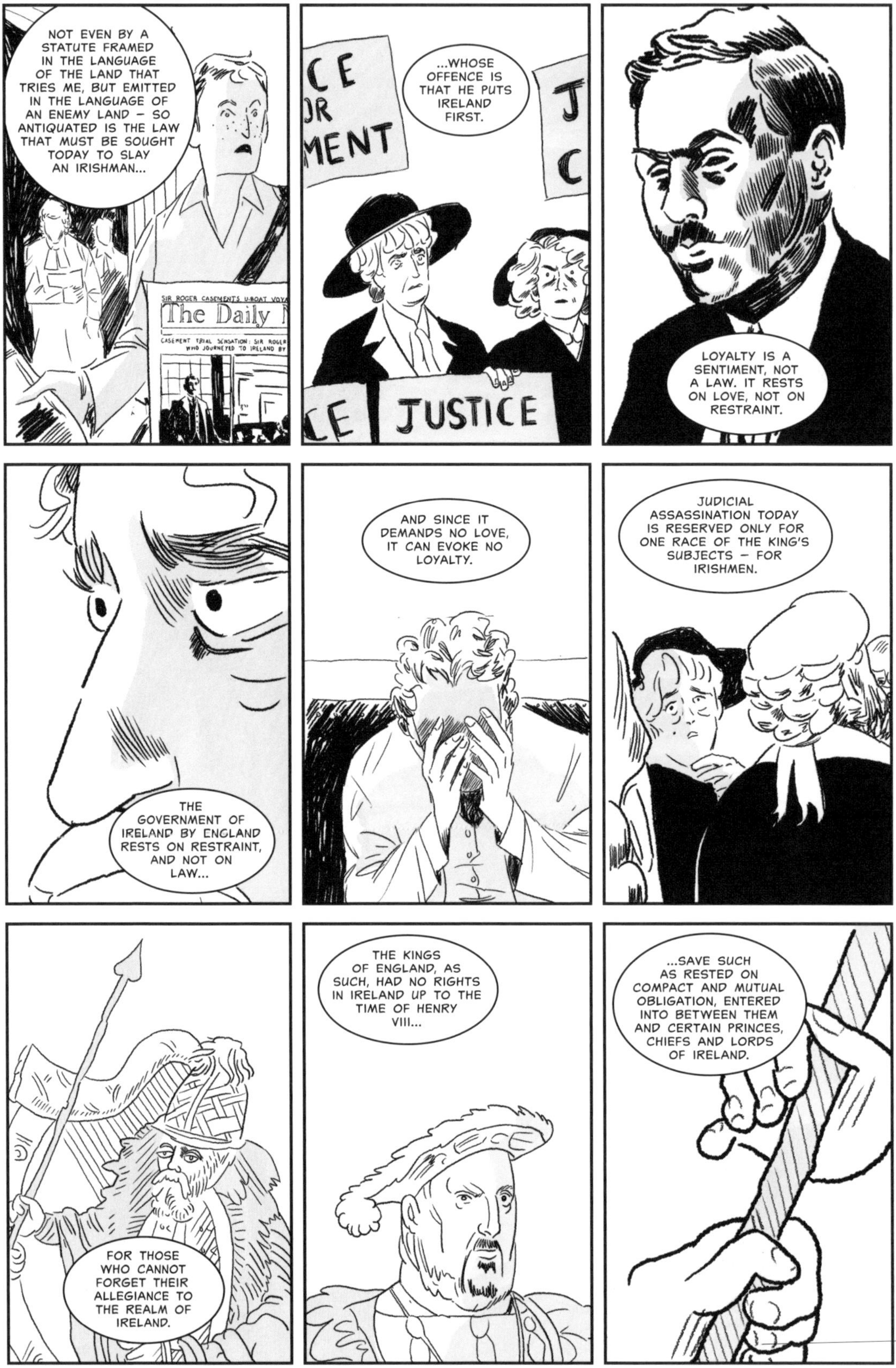
NOT EVEN BY A STATUTE FRAMED IN THE LANGUAGE OF THE LAND THAT TRIES ME, BUT EMITTED IN THE LANGUAGE OF AN ENEMY LAND – SO ANTIQUATED IS THE LAW THAT MUST BE SOUGHT TODAY TO SLAY AN IRISHMAN...
...WHOSE OFFENCE IS THAT HE PUTS IRELAND FIRST.
JUSTICE
LOYALTY IS A SENTIMENT, NOT A LAW. IT RESTS ON LOVE, NOT ON RESTRAINT.
THE GOVERNMENT OF IRELAND BY ENGLAND RESTS ON RESTRAINT, AND NOT ON LAW...
AND SINCE IT DEMANDS NO LOVE, IT CAN EVOKE NO LOYALTY.
JUDICIAL ASSASSINATION TODAY IS RESERVED ONLY FOR ONE RACE OF THE KING'S SUBJECTS – FOR IRISHMEN.
FOR THOSE WHO CANNOT FORGET THEIR ALLEGIANCE TO THE REALM OF IRELAND.
THE KINGS OF ENGLAND, AS SUCH, HAD NO RIGHTS IN IRELAND UP TO THE TIME OF HENRY VIII...
...SAVE SUCH AS RESTED ON COMPACT AND MUTUAL OBLIGATION, ENTERED INTO BETWEEN THEM AND CERTAIN PRINCES, CHIEFS AND LORDS OF IRELAND.

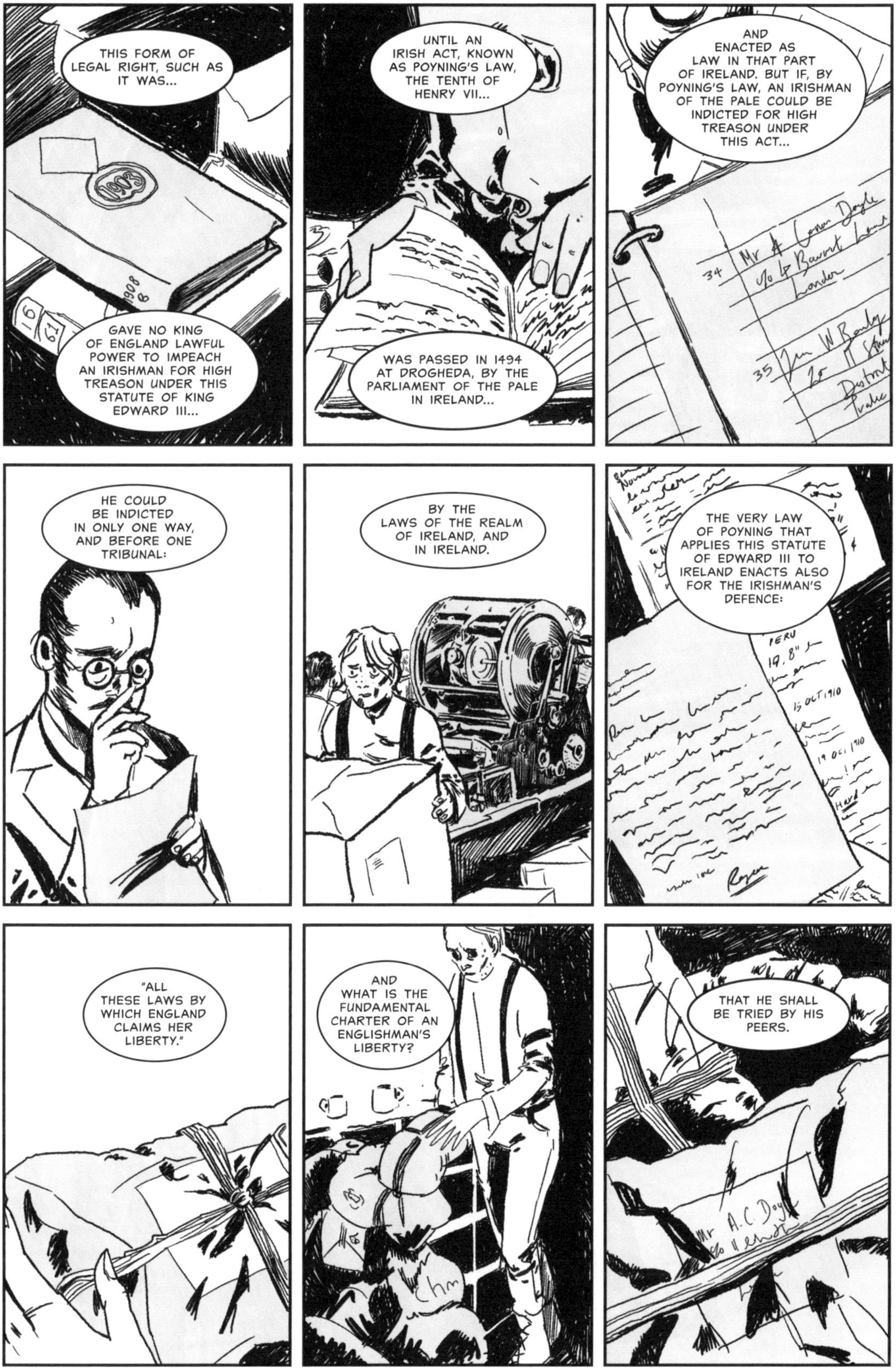
THIS FORM OF LEGAL RIGHT, SUCH AS IT WAS...
GAVE NO KING OF ENGLAND LAWFUL POWER TO IMPEACH AN IRISHMAN FOR HIGH TREASON UNDER THIS STATUTE OF KING EDWARD III...
UNTIL AN IRISH ACT, KNOWN AS POYNING'S LAW, THE TENTH OF HENRY VII...
WAS PASSED IN 1494 AT DROGHEDA, BY THE PARLIAMENT OF THE PALE IN IRELAND...
AND ENACTED AS LAW IN THAT PART OF IRELAND. BUT IF, BY POYNING'S LAW, AN IRISHMAN OF THE PALE COULD BE INDICTED FOR HIGH TREASON UNDER THIS ACT...
HE COULD BE INDICTED IN ONLY ONE WAY, AND BEFORE ONE TRIBUNAL:
BY THE LAWS OF THE REALM OF IRELAND, AND IN IRELAND.
THE VERY LAW OF POYNING THAT APPLIES THIS STATUTE OF EDWARD III TO IRELAND ENACTS ALSO FOR THE IRISHMAN'S DEFENCE:
"ALL THESE LAWS BY WHICH ENGLAND CLAIMS HER LIBERTY."
AND WHAT IS THE FUNDAMENTAL CHARTER OF AN ENGLISHMAN'S LIBERTY?
THAT HE SHALL BE TRIED BY HIS PEERS.

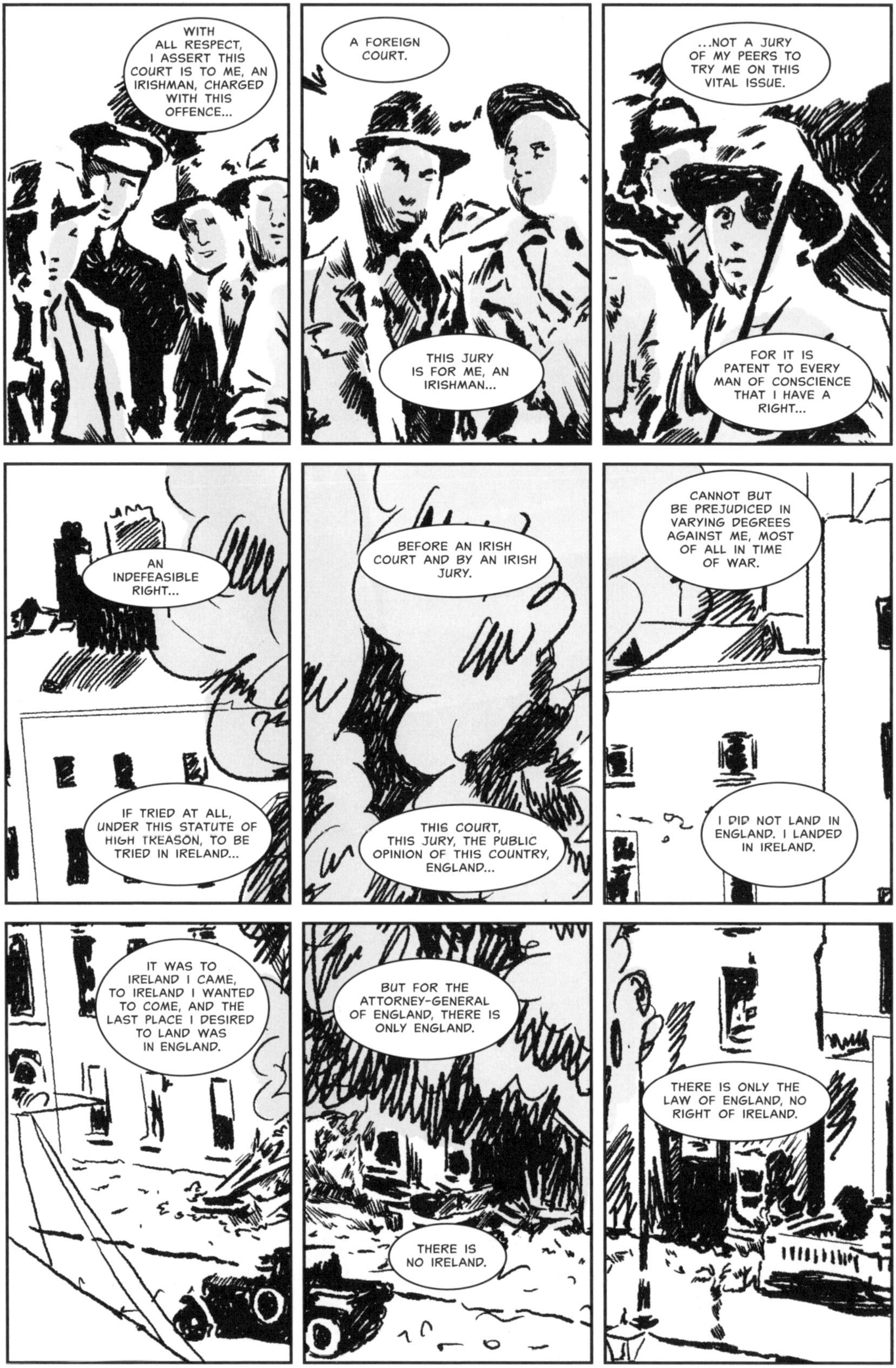
WITH ALL RESPECT, I ASSERT THIS COURT IS TO ME, AN IRISHMAN, CHARGED WITH THIS OFFENCE...
A FOREIGN COURT.
THIS JURY IS FOR ME, AN IRISHMAN...
...NOT A JURY OF MY PEERS TO TRY ME ON THIS VITAL ISSUE.
FOR IT IS PATENT TO EVERY MAN OF CONSCIENCE THAT I HAVE A RIGHT...
AN INDEFEASIBLE RIGHT...
IF TRIED AT ALL, UNDER THIS STATUTE OF HIGH TREASON, TO BE TRIED IN IRELAND...
BEFORE AN IRISH COURT AND BY AN IRISH JURY.
THIS COURT, THIS JURY, THE PUBLIC OPINION OF THIS COUNTRY, ENGLAND...
CANNOT BUT BE PREJUDICED IN VARYING DEGREES AGAINST ME, MOST OF ALL IN TIME OF WAR.
I DID NOT LAND IN ENGLAND. I LANDED IN IRELAND.
IT WAS TO IRELAND I CAME, TO IRELAND I WANTED TO COME, AND THE LAST PLACE I DESIRED TO LAND WAS IN ENGLAND.
BUT FOR THE ATTORNEY-GENERAL OF ENGLAND, THERE IS ONLY ENGLAND.
THERE IS NO IRELAND.
THERE IS ONLY THE LAW OF ENGLAND, NO RIGHT OF IRELAND.

THE LIBERTY OF IRELAND AND OF AN IRISHMAN IS TO BE JUDGED BY THE POWER OF ENGLAND.

P H PEARSE "President" of the Republic has been executed.

YET FOR ME, THE IRISH OUTLAW...

THERE IS A LAND OF IRELAND, A RIGHT OF IRELAND...

THOMAS MacDONAGH, one of the "Provisional Government" has been executed.

AND A CHARTER FOR ALL IRISHMEN TO APPEAL TO IN THE LAST RESORT...

A CHARTER THAT EVEN THE VERY STATUTES OF ENGLAND ITSELF CANNOT DEPRIVE US OF...

THOMAS J. CLARKE, one of the "Provisional Government" and an old Fenian, has been executed.

NAY, MORE...

A CHARTER THAT ENGLISHMEN THEMSELVES ASSERT AS THE FUNDAMENTAL BOND OF LAW THAT CONNECTS THE TWO KINGDOMS.

EDWARD DALY, commander of the rebels at the Four Courts, has been executed.

THIS CHARGE OF HIGH TREASON INVOLVES A MORAL RESPONSIBILITY...

M O'HANRAHAN one of the clerical staff of the rebel headquarters, has been executed.

AS THE VERY TERMS OF THE INDICTMENT AGAINST MYSELF RECITE, INASMUCH AS I COMMITTED THE ACTS I AM CHARGED WITH TO THE "EVIL EXAMPLE OF OTHERS IN LIKE CASE".

JOHN McBRIDE, commander of the rebels in Jacob's factory, has been executed.

WHAT WAS THE EVIL EXAMPLE I SET TO OTHERS IN THE LIKE CASE, AND WHO WERE THESE OTHERS?

THE "EVIL EXAMPLE" CHARGED IS THAT I ASSERTED THE RIGHT OF MY OWN COUNTRY...

JOSEPH PLUNKETT, one of the "Provisional Government", was married in prison before being executed.

CORNELIUS COLBERT who took a very prominent part in the rebellion has been executed.

AND THE "OTHERS" I APPEALED TO, TO AID MY ENDEAVOUR, WERE MY OWN COUNTRYMEN.

JAMES CONNOLLY, "Commander General" of the Dublin Division was wounded in the fighting and has now been executed.

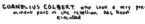

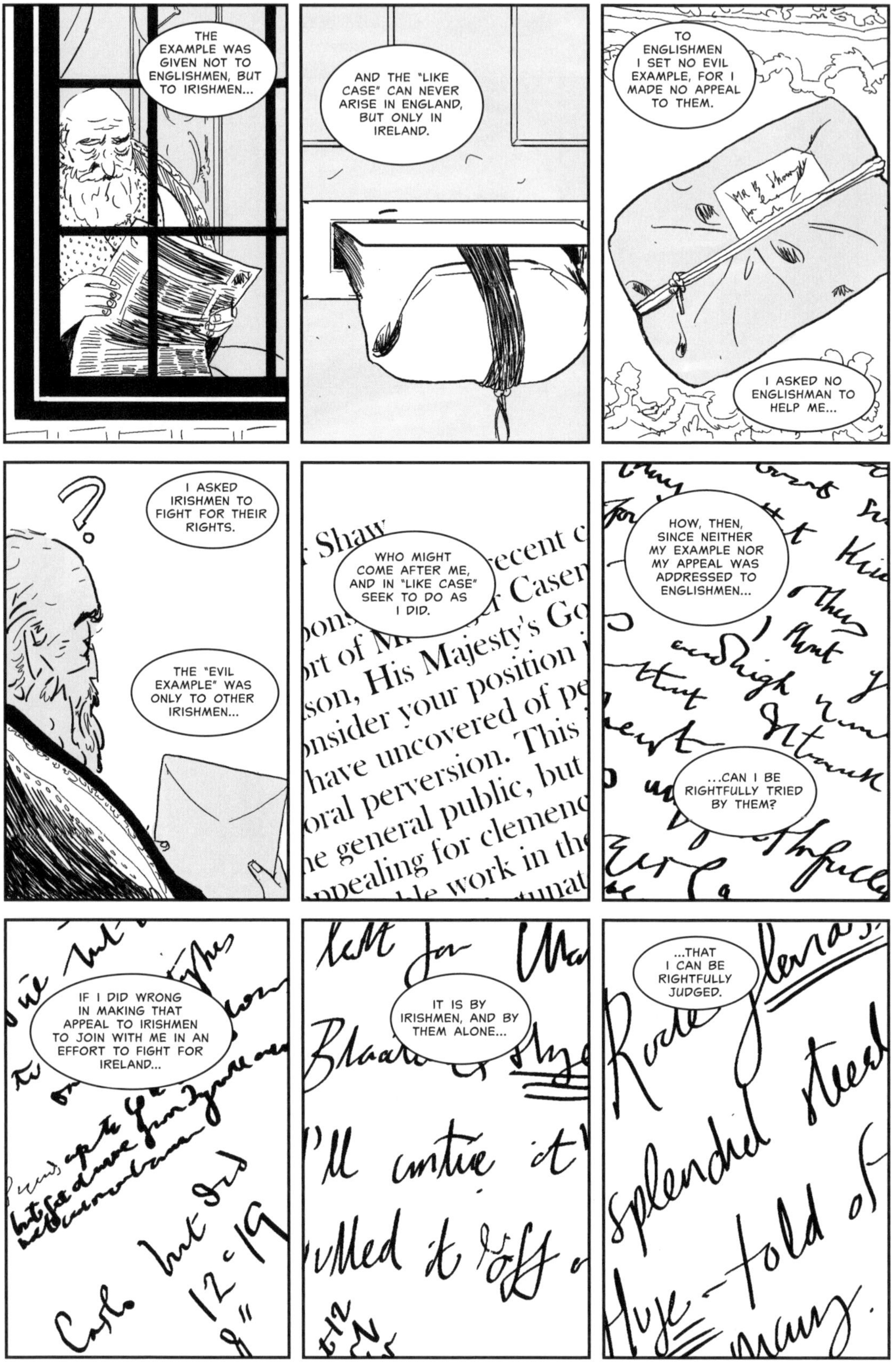
THE EXAMPLE WAS GIVEN NOT TO ENGLISHMEN, BUT TO IRISHMEN...
AND THE "LIKE CASE" CAN NEVER ARISE IN ENGLAND, BUT ONLY IN IRELAND.
TO ENGLISHMEN I SET NO EVIL EXAMPLE, FOR I MADE NO APPEAL TO THEM.
I ASKED NO ENGLISHMAN TO HELP ME...
I ASKED IRISHMEN TO FIGHT FOR THEIR RIGHTS.
THE "EVIL EXAMPLE" WAS ONLY TO OTHER IRISHMEN...
WHO MIGHT COME AFTER ME, AND IN "LIKE CASE" SEEK TO DO AS I DID.
HOW, THEN, SINCE NEITHER MY EXAMPLE NOR MY APPEAL WAS ADDRESSED TO ENGLISHMEN...
...CAN I BE RIGHTFULLY TRIED BY THEM?
IF I DID WRONG IN MAKING THAT APPEAL TO IRISHMEN TO JOIN WITH ME IN AN EFFORT TO FIGHT FOR IRELAND...
IT IS BY IRISHMEN, AND BY THEM ALONE...
...THAT I CAN BE RIGHTFULLY JUDGED.

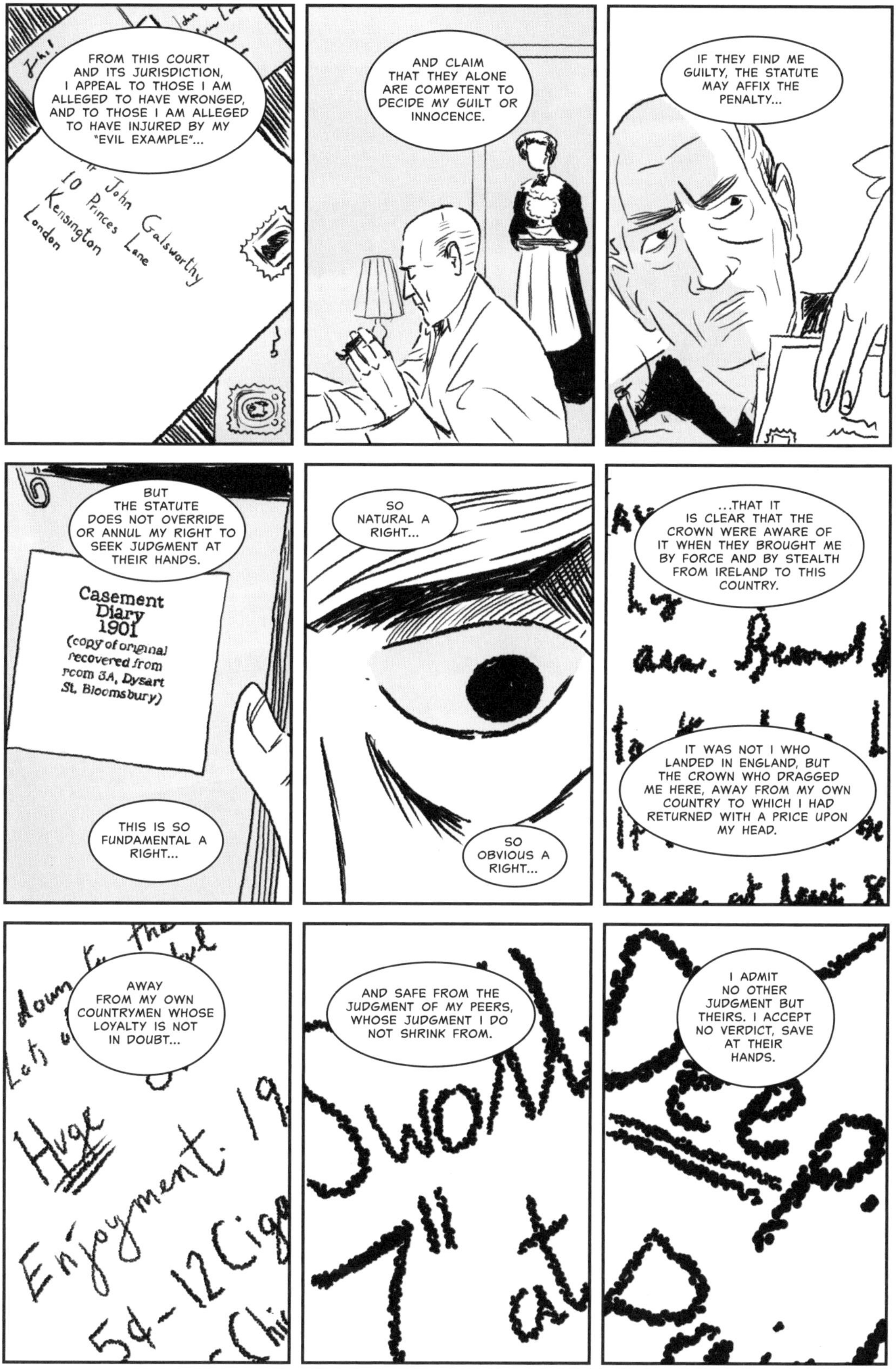
FROM THIS COURT AND ITS JURISDICTION, I APPEAL TO THOSE I AM ALLEGED TO HAVE WRONGED, AND TO THOSE I AM ALLEGED TO HAVE INJURED BY MY "EVIL EXAMPLE"...
John Galsworthy
10 Princes Lane
Kensington
London
AND CLAIM THAT THEY ALONE ARE COMPETENT TO DECIDE MY GUILT OR INNOCENCE.
IF THEY FIND ME GUILTY, THE STATUTE MAY AFFIX THE PENALTY...
BUT THE STATUTE DOES NOT OVERRIDE OR ANNUL MY RIGHT TO SEEK JUDGMENT AT THEIR HANDS.
Casement Diary 1901
(copy of original recovered from room 3A, Dysart St, Bloomsbury)
THIS IS SO FUNDAMENTAL A RIGHT...
SO NATURAL A RIGHT...
SO OBVIOUS A RIGHT...
...THAT IT IS CLEAR THAT THE CROWN WERE AWARE OF IT WHEN THEY BROUGHT ME BY FORCE AND BY STEALTH FROM IRELAND TO THIS COUNTRY.
IT WAS NOT I WHO LANDED IN ENGLAND, BUT THE CROWN WHO DRAGGED ME HERE, AWAY FROM MY OWN COUNTRY TO WHICH I HAD RETURNED WITH A PRICE UPON MY HEAD.
AWAY FROM MY OWN COUNTRYMEN WHOSE LOYALTY IS NOT IN DOUBT...
Huge
Enjoyment. 19
54-12 Cig
AND SAFE FROM THE JUDGMENT OF MY PEERS, WHOSE JUDGMENT I DO NOT SHRINK FROM.
I ADMIT NO OTHER JUDGMENT BUT THEIRS. I ACCEPT NO VERDICT, SAVE AT THEIR HANDS.

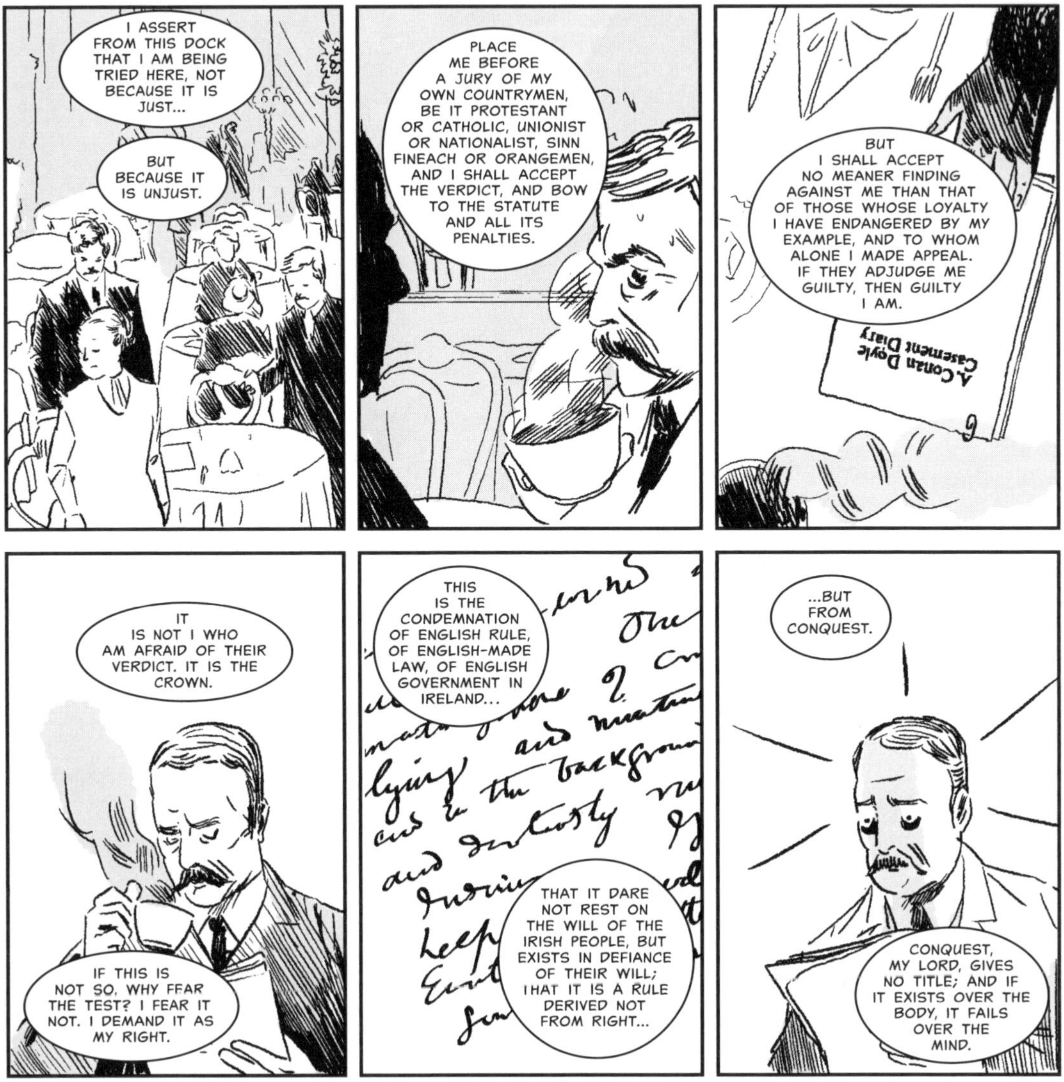
I ASSERT FROM THIS DOCK THAT I AM BEING TRIED HERE, NOT BECAUSE IT IS JUST...
BUT BECAUSE IT IS UNJUST.
PLACE ME BEFORE A JURY OF MY OWN COUNTRYMEN, BE IT PROTESTANT OR CATHOLIC, UNIONIST OR NATIONALIST, SINN FINEACH OR ORANGEMEN, AND I SHALL ACCEPT THE VERDICT, AND BOW TO THE STATUTE AND ALL ITS PENALTIES.
BUT I SHALL ACCEPT NO MEANER FINDING AGAINST ME THAN THAT OF THOSE WHOSE LOYALTY I HAVE ENDANGERED BY MY EXAMPLE, AND TO WHOM ALONE I MADE APPEAL. IF THEY ADJUDGE ME GUILTY, THEN GUILTY I AM.
IT IS NOT I WHO AM AFRAID OF THEIR VERDICT. IT IS THE CROWN.
IF THIS IS NOT SO, WHY FEAR THE TEST? I FEAR IT NOT. I DEMAND IT AS MY RIGHT.
THIS IS THE CONDEMNATION OF ENGLISH RULE, OF ENGLISH-MADE LAW, OF ENGLISH GOVERNMENT IN IRELAND...
THAT IT DARE NOT REST ON THE WILL OF THE IRISH PEOPLE, BUT EXISTS IN DEFIANCE OF THEIR WILL; THAT IT IS A RULE DERIVED NOT FROM RIGHT...
...BUT FROM CONQUEST.
CONQUEST, MY LORD, GIVES NO TITLE; AND IF IT EXISTS OVER THE BODY, IT FAILS OVER THE MIND.
IT CAN EXERT NO EMPIRE OVER MEN'S REASON AND JUDGMENT AND AFFECTIONS; AND IT IS FROM THIS LAW OF CONQUEST WITHOUT TITLE TO THE REASON, JUDGMENT AND AFFECTION OF MY OWN COUNTRYMEN THAT I APPEAL.
I CAN ANSWER FOR MY OWN ACTS AND SPEECHES.
WHILE ONE ENGLISH PARTY WAS RESPONSIBLE FOR PREACHING A DOCTRINE OF HATRED, DESIGNED TO BRING ABOUT CIVIL WAR IN IRELAND, THE OTHER, AND THAT THE PARTY IN POWER...

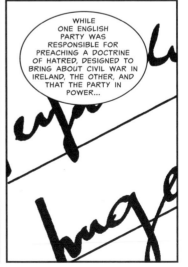

TOOK NO ACTIVE STEPS TO RESTRAIN A PROPAGANDA THAT FOUND ITS ADVOCATES IN THE ARMY, NAVY AND PRIVY COUNCIL...

IN THE HOUSES OF PARLIAMENT AND IN THE STATE CHURCH...

A PROPAGANDA THE METHODS OF WHOSE EXPRESSION WERE SO GROSSLY ILLEGAL AND UTTERLY UNCONSTITUTIONAL...

THAT EVEN THE LORD CHANCELLOR OF ENGLAND COULD FIND ONLY WORDS AND NO REPRESSIVE ACTION TO APPLY TO THEM.

SINCE LAWLESSNESS SAT IN HIGH PLACES IN ENGLAND, AND LAUGHED AT THE LAW AS AT THE CUSTODIANS OF THE LAW...

WHAT WONDER WAS IT THAT IRISHMEN SHOULD REFUSE TO ACCEPT THE VERBAL PROTESTATIONS OF AN ENGLISH LORD CHANCELLOR AS A SUFFICIENT SAFEGUARD FOR THEIR LIVES AND LIBERTIES?

I KNOW NOT HOW ALL MY COLLEAGUES ON THE VOLUNTEER COMMITTEE IN DUBLIN REVIEWED THE GROWING MENACE...

BUT THOSE WITH WHOM I WAS IN CLOSEST CO-OPERATION REDOUBLED, IN FACE OF THESE THREATS FROM WITHOUT, OUR EFFORTS TO UNITE ALL IRISHMEN FROM WITHIN.

OUR APPEALS WERE MADE TO PROTESTANT AND UNIONIST AS MUCH ALMOST AS TO CATHOLIC AND NATIONALIST IRISHMEN.

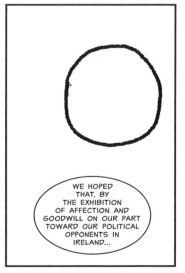

WE HOPED THAT, BY THE EXHIBITION OF AFFECTION AND GOODWILL ON OUR PART TOWARD OUR POLITICAL OPPONENTS IN IRELAND...

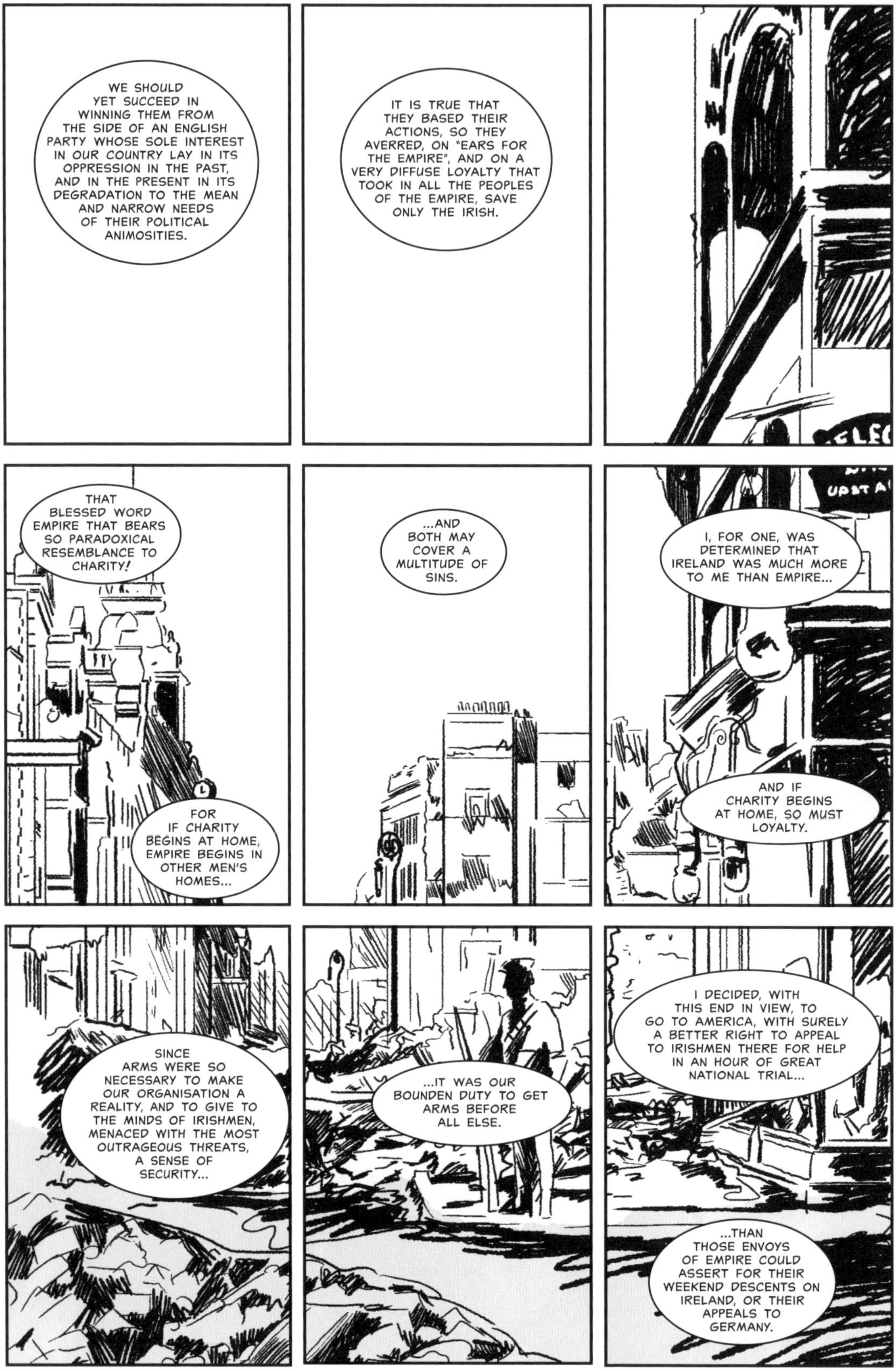
WE SHOULD YET SUCCEED IN WINNING THEM FROM THE SIDE OF AN ENGLISH PARTY WHOSE SOLE INTEREST IN OUR COUNTRY LAY IN ITS OPPRESSION IN THE PAST, AND IN THE PRESENT IN ITS DEGRADATION TO THE MEAN AND NARROW NEEDS OF THEIR POLITICAL ANIMOSITIES.
IT IS TRUE THAT THEY BASED THEIR ACTIONS, SO THEY AVERRED, ON "EARS FOR THE EMPIRE", AND ON A VERY DIFFUSE LOYALTY THAT TOOK IN ALL THE PEOPLES OF THE EMPIRE, SAVE ONLY THE IRISH.
THAT BLESSED WORD EMPIRE THAT BEARS SO PARADOXICAL RESEMBLANCE TO CHARITY!
FOR IF CHARITY BEGINS AT HOME, EMPIRE BEGINS IN OTHER MEN'S HOMES...
...AND BOTH MAY COVER A MULTITUDE OF SINS.
I, FOR ONE, WAS DETERMINED THAT IRELAND WAS MUCH MORE TO ME THAN EMPIRE...
AND IF CHARITY BEGINS AT HOME, SO MUST LOYALTY.
SINCE ARMS WERE SO NECESSARY TO MAKE OUR ORGANISATION A REALITY, AND TO GIVE TO THE MINDS OF IRISHMEN, MENACED WITH THE MOST OUTRAGEOUS THREATS, A SENSE OF SECURITY...
...IT WAS OUR BOUNDEN DUTY TO GET ARMS BEFORE ALL ELSE.
I DECIDED, WITH THIS END IN VIEW, TO GO TO AMERICA, WITH SURELY A BETTER RIGHT TO APPEAL TO IRISHMEN THERE FOR HELP IN AN HOUR OF GREAT NATIONAL TRIAL...
...THAN THOSE ENVOYS OF EMPIRE COULD ASSERT FOR THEIR WEEKEND DESCENTS ON IRELAND, OR THEIR APPEALS TO GERMANY.

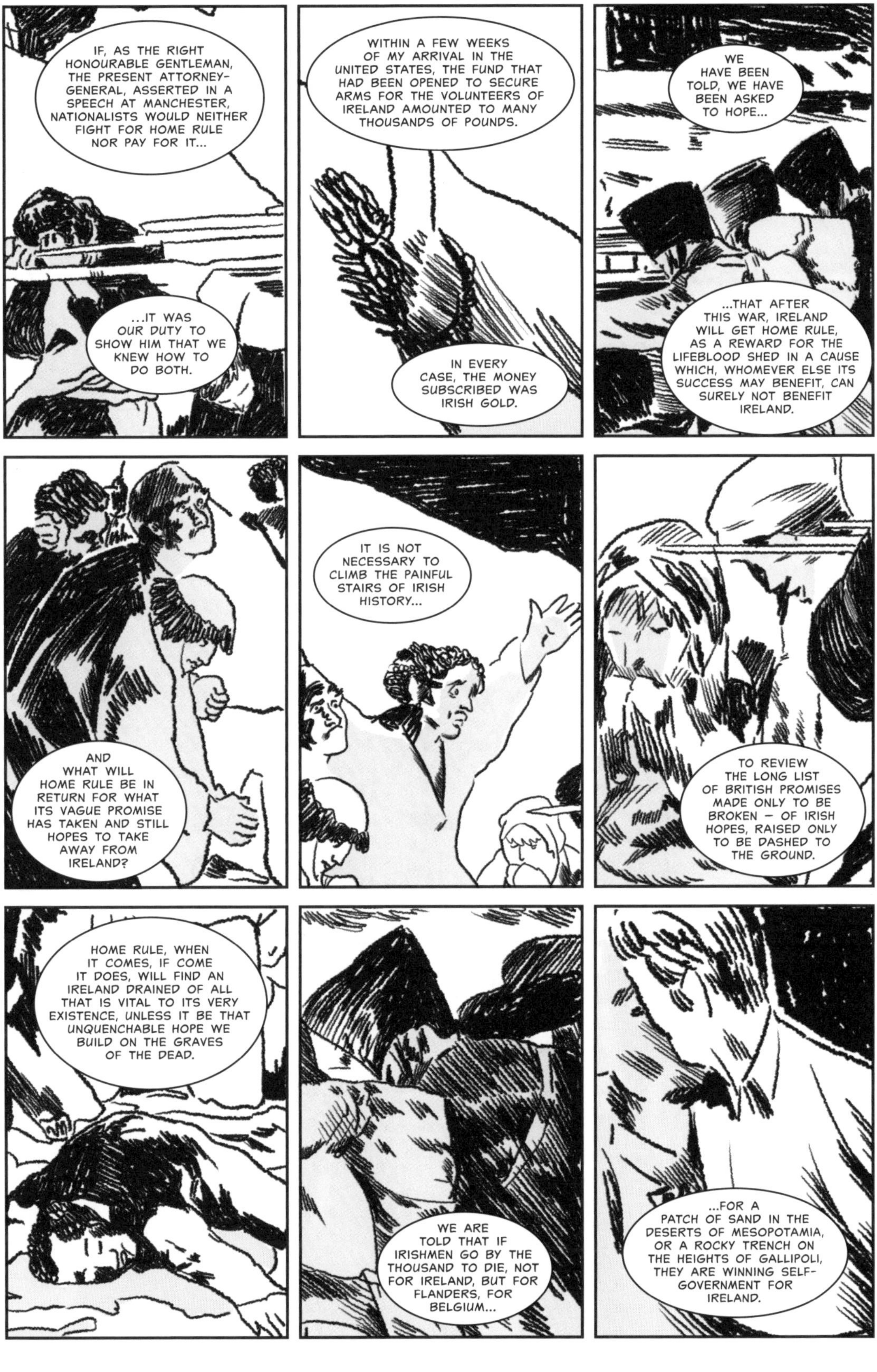
IF, AS THE RIGHT HONOURABLE GENTLEMAN, THE PRESENT ATTORNEY-GENERAL, ASSERTED IN A SPEECH AT MANCHESTER, NATIONALISTS WOULD NEITHER FIGHT FOR HOME RULE NOR PAY FOR IT...
...IT WAS OUR DUTY TO SHOW HIM THAT WE KNEW HOW TO DO BOTH.
WITHIN A FEW WEEKS OF MY ARRIVAL IN THE UNITED STATES, THE FUND THAT HAD BEEN OPENED TO SECURE ARMS FOR THE VOLUNTEERS OF IRELAND AMOUNTED TO MANY THOUSANDS OF POUNDS.
IN EVERY CASE, THE MONEY SUBSCRIBED WAS IRISH GOLD.
WE HAVE BEEN TOLD, WE HAVE BEEN ASKED TO HOPE...
...THAT AFTER THIS WAR, IRELAND WILL GET HOME RULE, AS A REWARD FOR THE LIFEBLOOD SHED IN A CAUSE WHICH, WHOMEVER ELSE ITS SUCCESS MAY BENEFIT, CAN SURELY NOT BENEFIT IRELAND.
AND WHAT WILL HOME RULE BE IN RETURN FOR WHAT ITS VAGUE PROMISE HAS TAKEN AND STILL HOPES TO TAKE AWAY FROM IRELAND?
IT IS NOT NECESSARY TO CLIMB THE PAINFUL STAIRS OF IRISH HISTORY...
TO REVIEW THE LONG LIST OF BRITISH PROMISES MADE ONLY TO BE BROKEN – OF IRISH HOPES, RAISED ONLY TO BE DASHED TO THE GROUND.
HOME RULE, WHEN IT COMES, IF COME IT DOES, WILL FIND AN IRELAND DRAINED OF ALL THAT IS VITAL TO ITS VERY EXISTENCE, UNLESS IT BE THAT UNQUENCHABLE HOPE WE BUILD ON THE GRAVES OF THE DEAD.
WE ARE TOLD THAT IF IRISHMEN GO BY THE THOUSAND TO DIE, NOT FOR IRELAND, BUT FOR FLANDERS, FOR BELGIUM...
...FOR A PATCH OF SAND IN THE DESERTS OF MESOPOTAMIA, OR A ROCKY TRENCH ON THE HEIGHTS OF GALLIPOLI, THEY ARE WINNING SELF-GOVERNMENT FOR IRELAND.

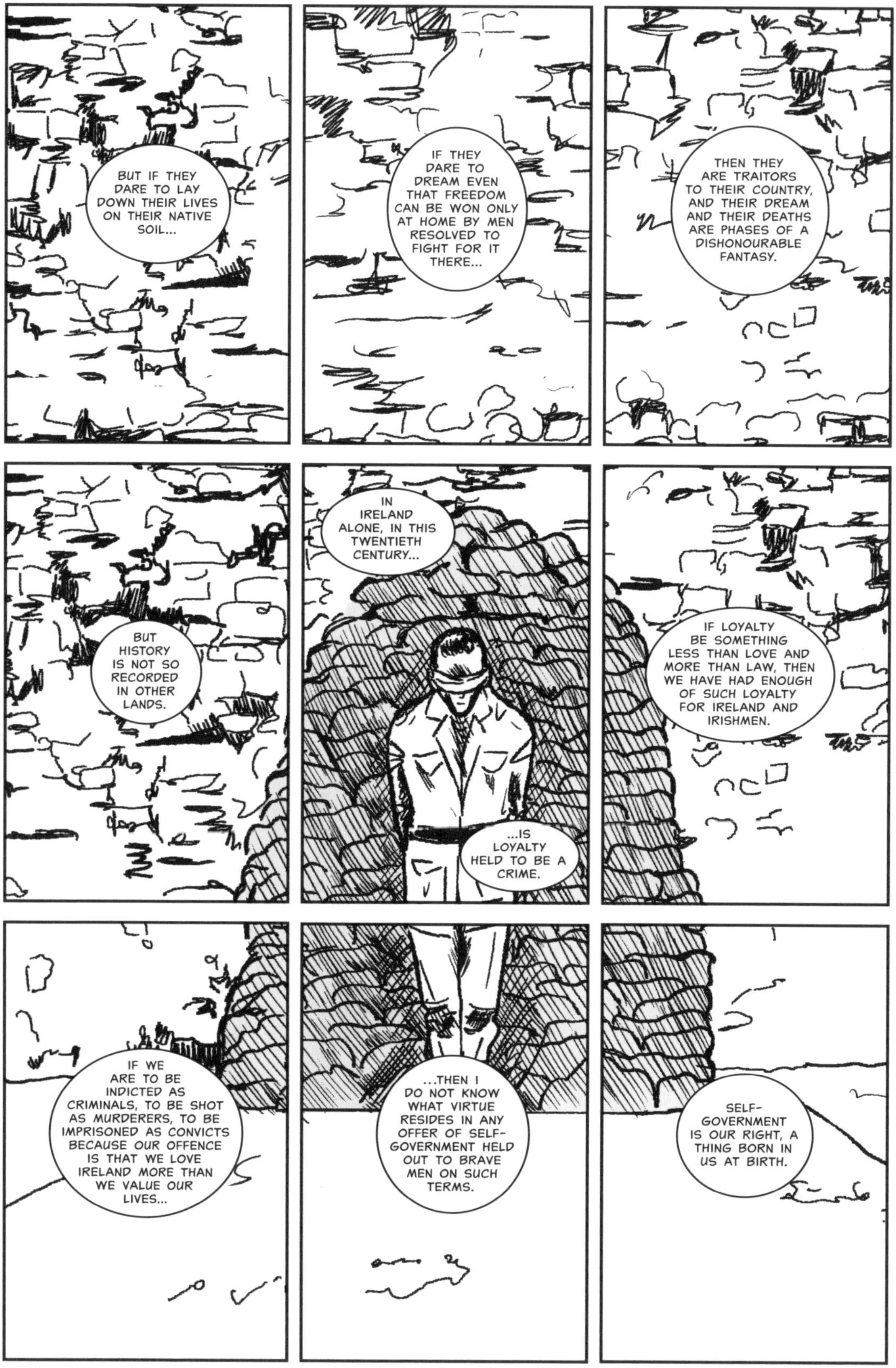

BUT IF THEY DARE TO LAY DOWN THEIR LIVES ON THEIR NATIVE SOIL...
IF THEY DARE TO DREAM EVEN THAT FREEDOM CAN BE WON ONLY AT HOME BY MEN RESOLVED TO FIGHT FOR IT THERE...
THEN THEY ARE TRAITORS TO THEIR COUNTRY, AND THEIR DREAM AND THEIR DEATHS ARE PHASES OF A DISHONOURABLE FANTASY.
BUT HISTORY IS NOT SO RECORDED IN OTHER LANDS.
IN IRELAND ALONE, IN THIS TWENTIETH CENTURY...
...IS LOYALTY HELD TO BE A CRIME.
IF LOYALTY BE SOMETHING LESS THAN LOVE AND MORE THAN LAW, THEN WE HAVE HAD ENOUGH OF SUCH LOYALTY FOR IRELAND AND IRISHMEN.
IF WE ARE TO BE INDICTED AS CRIMINALS, TO BE SHOT AS MURDERERS, TO BE IMPRISONED AS CONVICTS BECAUSE OUR OFFENCE IS THAT WE LOVE IRELAND MORE THAN WE VALUE OUR LIVES...
...THEN I DO NOT KNOW WHAT VIRTUE RESIDES IN ANY OFFER OF SELF-GOVERNMENT HELD OUT TO BRAVE MEN ON SUCH TERMS.
SELF-GOVERNMENT IS OUR RIGHT, A THING BORN IN US AT BIRTH.

A THING NO MORE TO BE DOLED OUT TO US, OR WITHHELD FROM US, BY ANOTHER PEOPLE THAN THE RIGHT TO LIFE ITSELF...

THAN THE RIGHT TO FEEL THE SUN, OR SMELL THE FLOWERS...

OR TO LOVE OUR KIND.

IT IS ONLY FROM THE CONVICT THESE THINGS ARE WITHHELD, FOR CRIME COMMITTED AND PROVEN...

485 CIVILIANS DEAD IN FIGHTING

AND IRELAND, THAT HAS WRONGED NO MAN, HAS INJURED NO LAND, THAT HAS SOUGHT NO DOMINION OVER OTHERS...

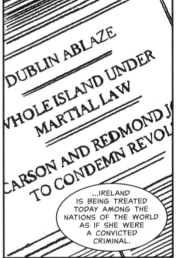

DUBLIN ABLAZE

WHOLE ISLAND UNDER MARTIAL LAW

CARSON AND REDMOND J TO CONDEMN REVOL

...IRELAND IS BEING TREATED TODAY AMONG THE NATIONS OF THE WORLD AS IF SHE WERE A CONVICTED CRIMINAL.

IF IT BE TREASON TO FIGHT AGAINST SUCH AN UNNATURAL FATE AS THIS...

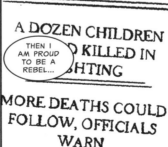

A DOZEN CHILDREN
[KILLE]D KILLED IN
[FIG]HTING

THEN I AM PROUD TO BE A REBEL...

MORE DEATHS COULD FOLLOW, OFFICIALS WARN

[C]ITIZENS ADVISED TO [P]ROCEED ABOUT CITY WITH CAUTION

AND SHALL CLING TO MY "REBELLION" WITH THE LAST DROP OF MY BLOOD.

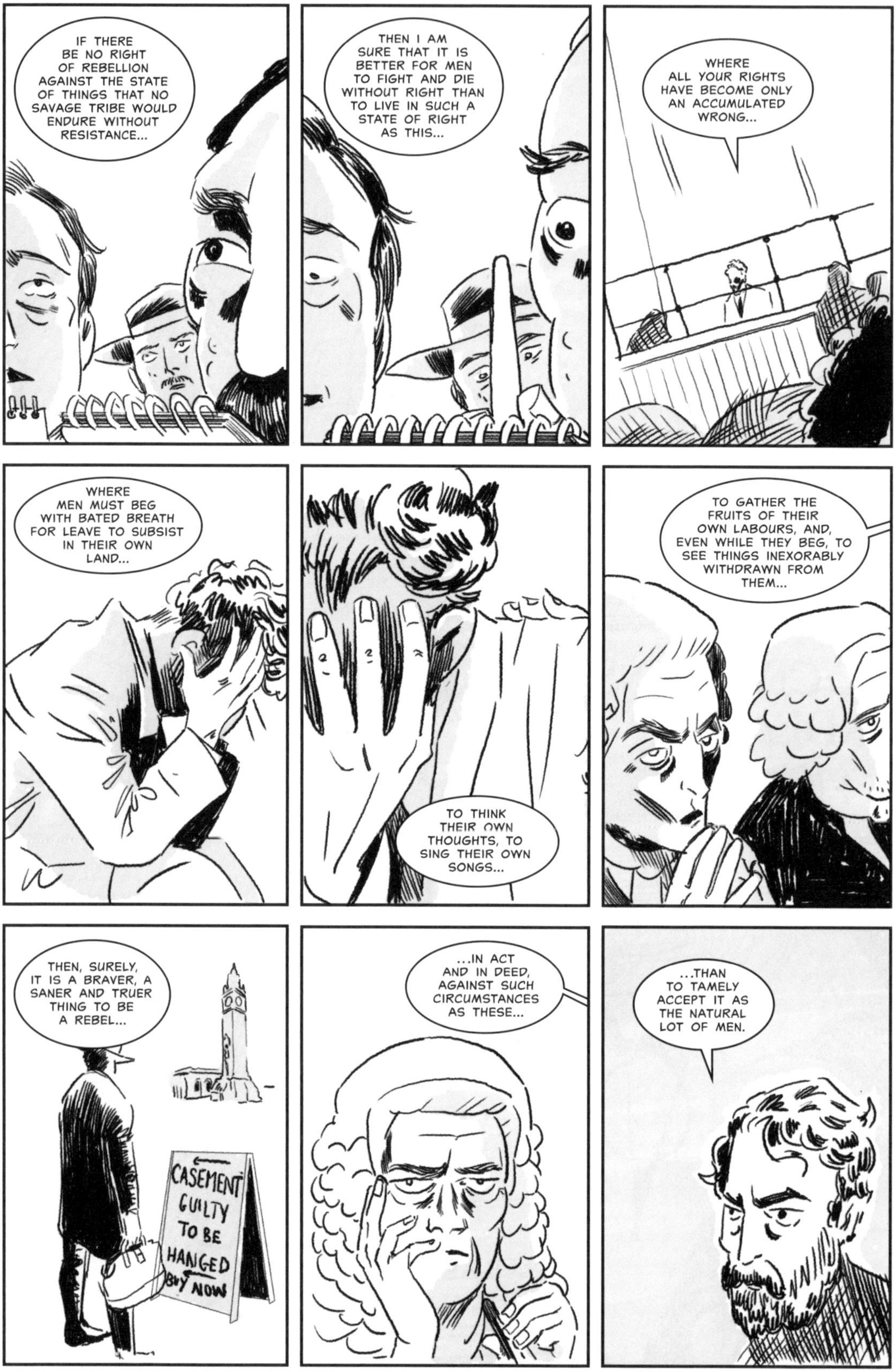
IF THERE BE NO RIGHT OF REBELLION AGAINST THE STATE OF THINGS THAT NO SAVAGE TRIBE WOULD ENDURE WITHOUT RESISTANCE...
THEN I AM SURE THAT IT IS BETTER FOR MEN TO FIGHT AND DIE WITHOUT RIGHT THAN TO LIVE IN SUCH A STATE OF RIGHT AS THIS...
WHERE ALL YOUR RIGHTS HAVE BECOME ONLY AN ACCUMULATED WRONG...
WHERE MEN MUST BEG WITH BATED BREATH FOR LEAVE TO SUBSIST IN THEIR OWN LAND...
TO THINK THEIR OWN THOUGHTS, TO SING THEIR OWN SONGS...
TO GATHER THE FRUITS OF THEIR OWN LABOURS, AND, EVEN WHILE THEY BEG, TO SEE THINGS INEXORABLY WITHDRAWN FROM THEM...
THEN, SURELY, IT IS A BRAVER, A SANER AND TRUER THING TO BE A REBEL...
CASEMENT GUILTY TO BE HANGED BUY NOW
...IN ACT AND IN DEED, AGAINST SUCH CIRCUMSTANCES AS THESE...
...THAN TO TAMELY ACCEPT IT AS THE NATURAL LOT OF MEN.

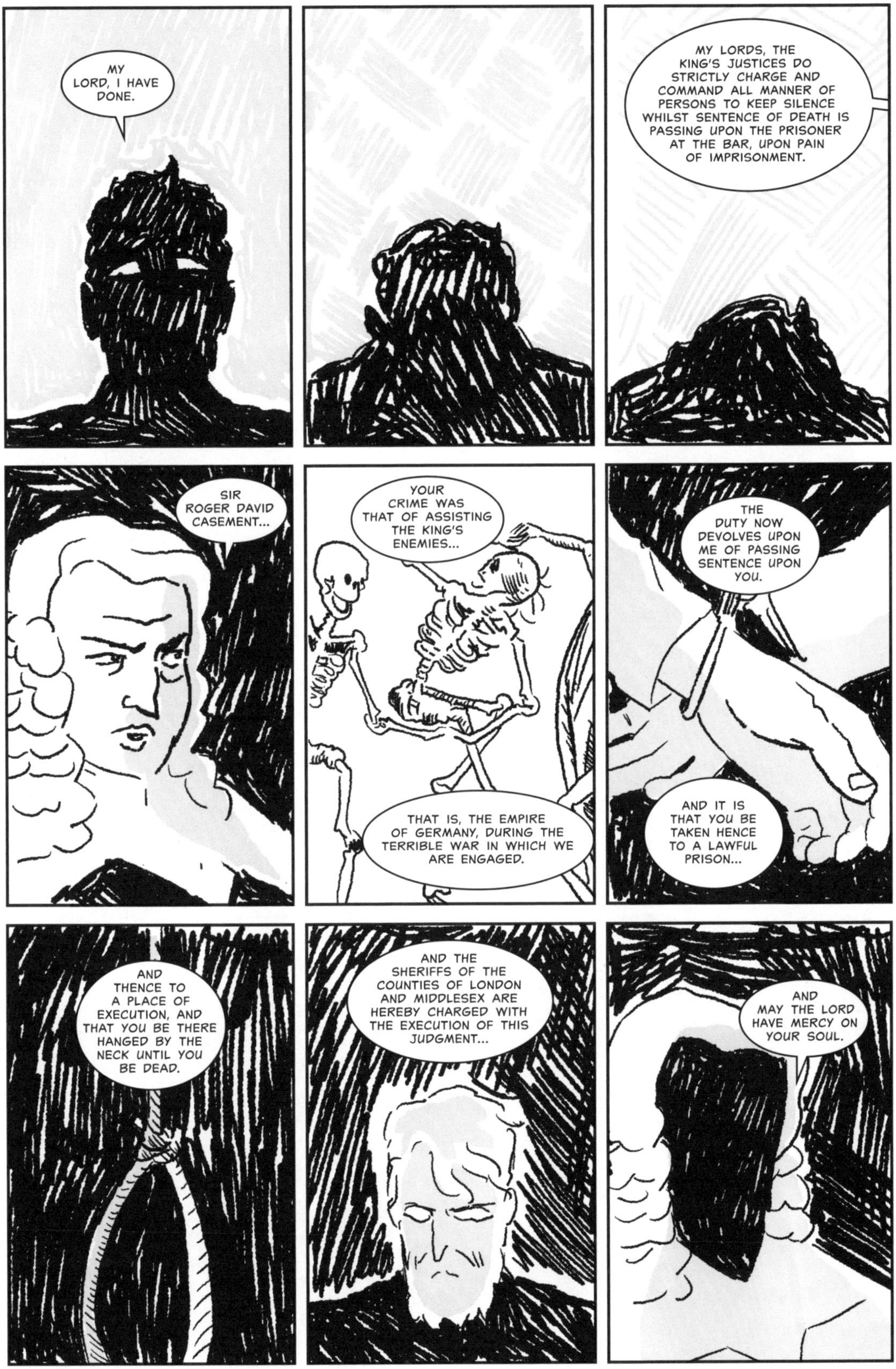
MY LORD, I HAVE DONE.
MY LORDS, THE KING'S JUSTICES DO STRICTLY CHARGE AND COMMAND ALL MANNER OF PERSONS TO KEEP SILENCE WHILST SENTENCE OF DEATH IS PASSING UPON THE PRISONER AT THE BAR, UPON PAIN OF IMPRISONMENT.
SIR ROGER DAVID CASEMENT...
YOUR CRIME WAS THAT OF ASSISTING THE KING'S ENEMIES...
THAT IS, THE EMPIRE OF GERMANY, DURING THE TERRIBLE WAR IN WHICH WE ARE ENGAGED.
THE DUTY NOW DEVOLVES UPON ME OF PASSING SENTENCE UPON YOU.
AND IT IS THAT YOU BE TAKEN HENCE TO A LAWFUL PRISON...
AND THENCE TO A PLACE OF EXECUTION, AND THAT YOU BE THERE HANGED BY THE NECK UNTIL YOU BE DEAD.
AND THE SHERIFFS OF THE COUNTIES OF LONDON AND MIDDLESEX ARE HEREBY CHARGED WITH THE EXECUTION OF THIS JUDGMENT...
AND MAY THE LORD HAVE MERCY ON YOUR SOUL.

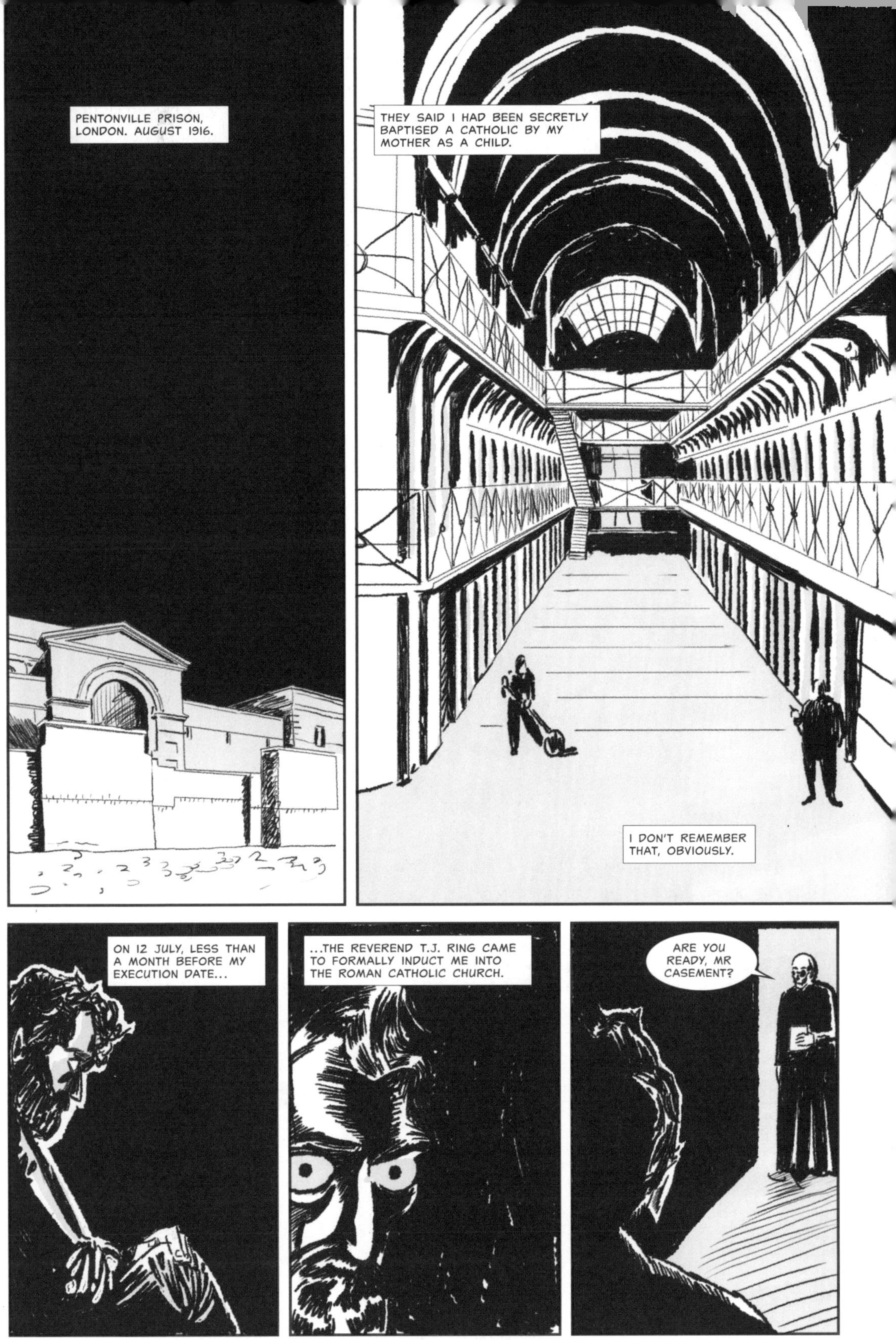
PENTONVILLE PRISON, LONDON. AUGUST 1916.
THEY SAID I HAD BEEN SECRETLY BAPTISED A CATHOLIC BY MY MOTHER AS A CHILD.
I DON'T REMEMBER THAT, OBVIOUSLY.
ON 12 JULY, LESS THAN A MONTH BEFORE MY EXECUTION DATE...
...THE REVEREND T.J. RING CAME TO FORMALLY INDUCT ME INTO THE ROMAN CATHOLIC CHURCH.
ARE YOU READY, MR CASEMENT?

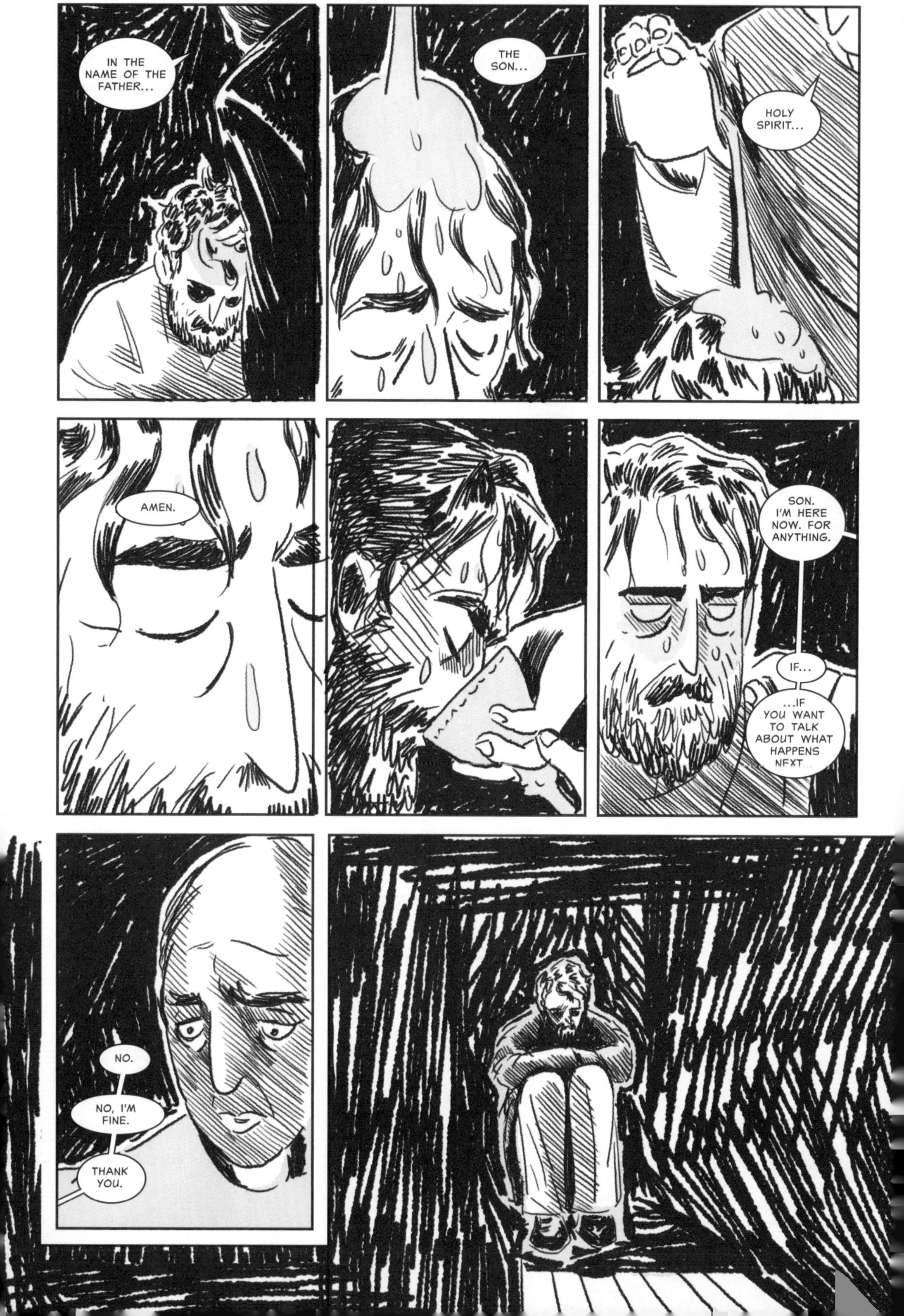
IN THE NAME OF THE FATHER...
THE SON...
HOLY SPIRIT...
AMEN.
SON. I'M HERE NOW. FOR ANYTHING.
IF...
...IF YOU WANT TO TALK ABOUT WHAT HAPPENS NEXT...
NO.
NO, I'M FINE.
THANK YOU.

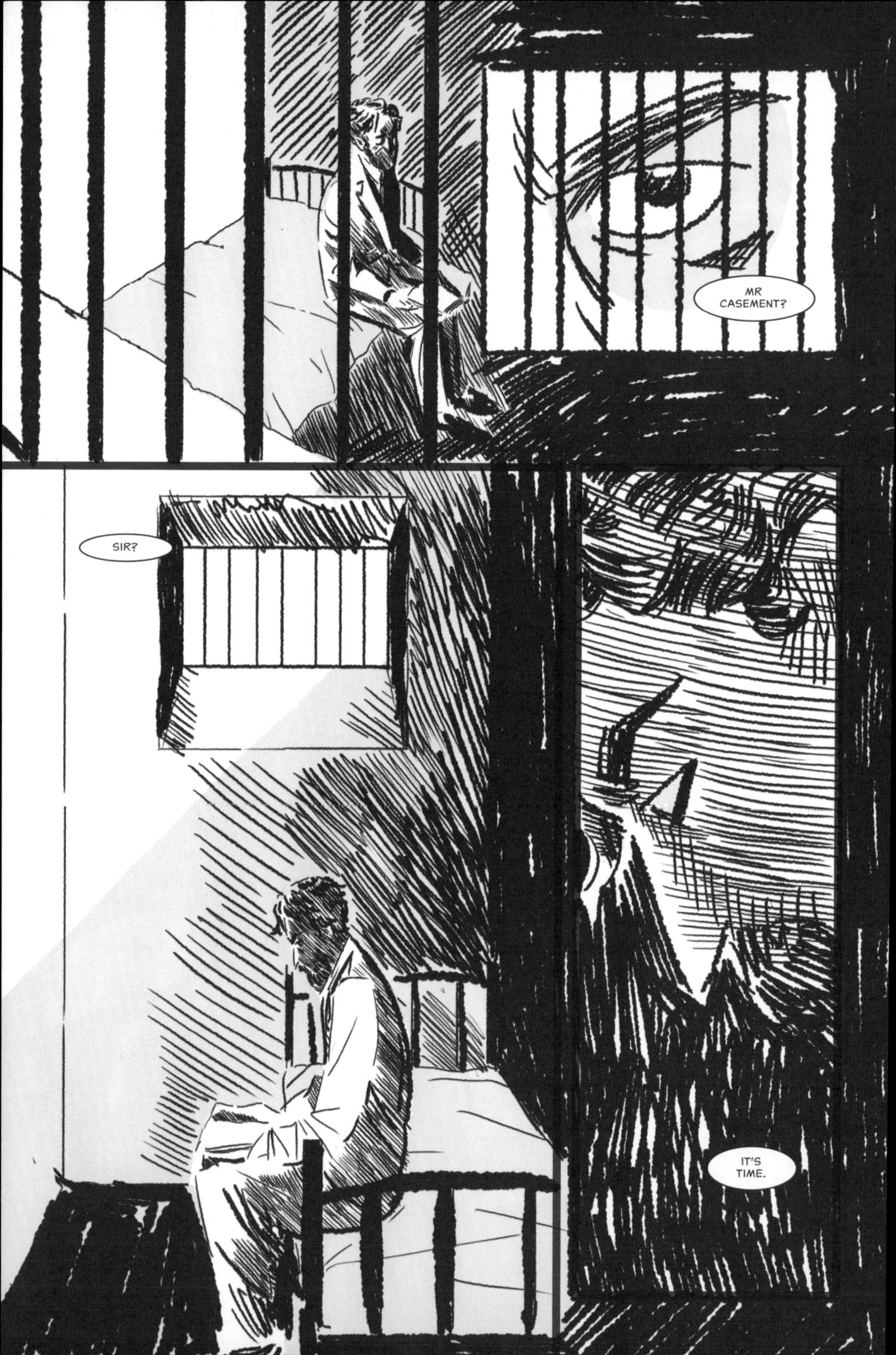
MR CASEMENT?
SIR?
IT'S TIME.

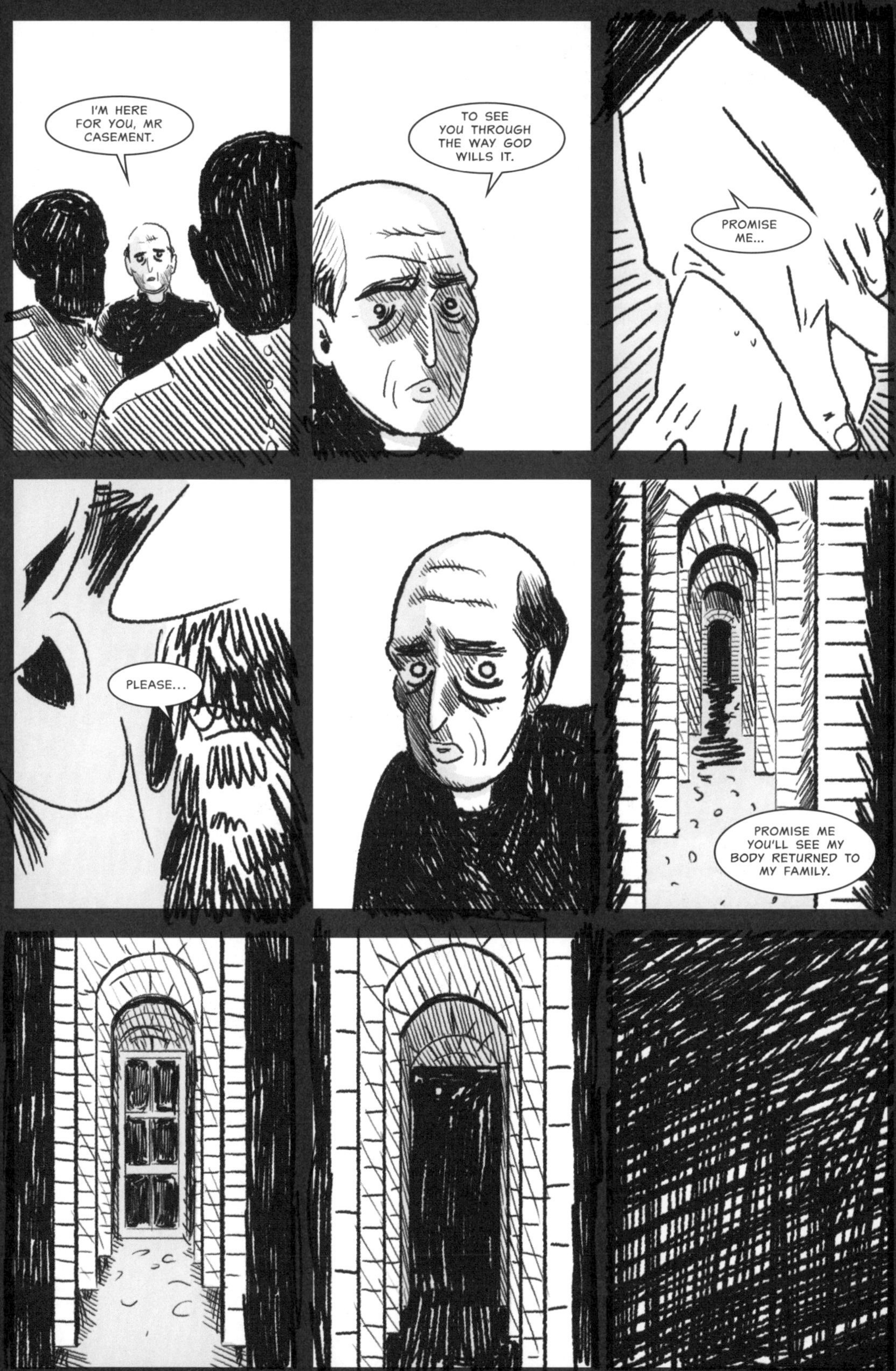
I'M HERE FOR YOU, MR CASEMENT.
TO SEE YOU THROUGH THE WAY GOD WILLS IT.
PROMISE ME...
PLEASE...
PROMISE ME YOU'LL SEE MY BODY RETURNED TO MY FAMILY.

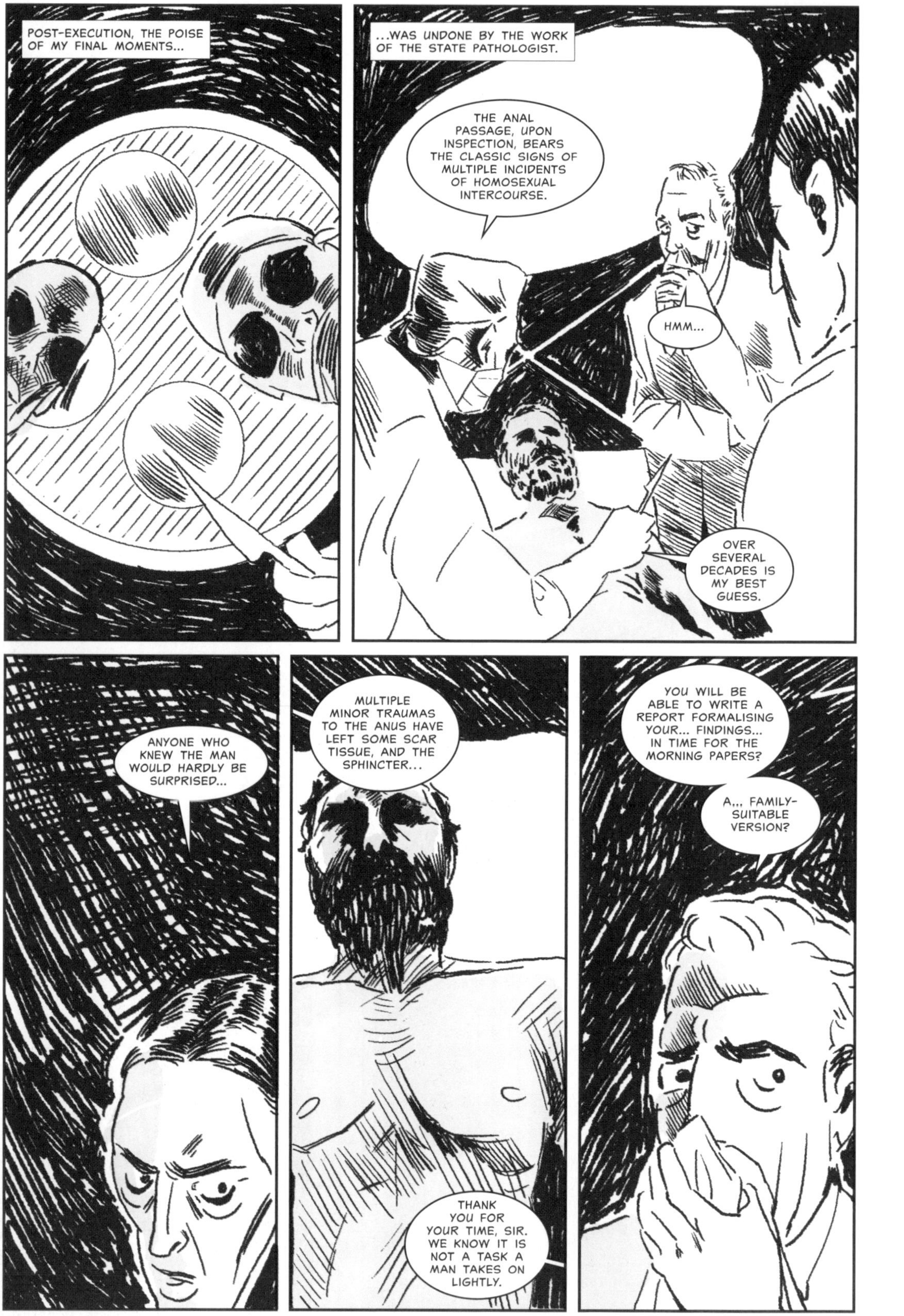
POST-EXECUTION, THE POISE OF MY FINAL MOMENTS...
...WAS UNDONE BY THE WORK OF THE STATE PATHOLOGIST.
THE ANAL PASSAGE, UPON INSPECTION, BEARS THE CLASSIC SIGNS OF MULTIPLE INCIDENTS OF HOMOSEXUAL INTERCOURSE.
HMM...
OVER SEVERAL DECADES IS MY BEST GUESS.
ANYONE WHO KNEW THE MAN WOULD HARDLY BE SURPRISED...
MULTIPLE MINOR TRAUMAS TO THE ANUS HAVE LEFT SOME SCAR TISSUE, AND THE SPHINCTER...
THANK YOU FOR YOUR TIME, SIR. WE KNOW IT IS NOT A TASK A MAN TAKES ON LIGHTLY.
YOU WILL BE ABLE TO WRITE A REPORT FORMALISING YOUR... FINDINGS... IN TIME FOR THE MORNING PAPERS?
A... FAMILY-SUITABLE VERSION?

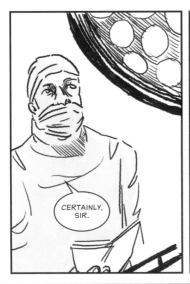

CERTAINLY, SIR.

HAVE IT WIRED TO THE TIMES AS SOON AS YOU'RE FINISHED.

AND MAKE SURE THAT SHERLOCK-WRITING PILLOCK GETS A COPY.

A BIT HARSH.

I LIKED THE LAST SHERLOCK HOLMES NOVEL.

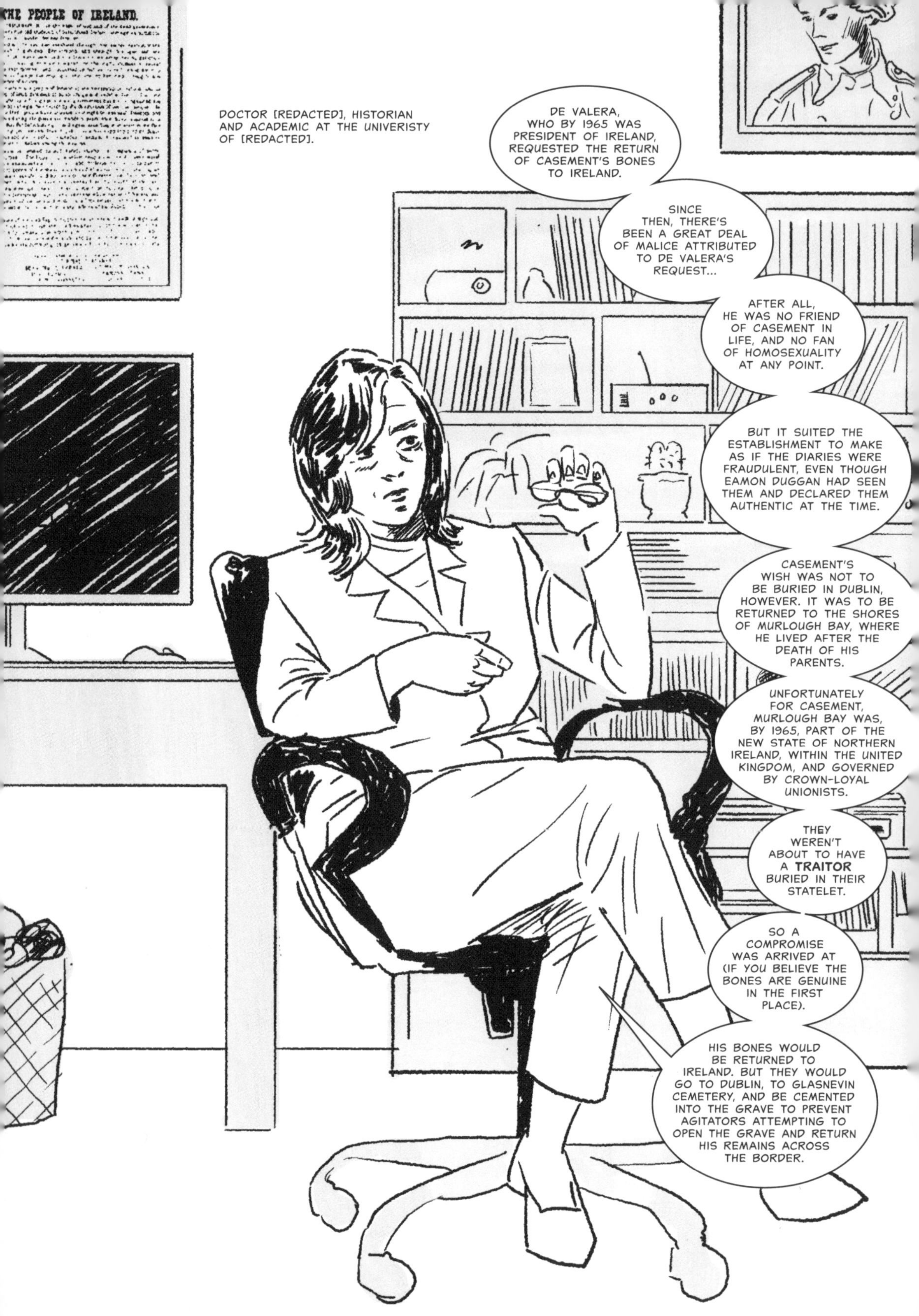
DOCTOR [REDACTED], HISTORIAN AND ACADEMIC AT THE UNIVERISTY OF [REDACTED].
DE VALERA, WHO BY 1965 WAS PRESIDENT OF IRELAND, REQUESTED THE RETURN OF CASEMENT'S BONES TO IRELAND.
SINCE THEN, THERE'S BEEN A GREAT DEAL OF MALICE ATTRIBUTED TO DE VALERA'S REQUEST...
AFTER ALL, HE WAS NO FRIEND OF CASEMENT IN LIFE, AND NO FAN OF HOMOSEXUALITY AT ANY POINT.
BUT IT SUITED THE ESTABLISHMENT TO MAKE AS IF THE DIARIES WERE FRAUDULENT, EVEN THOUGH EAMON DUGGAN HAD SEEN THEM AND DECLARED THEM AUTHENTIC AT THE TIME.
CASEMENT'S WISH WAS NOT TO BE BURIED IN DUBLIN, HOWEVER. IT WAS TO BE RETURNED TO THE SHORES OF MURLOUGH BAY, WHERE HE LIVED AFTER THE DEATH OF HIS PARENTS.
UNFORTUNATELY FOR CASEMENT, MURLOUGH BAY WAS, BY 1965, PART OF THE NEW STATE OF NORTHERN IRELAND, WITHIN THE UNITED KINGDOM, AND GOVERNED BY CROWN-LOYAL UNIONISTS.
THEY WEREN'T ABOUT TO HAVE A **TRAITOR** BURIED IN THEIR STATELET.
SO A COMPROMISE WAS ARRIVED AT (IF YOU BELIEVE THE BONES ARE GENUINE IN THE FIRST PLACE).
HIS BONES WOULD BE RETURNED TO IRELAND. BUT THEY WOULD GO TO DUBLIN, TO GLASNEVIN CEMETERY, AND BE CEMENTED INTO THE GRAVE TO PREVENT AGITATORS ATTEMPTING TO OPEN THE GRAVE AND RETURN HIS REMAINS ACROSS THE BORDER.
THE PEOPLE OF IRELAND.

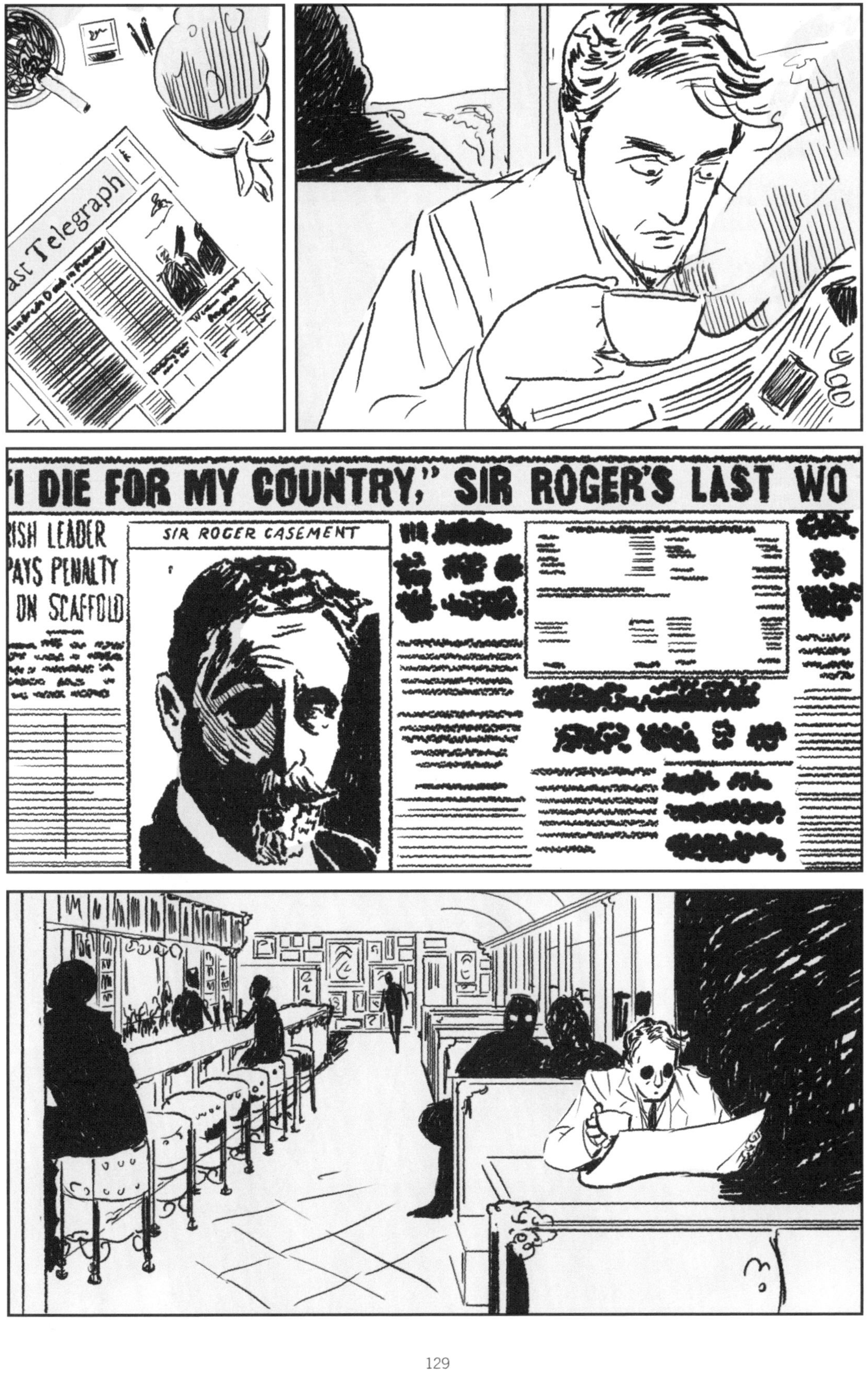
ast Telegraph
"I DIE FOR MY COUNTRY," SIR ROGER'S LAST WO
ISH LEADER
PAYS PENALTY
ON SCAFFOLD
SIR ROGER CASEMENT

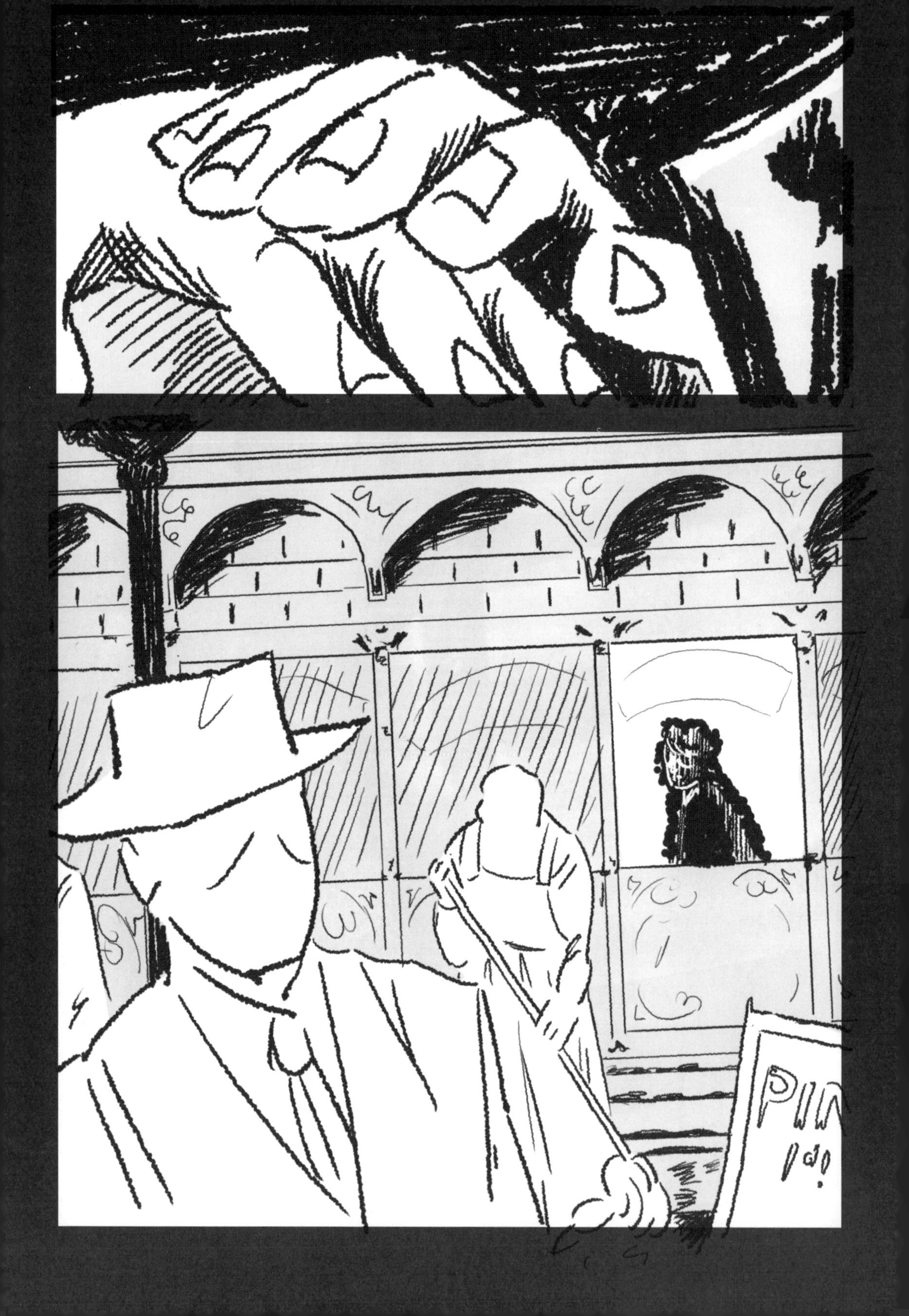

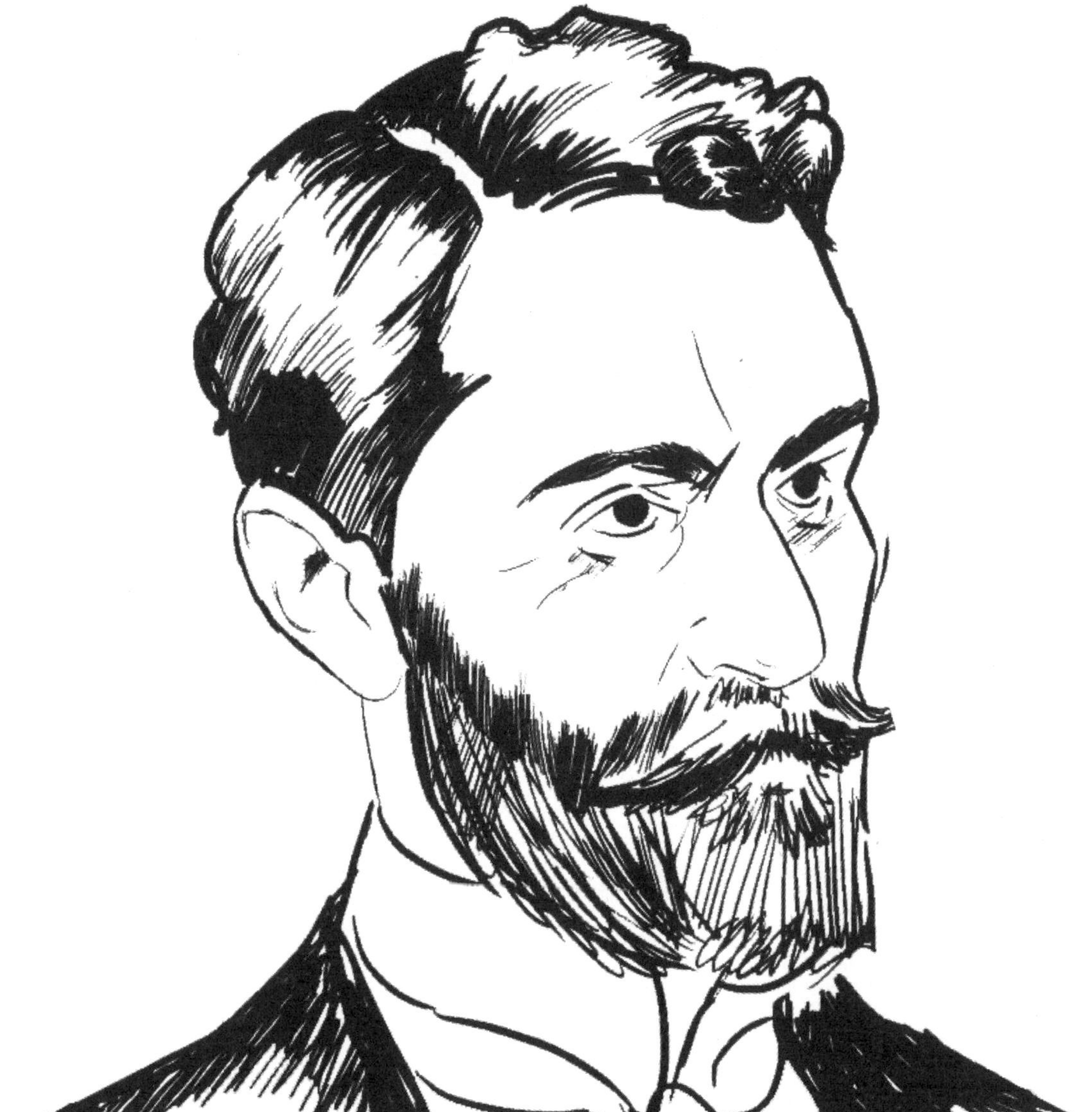

TIMELINE

1864
Roger David Casement is born in Sandycove, Dublin, to Roger Casement and Anne Jephson.

1868
It is rumoured that Casement is secretly baptised as a Roman Catholic in Rhyl, Wales by his mother.

1873
Casement's mother dies in childbirth in Worthing, England. The family returns to Ireland.

1877
Casement's father dies. Together with his older siblings – Charles, Tom and Agnes (known as Nina) – Casement becomes a ward of paternal relatives at Murlough Bay in County Antrim.

1880
Casement leaves the Diocesan School in Ballymena at the age of 16. He goes to England to work as a clerk for Liverpool shipping company Elder Dempster.

1884–1890
Casement's work takes him to Africa, where he carries out a number of roles for the International African Association in the Congo. This supposedly humanitarian organisation had rapidly devolved into a commercial colonisation tool as part of the European 'Scramble for Africa'; in the Congo basin, this allowed King Leopold II of Belgium to assume private ownership of the then Congo Free State (now known as the Democratic Republic of Congo) and its natural resources, including ivory, minerals and rubber. Casement meets Joseph Conrad, who would combine his own experiences with Casement's recollections to explore the 'civilising' nature of Western rule in *Heart of Darkness*.

1890s
Casement joins the British Consular Service, working his way from clerk to consul in various African territories held by Britain, Portugal and France.

1903
Following years of speculation about the situation in the Congo, the British government instructs Casement – by now the British consul in the Congo Free State capital, Boma – to investigate human rights abuses and exploitation under King Leopold's administration. Casement begins his inquiry in July, travelling extensively to interview people throughout the region.

1904
On 15 February, Casement's findings are published in what swiftly becomes known as the *Casement Report*. Detailing enslavement, mass killings, beatings, mutilations and kidnappings carried out by Leopold's private army (the Force Publique) and private companies, the report prompts international outrage against the Belgian Crown and further investigations into Leopold's brutal Congolese policy.

Meanwhile, in Ireland, Casement joins the Gaelic League, established to preserve the Irish language.

1905
An independent Belgian inquiry confirms the veracity of the *Casement Report*, leading to arrest and punishment for some officials implicated in the investigation.

Casement is appointed Companion of the Order of St Michael and St George for his part in exposing these atrocities. The same year, he joins the newly formed Sinn Féin party in Ireland, which aims to bring about Irish independence through non-violent means.

1906
Casement is transferred by the Foreign Office to Brazil.

1908
The Belgian parliament annexes the Congo Free State from Leopold and takes over the administration of the newly named Belgian Congo. Despite improvements in certain

respects – including a curbing of the systemic and arbitrary violence that Casement had highlighted – the exploitation of the Congo's population and resources continues.

1910
Since 1909, rumours had been circulating of slavery and mistreatment by the Peruvian Amazon Company (PAC), a British-registered company operating out of Iquitos, Peru, under the control of rubber baron Julio Arana. The British government sends Casement to Iquitos to investigate reports of abuse, and he subsequently travels deep into the Amazon basin to witness PAC's treatment of the indigenous population in the Putumayo district. He uncovers a pattern of abuse, which included forced labour, rape, murder, branding and starvation. Casement's first reports on this situation drive PAC's British board members to demand change from both Arana and the Peruvian government.

1911
Casement returns to Iquitos and Putumayo, only to find that promised reforms have not been put into action. While some of the men Casement had exposed have been imprisoned, beatings, torture and the starvation of the native workers remain standard. On his return to Britain, Casement campaigns with the Anti-Slavery Society to put further pressure on the Peruvian government. The scandal of these atrocities leads to PAC's eventual collapse.

On 6 July, Casement is knighted by King George V.

1912
On 13 July, Casement's eloquent *Putumayo Report* is published.

1913
Disillusioned with imperialism and its consequences, Casement retires from British consular service. By the end of the year, he is party to the formation of the Irish Volunteers, a military force intended to maintain Irish rights and liberties in the face of the recently formed Ulster Volunteers. This unionist organisation had been established earlier in the year to resist the granting of Home Rule for Ireland.

1914
In July, Casement travels to the US to raise money and support for the Volunteers from Irish communities there, making contact via friends in the secretive Irish Republican Brotherhood (IRB) with exiled republican groups including Clan na Gael. He meets a seemingly stranded Norwegian sailor, Eivind Adler Christensen, on Times Square. Christensen becomes his companion, valet and, it is rumoured, lover.

On 28 July, World War One begins.

In October, Casement travels to Germany via Norway, where Christensen is offered £5,000 by the British diplomat Mansfeldt Findlay to betray Casement, amid rumours that the two are in a homosexual relationship. Christensen refuses. An alternative version of this story suggests that Christensen himself instigates the deal with the British before backing out. The British Embassy will later obtain sworn affidavits from hotel staff in Christiania stating that Casement and Christensen practised sodomy during their stay.

On 31 October, Casement arrives in Berlin, hoping to secure a German declaration of support for an independent Ireland. The mutually beneficial plan he presents proposes the receipt of arms, training and personnel from Germany in exchange for an Irish revolt against England to divert troops from the war effort. While there, he addresses Irish prisoners of war in a largely unsuccessful attempt to raise a rebel brigade.

1915
Casement remains in Germany negotiating with the authorities. In November, Christensen returns to the US. In Ireland, preparations for an uprising are gaining pace.

1916
News arrives in March that the date for the republican uprising has been set for 23 April – Easter Sunday. On 15 April, Casement, Robert

Monteith and Daniel Bailey, an Irish Brigade sergeant, leave for Ireland aboard a German submarine. They aim to rendezvous with the *Aud*, a ship carrying German weapons, off the coast.

On 21 April, Good Friday, Casement lands at Banna Strand, Curraghane, County Kerry, but is soon arrested. On the same day, the *Aud* is intercepted by the Royal Navy before it can make contact with the Irish rebels. Casement is swiftly transferred to London.

On 24 April, Easter Monday, the Easter Rising (also known as the Sinn Féin Rebellion) begins a day later than planned in Dublin, lasting for 6 days. It is brutally suppressed, and will have wide-ranging repercussions for both Ireland and Britain.

On 26 June, Casement's trial for treason begins.

On 29 June, he is found guilty and sentenced to death by hanging.

Following his conviction, the British government leaks details of Casement's journals. These documents, known as the Black Diaries, contain numerous explicit references to Casement's homosexual activity. Their circulation among a homophobic population undermines support for any appeal for clemency.

On 3 August, Casement reaffirms his allegiance to the Catholic faith. He expresses his desire to be buried at Murlough Bay, his childhood home. He is hanged at Pentonville Prison by John Ellis. Following an autopsy which confirms sodomy, his body is thrown into the quicklime pit in the prison cemetery.

1932
John Ellis, Casement's executioner, cuts his own throat with a razor.

1960
The Belgian Congo gains independence, renaming itself the Republic of Congo. Within the year, two provinces secede

and a constitutional crisis emerges between the President and Prime Minister. The country descends into instability and civil war.

1965
Following decades of refusals, the British government agrees to repatriate Casement's remains to Ireland. On his return, he is given a state funeral and is buried with full military honours in Glasnevin Cemetery, Dublin. The ceremony is attended by an estimated 30,000 people. As a condition of return, his coffin is cemented into the plot to prevent repatriation to Murlough Bay.

2002
Controversy has surrounded the Black Diaries since their first circulation, with some claiming them to be forgeries created by British intelligence to tarnish Casement's reputation and, by extension, his cause. On 12 March, the results of the first fully independent forensic examination of the Black Diaries are released by the Giles Document Laboratory through the BBC documentary *Secrets of the Black Diaries*. Their conclusion, based largely on handwriting analysis, is that the diaries had all been written in Casement's hand.

2016
On 21 April, a formal state ceremony in Casement's honour takes place at Banna Strand, featuring a reading of the impassioned speech that Casement gave upon his conviction.